FEMINIST CHRISTIAN ENCOUNTERS

Feminist discourses have focused sustained and sometimes devastating critical attention on Christianity over the last fifty years. Today feminisms remain significant but often ambiguous forces in contemporary Christian theology.

At a time in which questions about the success and viability of feminisms are increasingly posed, *Feminist Christian Encounters* makes a unique contribution to the ongoing investigation into the creative relationship between feminisms and Christianity. Angela Pears identifies some of the key theological and methodological mechanisms by which Christian feminist theologies are informed, sustained, and made possible by feminist values and critiques. Pears argues that certain strategies characterize the facilitation of this dialogue in contemporary Christian feminist theologies, enabling theologians to accept the values and critiques of feminisms whilst at the same time proclaim some level of commitment to Christianity. Engaging in a process of deconstruction of the methodologies of key Christian theological thinkers who have made use of feminisms in their theologies, this book reveals the mechanisms of feminist Christian encounter at work.

Feminist Christian Encounters
The Methods and Strategies of Feminist Informed Christian Theologies

ANGELA PEARS
Oxford Brookes University, UK

LONDON AND NEW YORK

First published 2004 by Ashgate Publishing

Reissued 2019 by Routledge
2 Park Square, Milton Park, Abingdon, Oxon, OX1 4 4RN
52 Vanderbilt Avenue, New York, NY 10017

Routledge is an imprint of the Taylor & Francis Group, an informa business

Copyright © Angela Pears 2004

The author has asserted her moral right under the Copyright, Designs and Patents Act, 1988, to be identified as the author of this work.

All rights reserved. No part of this book may be reprinted or reproduced or utilised in any form or by any electronic, mechanical, or other means, now known or hereafter invented, including photocopying and recording, or in any information storage or retrieval system, without permission in writing from the publishers.

Notice:
Product or corporate names may be trademarks or registered trademarks, and are used only for identification and explanation without intent to infringe.

Publisher's Note
The publisher has gone to great lengths to ensure the quality of this reprint but points out that some imperfections in the original copies may be apparent.

Disclaimer
The publisher has made every effort to trace copyright holders and welcomes correspondence from those they have been unable to contact.

A Library of Congress record exists under LC control number:

ISBN 13: 978-0-8153-8900-2 (hbk)
ISBN 13: 978-0-367-19802-2 (pbk)
ISBN 13: 978-0-429-24335-6 (ebk)

Contents

Acknowledgements		*vi*
Introduction		1
1	The Contours of Christian Feminist Theologies	9
2	Feminist Rejections of Christianity	40
3	Christology and Passionate Mutuality: The Feminist Theology of Carter Heyward	69
4	Remembering and Valuing: Elisabeth Schüssler Fiorenza	101
5	In Context and in Dialogue: Being Indecent With Marcella Althaus-Reid	134
6	Christian Tradition, Authority and Feminisms	163
Bibliography		*184*
Index		*197*

Acknowledgements

This book represents some explorations in issues of gender, Christian theological method and encounters between feminisms and Christianity. At the heart of its progress through to completion I have been fortunate enough to be engaged in dialogue with a number of people whose critical but sustaining input has been vital to the development of my thinking. To this end I am particularly indebted to Graeme Smith whose friendship and probing theological mind have provided crucial feedback at key points. I am also grateful to students and colleagues at Oxford Brookes University; in particular, thanks go to Dom Corrywright, Ailsa Clarke, Brian Marshall, Bev Clack and Martin Groves. The sabbatical that I was awarded enabled me to begin research for this book. Colleagues' generous support here was much appreciated. My thanks also to the editorial team at Ashgate for their advice and patience, especially Sarah Lloyd.

Finally, thanks to my friends and family, especially to Deb, Jo, Jessie, Shaun, Erin, Ella and Keira.

Introduction

Feminisms are a feature of life in the twenty-first century. They are sometimes considered to be groundbreaking, sometimes unremarkable and sometimes dangerous, but whatever the perspective taken on the value or effectiveness of feminisms there is a persistence in their varied and often troubled presence. Whether they are accepted, rejected or disputed, feminisms can be seen to inform many different aspects and contexts of human living. Such an influence and critical presence has been effected through a variety of encounters in which feminist informed perspectives and criteria have been employed as the basis of critical and transformative engagement. And this diversity of encounters, along with the diversity of contexts in which such encounters take place, make it necessary to now talk of "feminisms", in the plural, rather than a singular "feminism". Since the 1960s the creative encountering of feminisms has significantly influenced the shape of contemporary theological engagement. For Christian theology the impact of this encounter has been varied but irrefutable as almost every aspect of the doctrinal, organisational and conceptual identities of Christianity has been subject to some level of feminist enquiry. The nature and depth of this enquiry has often proved to be deeply challenging and sometimes transformative of Christianity. And has resulted in the emergence of what is largely considered to be an identifiable and often radical discourse 'feminist theology'. The years since 1968 have seen the destabilising and reconfiguring of central theological constituents, the result of which is an ongoing and increasingly diverse if not disparate feminist Christian encounter. Some of the most significant aspects of this theological movement and encounter include, the politicising of issues of gender and Christianity; the explosion of women's scholarship that refuses to recognise and comply with traditional theological and religious boundaries; the painful passage away from religious and theological institutions; the theological articulation of boundary Christian living; the recovering, naming and reconstruction of women's historical and religious selves; and also, the apparent exclusion and marginalisation of women by the very ideas and structures of feminisms that have spoken in such promising terms of justice.

Given such a vital encountering of Christian theology and feminisms there have been many attempts to evaluate its theological impact and implications for Christian belief and practice. However, the historical patterns of the development of Christian feminist theologies are such that studies have tended to focus on responding to the fundamental but often devastating feminist critique of Christianity as patriarchal and oppressive to women. And, most importantly, as intrinsically incompatible with feminist values and visions. The binary differential between feminisms as compatible with Christianity, and feminisms as incompatible with Christianity, has had a determinate influence on Christian feminist theologies and on critical evaluation of these theologies. Evaluative critique of Christian feminist positions has often entailed or been motivated by the assertion of one religious feminist perspective over another and this has diverted attention away from detailed critical work. In short, critical energy has been taken up with what has emerged as the apparently complex and demanding issue of the compatibility of feminisms and Christianity. The result of this understandable but nevertheless distracting preoccupation is a clear lack of critical evaluative study of Christian feminist theologies that focuses on the methodological mechanisms by which Christian theologies have come to be informed by feminist values and critique. Broadly speaking, contemporary Christian feminist theologies, from their emergence in the 1960s, have largely comprised four areas of enquiry.

1. The first area of enquiry is theological explorations of the possibilities of incorporating feminist critique and praxis into Christianity, and recent key texts here include, Denise L. Carmody *Christian Feminist Theology: A Constructive Response*[1] (1995) and Daphne Hampson (ed.) *Swallowing a Fishbone?: Feminist Theologians Debate Christianity*[2] (1996). Such texts have raised and addressed questions about the underlying issues of the compatibility/incompatibility of feminisms and Christianity.
2. The second area of enquiry, and by far the largest, has focused on the theological and ethical outworking of this feminist Christian encounter. Important texts here include for example, Carter Heyward *Our Passion for Justice: Images of Power, Sexuality and Liberation*[3] (1984), Katie Cannon *Black Womanist Ethics* (1988), Sharon Welch *A Feminist Ethic of Risk*[4] (1990), Susan F. Parsons *Feminism and Christian Ethics*[5] (1998), Rosemary Radford Ruether *Women and Redemption: A Theological History*[6] (1997), Ada María Isasi-Díaz *Mujerista Theology: A Theology for the Twenty-First Century*[7] (1997), Elisabeth Schüssler Fiorenza *Rhetoric and Ethic: The Politics of Biblical Studies*[8] (1999), Marcella Althaus-Reid *Indecent Theology: Theological Perversions in Sex, Gender and Politics*[9] (2000) and Mary Grey *Introducing Feminist Images of God*[10] (2001). Here, concern is with a more detailed working out of the theological and ethical implications of a feminist informed approach for Christianity and such theologies may advocate the merits of feminist informed theologies often also offer committed perspectives on the implications of feminisms for Christianity.
3. The third area is the questioning and refuting of the possibilities and legitimacy of Christian feminist theologies. Texts here include Mary Daly *Beyond God the Father*[11] (1973), Naomi Goldenberg *Changing the Gods: The End of Traditional Religion*[12] (1979), and Daphne Hampson *After Christianity*[13] (1996). Such texts have a direct concern with presenting a committed feminist informed rejection of the possibilities of any kind of feminist based reformation of Christianity.
4. The fourth, and most recently developed, of the areas of enquiries, is a critical concern with the possibilities of feminist informed theology in the light of issues raised by a number of significant developments including a) the diversification of gender aware and feminist informed theologies;

b) the development of poststructuralist thought; and c) the development of postcolonial analysis. Key texts here include, Mary McClintock Fulkerson *Changing the Subject: Women's Discourses and Feminist Theology*[14] (1994), Deborah Sawyer and Diana Collier (eds.) *Is There a Future for Feminist Theology*[15] (1999), Ellen Armour *Deconstruction, Feminist Theology, and the Problem of Difference: Subverting the Race/Gender Divide*[16] (1999). These studies are accepting the problematising of feminisms and feminist theologies and are engaging in explorations of a more self-reflexive feminist informed theological approach.

All four of these are interdependent aspects of Christian feminist enquiry and constitute a diverse and dynamic discourse, the language and values of which, are discernibly both Christian and feminist. As such, these four areas identified overlap in concern and approach, and are not proposed as a restrictive or contained definition of feminist theologies so far. For example, texts such as Marcella Althaus-Reid *Indecent Theology* (2000) might well be said to be an example of the theological and ethical outworking of this feminist Christian encounter, described as the second area of enquiry above, as well as an example of the fourth named area of enquiry, that of a critical concern with the possibilities of feminist informed theology in the light of issues raised by poststructuralist, postcolonial analysis and the general diversification of feminist informed approaches to Christian theology. At the same time many texts within each of these broad areas have an underlying address to the issue of the compatibility/incompatibility of feminisms and Christianity. Even the few studies that do focus on the methods of Christian feminist theologies demonstrate a similar concern with the issue of compatibility. Pamela Dickey Young, for example, in *Feminist Theology/Christian Theology: In Search of Method*[17] reflects just such a concern by beginning her study with the question, "Can one be both Christian and feminist at the same time?",[18] and she explains the crucial positioning of this question at the outset of her study with the claim that, "This question is still one of the central issues for feminist theology"[19].

The imperative for detailed evaluation that marks out the methodological processes of the engagement of feminisms and Christianity is becoming increasingly significant as the presence of feminisms in Christian theologies not only persists, but also fragments and is being questioned by those opposing the underlying values of feminisms as well as by some of those who have traditionally identified themselves with the underlying feminist concerns. Evidence for both the beginnings of such evaluation and the impact and significance this evaluation might bring for feminist theological discourse comes with the 1997 collection *Horizons in Feminist Theology*[20] edited by Rebecca Chopp and Sheila Greeve Davaney. This text marks the emergent questioning of the theoretical identity and perspectives of feminist theologies along with recognition of the ambiguous status of such questioning. Critical evaluation now needs to move on from the question of the compatibility of Christianity and feminisms to identify and assess the types and success of particular strategies that have been developed by different Christian theologians to enable the creative encountering of feminisms and Christianity. As part of this a diverse range of motivations and perspectives needs to be recognised as resourcing and shaping feminist theologies. Feminist theological discourse needs to embrace variously motivated detailed critical interrogation that asks probing questions of the methodological identity of feminist theologies, questions that will sit alongside questions of content. Methodological questions are necessarily a part of understanding the development and identity of Christian feminist theologies.

Feminist Christian Encounters incorporates such a shift of focus away from a discourse characterised by questions of the compatibility or incompatibility of Christianity and feminisms, to one characterised by a focus on method. It identifies some of the key theological and methodological mechanisms by which Christian feminist theologies are informed, sustained and made possible by feminist values and critiques. It argues that certain strategies characterise the facilitation of this dialogue in contemporary Christian feminist theologies, enabling theologians to accept the values and critiques of feminisms whilst at the same time proclaim some level of commitment to Christianity. This, then, moves to a more functional critical approach to Christian feminist theologies, bypassing seemingly immutable questions of the compatibility/incompatibility of feminisms and Christianity. It works from the evidence of existing theologies and it investigates *how* apparently creative and constructive relationships are maintained between feminisms and Christian theology and tradition, rather than theorises about *if* such relationships are possible. In order to do this it engages in a process of uncovering, of deconstruction of the methodologies of key Christian theological thinkers who have made use of feminisms in their theologies, in order to reveal the mechanisms of feminist Christian encounter at work. A diversity of methodological explanations and terms could, and have been elsewhere, given to approaches of the feminist informed theologians whose work will be studied here. Also, a different approach to the whole issue of method in feminist informed Christian theology could have been taken. For example, elsewhere descriptions have been made using the following categorisations of feminist informed theologies: reformist, revolutionary, revisionist, post-traditional, radical, neo-orthodox, liberal, traditional, post-structural, post-colonial and orthodox. And whilst this study will make some reference to such terms, on the whole it takes a more functional approach to describe the strategies employed. In order to carry out this study of the mechanisms of feminist Christian encounter the approach here will be to employ in effect a three-part methodology in which the strategies of feminist Christian encounter are identified and unpacked primarily in relation to theological texts. Whilst recognition is given to the problems facing women, and particular certain groups of women, seeking publication, the focus on texts is because of their accessibility and because, as Mary Hunt commented in 2000 when reflecting on 15 years of *The Journal of Feminist Studies in Religion*, feminist publishing is regarded by feminist informed theologians as feminist praxis.[21]

The emergence of feminisms as a distinct presence in theology will be traced and the dominance of the issue of the compatibility/incompatibility of feminisms and Christianity established. In chapter one the emergence of the historical and conceptual identities of Christian feminist theological discourse will be mapped out. This will involve a detailed consideration of key early feminist theological writings that influenced or characterised the development of Christian feminist theologies. In tracing and evaluating such writings it explores the emerging identity of what has come to be labelled "Christian feminist theology". This will establish a framework for investigating the strategies of feminist Christian encounter in the rest of the study. One of the key points to be established in the historical overview of chapter one is the persistently diverse and vital nature of feminist Christian encounter. The specific and contextual nature of feminist theologies has resulted in problems of exclusion that call for the deconstruction of key concepts and underlying presuppositions of Christian feminist theologies. The diverse picture of feminist Christian encounter in the early twenty-first century is one enriched and challenged by explicit feminist presence and development in a wide variety of social, ethnic and denominational contexts, of which mujerista, womanist and Asian theologies are just some examples.

Chapter two examines in detail one particular and highly significant aspect of the emergence of Christian feminist theologies as outlined in chapter one. It focuses in depth on the Postchristian feminist rejection of Christianity found in the work of influential feminist writers such as Mary Daly, Carol Christ, and Daphne Hampson. It explores the forms and implications of their variously stressed claims that Christianity and feminisms are fundamentally incompatible. This then details the influential discourse of feminist rejection of traditional religions. It argues that the issue of compatibility/incompatibility has dominated not only dialogue between Christian and Postchristian feminists but also Christian feminist theological writings, and critical evaluation of feminist theologies. A key insight here is that the form and content of the Postchristian feminist rejection of Christianity amounts in some cases to a feminist ethical imperative for women to leave traditional religions. Addressing and refuting this alignment of feminisms with the rejection of Christianity underlies and influences many Christian feminist theologies, so that the strategies employed by Christian feminist theologians have an implicit address to these critiques.

Following this *Feminist Christian Encounters* then moves the study of Christian feminist theologies on by exploring in detail the characterising methodologies or strategies of contemporary Christian feminist engagement. Chapters three, four and five each focus on one of three key methods or strategies by which feminist Christian encounter can be seen to be facilitated in contemporary Christian feminist theologies. These three strategies are those of (1) radical reinterpretation, (2) recovery and reconstruction of authentic or original Christianity, and (3) radically contextual queering of Christianity. It will argue that whilst recognising some overlap and diversification of approach that these three strategies are significant to the patterns of feminist Christian encounter to date. In order to engage fully with the radically contextual and specific nature of feminist theologies each of these strategies or methods will be explored primarily in relation to the work of one influential theologian, and their particular use of this strategy unpacked. The identification of these three strategies is not meant as an exercise in defining the whole spectrum of feminist informed Christian theological approaches. Such a task, if possible at all, is clearly beyond the scope of this study.

Also, the contextual range of the theologies explored is limited; for example, there is no sustained study of mujerista or womanist theologies. In that two of the theologians to be featured, Carter Heyward and Elisabeth Schüssler Fiorenza are North American based and one, Marcella Althaus-Reid, is British based and who describes herself as a Latin American theologian in diaspora. The choice of these particular theologians, however, relates to the influence that they have exercised over the range of feminist informed theologies and the groundbreaking impact of their writings.

Chapter three will focus on the strategy of radical reinterpretation that has come to be employed by many different Christian feminist theologians. This approach sees a feminist informed, and often necessarily radical reinterpretation of Christian symbols and traditions that is effective in maintaining what is claimed as a clear conceptual relationship to the traditions of Christianity, whilst at the same time offering a feminist rereading or reinterpretation of the meaning and relevance of these traditions. Here, this approach will be explored through the work of Carter Heyward and particularly her feminist arguments for a compassionate christology of mutual relationship. It will deconstruct the way in which her emphasis on connection and mutual relationship brings Heyward to a feminist reinterpretation of the symbols and traditions of Christianity. Her sustained feminist critical focus on the traditions and images of Jesus brings a radical shift from a theology that stresses the unique revelatory and redemptive significance of Jesus to a theology that emphasises the possibilities of mutuality as evidenced in the life and teachings of Jesus. Heyward's feminist theology, then, through radical reinterpretation of christology and characterised by feminist values of relationship, connection and mutuality, becomes a relational theology of justice that aims to overcome all forms of alienation and injustice, but has particular address to gender and sexual based injustices.

In chapter four the strategy of feminist recovery is identified and explored in relation to the work of Elisabeth Schüssler Fiorenza, and in particular her feminist reconstructionist approach to the recovery and elaboration of the Christian tradition. Schüssler Fiorenza's theology appeals to an understanding of an original or authentic Christian message of equality that she argues has been marginalised and silenced by the patriarchal movements of recorded history and societal and religious development. Her feminist reconstructionist model aims to identify and liberate the egalitarian impulses of the early Christian movement and engage them constructively in contemporary contexts. This egalitarian vision is incorporated and maintained by feminist visions and values. The critical process of discerning or uncovering this egalitarian Christian tradition is guided by women's experiences and feminist informed interpretation of this experience. In Schüssler Fiorenza's feminist approach to the early Christian traditions women's experiences and feminist values are the determining factor in assessing what is and what is not liberating and so, according to her understanding, what is and what is not authentically Christian.

Chapter five details the third key strategy of feminist theological engagement to be identified here, that of the radically contextual queering of Christianity that will be examined with specific reference to the indecenting theology of Marcella Althaus-Reid. Indecent theology argues that Christian theology functions in a constraining way to compel people to behave according to determined orders of (heterosexual) decency. Marcella Althaus-Reid is concerned to queer Christian theology and reveal the underlying orders of decency. Feminisms sit alongside other critical perspectives such as queer thinking, post-colonial thinking, sexual theologies and post-structuralist thinking, as tools of deconstruction. By which the orders of decency underpinned by Christian theology can be interrupted.

This study then moves on from the specific focus on key influential theologians who draw on feminist tools and visions, and begins to build up a picture of Christian feminist theological strategies. Chapter six will take an overview of the three strategies of feminist Christian encounter identified and ask of the roles and authority given to feminisms and Christianity or Christian tradition in each of the strategies in order to move to a clear understanding of how the encounter between feminisms and Christianity is being facilitated. As part of this it will also consider how the problematisation of feminisms is shaping the strategies of feminist Christian encounter. As the underlying "truth" or "liberation" agendas of both feminisms and feminist informed theologies are increasingly being scrutinised and challenged.

The timing of this study is particularly important given that the current climate is one in which multiple criticisms are being made of feminisms and feminist informed theologies. Questions are being asked not only of the effectiveness and future of feminisms and feminist informed theologies, but also of the underlying presuppositions and critical categories that seem to form the basis of such agendas. Most writings on feminist informed Christian theologies are written from a Christian or post-traditional perspective and so inevitably reflect and incorporate relationship to the Christian tradition, be it one of commitment or rejection. My own perspective is that I do not have, and never have had, a committed relationship to Christianity or any other faith tradition. And whilst of course recognising the inevitable influences of a Christian heritage given my context as a British white woman, my own interest and motivation for this study arises in part from a general contextual interest in the influence of organised religion on contemporary culture and society (and in particular Christianity), and also from an interest in the interaction of Christian theology and critical feminist informed perspectives. My concern is with investigating and uncovering the dependencies and relationships that underlie the feminist informed theological project. With the belief that the mechanisms of one of the most interesting (and perhaps transformative or threatening depending on one's perspective) theological developments of Christianity of the late twentieth and early twenty-first centuries have not as yet really been adequately deconstructed to reveal how the often radical critical and justice seeking bases of feminisms are informing Christian theologies. Interest, then, is with how the competing claims to authority of feminisms and Christianity are being organised, facilitated or possibly side stepped through these strategies of encounter. And how feminist informed theologies will respond, and indeed are responding, to the increasingly persistent and convincing criticisms that the Enlightenment inspired agendas of feminisms and feminist informed theologies are no longer viable in an age characterised by diversity, competing authorities and fluid, partial commitments.

Notes

[1] Carmody, D.L., (1995), *Christian Feminist Theology: A Constructive Response*, Oxford: Blackwell Publishers.
[2] Hampson, D., (ed.), (1996), *Swallowing a Fishbone?: Feminist Theologians Debate Christianity*, London: SPCK.
[3] Heyward, C., (1984), *Our Passion for Justice: Images of Power, Sexuality and Liberation*, Cleveland, Ohio: Pilgrim Press.
[4] Welch, S., (2000), *A Feminist Ethic of Risk*, Augsberg Fortress Publishers.
[5] Parsons, S., (1998), *Feminism and Christian Ethics*. Cambridge University Press.
[6] Ruether, R.R., (1997), *Women and Redemption: A Theological History*. SCM.
[7] Isasi-Diaz, A.M., (1997), *Mujerista Theology: A Theology for the Twenty-First Century*, New York: Maryknoll.
[8] Schussler Fiorenza, E., (1999), *Rhetoric and Ethic: The Politics of Biblical Studies*, Minneapolis: Fortress Press.
[9] Althaus-Reid, M., (2000), *Indecent Theology: Theological Perversions in Sex, Gender and Politics*, Routledge.
[10] Grey, M., (2001), *Introducing Feminist Images of God*, Cleveland, Ohio: The Pilgrim's Press.
[11] Daly, M., (1986), [1973], *Beyond God the Father: Towards a Philosophy of Women's Liberation*, London: The Women's Press.
[12] Goldenberg, N., (1979) *Changing of the Gods: Feminism and the End of Traditional Religion*, Boston: Beacon Press.
[13] Hampson, D., (1996), *After Christianity*, Continuum International Publishing Group.
[14] McClintock Fulkerson, M., (1994), *Changing the Subject: Women's Discourses and Feminist Theology*, Minneapolis: Fortress Press.
[15] Sawyer, D.F., and Collier, D.M., (eds.), (1999), *Is There a Future for Feminist Theology?*, Sheffield: Sheffield Academic Press.
[16] Armour, E., (1999), *Deconstruction, Feminist Theology, and the Problem of Difference: Subverting the Race/Gender Divide*, Chicago: The University of Chicago Press.
[17] Young, P.D., (1990), *Feminist Theology/Christian Theology: In Search of Method*, Eugene, OR: Wipf and Stock Publishers.
[18] Young, 1990:7.
[19] Young, 1990:7.
[20] Chopp, R.S., and Davaney, S.G., (eds.), (1997), *Horizons in Feminist Theology: Identity, Tradition and Norms*, Minneapolis: Fortress Press.
[21] Hunt, M.E., in Plaskow, J., et al, (2000), "Publish not perish: celebrating 15 years of struggle", *Journal of Feminist Studies in Religion*, 16(1), p.102.

Chapter One

The Contours of Christian Feminist Theologies

Introduction

In exploring the identity of Christian feminist theologies it is helpful to place the emergence and subsequent development of these theologies into some kind of historical perspective in order to establish an overall framework for analysis. The cultural, social and religious contexts out of which such theologies arose bear testimony to the shape and motivations of these theologies and so hold important clues to understanding their subsequent development and contemporary forms. But also, and perhaps more importantly here, an historical overview gives some sense of any stages or key moves which mark out the process of feminist Christian encounters, and especially early feminist Christian encounters. However, despite the benefits of such a mapping out project, historical perspectives on feminisms and feminist theologies are not easily established. Attempts to represent them accordingly into some kind of clear chronological order often remain at best ambiguous, if not actually misleading and problematic. The gendered silences of recorded history and the dangers of imposing inappropriate definitions and readings on women's experiences mean that the task of locating the historical beginnings of feminist theologies is uncertain and questionable for a number of reasons. Feminist historians and critics claim that the processes of recording history have largely been influenced, if not wholly determined by dominant male group perspectives and interests. So, the experiences, interests and achievements of women have not been recorded in the same way as male experiences and neither have they been given their appropriate place in cultural, social, political and religious history. As such, access to women's history, and to historical perspectives on feminisms, face many obstacles. As Pam Hirsch notes, "Women's lives and women's histories often look different, more diffuse and are (perhaps) harder to evaluate".[1] There is a need to avoid over-simplifying and homogenising the diverse experiences of women in order to present feminisms and feminist theologies into some kind of unified and coherent system, which is a tendency that has so far often proved irresistible and highly destructive, and in many ways has stifled the promise of feminisms and feminist theologies to the extent that some would even contend that it has lead to the end of feminisms as potentially liberative discourse or transformative social action. So, any attempt to locate something as fluid and evasive as "feminisms" or "feminist theologies" is inevitably challenging and potentially problematic. Also, it is possible to argue that there have always been individuals and groups who have displayed what might now be described as a "feminist" approach to religion and theology, and as such there might be said to be a long and substantial tradition of "feminist theologies". So, in this sense, talk of "beginnings" can clearly be misleading and even inaccurate. Given these factors, the task of identifying the "beginnings of feminist theologies" needs careful qualification and needs to be accompanied by a critical appreciation of the difficulties faced. Tension needs to be held throughout any such study between the need to uncover critically motivations and developments which shaped the emergence of feminisms and feminist theologies and the dangers of representing them in a unified whole. Also, any attempt to map out Christian feminist encounters is inevitably partial and selective.

Early Christian feminist encounters

The emergence of feminisms as discernible theological perspectives shadows the rise of feminisms generally. Like the wider feminist movement, feminist theologies are largely understood to have developed in two main impulses, the first in the late nineteenth century and the second beginning in the late 1960s and 1970s. Evidence for the emergence of feminist theologies, in their first phase, is often located with a number of key nineteenth-century writings which are variously celebrated as either heralding or anticipating feminist consciousness, Matilda Joslyn Gage's *Woman, Church and State*[2] (1893) and Elizabeth Cady Stanton's *The Woman's Bible*[3] (1895) are two such texts. Stanton and Gage, along with Susan B. Anthony, were influential figures in the nineteenth-century women's movement in North America and were involved with justice related issues of suffrage, temperance, anti-slavery, the ERA and especially women's rights. As part of their commitment to the promotion of justice, Stanton and Gage gave detailed attention to the causes and sites of gender based inequalities. In the process of such analysis they were particularly critical of the role of Christianity in establishing and perpetuating such injustices. For example, in *Woman, Church and State* Gage located considerable responsibility for gender based oppression with the Christian Church and raised a number of key issues surrounding questions of equality and hope, many of which have featured prominently in feminist theologies since. These focused on issues of priesthood, celibacy and marriage, the possibility and promises of matriarchal societies, and the apparently different codes of morality for men and women advocated by society. The challenges facing the Church, according to Gage were fundamental questions of human existence:

> The most important struggle in the history of the church is that of woman for liberty of thought and the right to give that thought to the world. As a spiritual force the church appealed to barbaric conception when it declared woman to have been made for man, first in sin and commanded to be under obedience. Holding as its chief tenet a belief in the inherent wickedness of woman, the originator of sin, as its sequence the sacrifice of a God becoming necessary, the church has

> treated her as alone under a "curse" for whose enforcement it declared itself the divine instrument. Woman's degradation under it dating back to its earliest history, while the nineteenth century still shows religious despotism to have its stronghold in the theory of woman's inferiority to man.[4]

Gage argued that doctrinal and theological authority legitimised and enforced various gender based oppressions of women, with the effect that women were seen as inherently sinful and morally inferior to men. The implication of Gage's analysis was that religious authority has been used to validate and sustain a gendered hierarchical anthropology and theology. Religion, and in particular Christianity (given Gage's own cultural and religious heritage) were not seen as incidental to gender based oppression but as a central causal factor.

Elizabeth Cady Stanton, like Gage, was an activist and was involved with planning the first women's rights convention in 1848 at Seneca Falls, New York. She too was committed to opposing perceived inequalities of women's lives and as part of this identified the particular significance of the Bible as a tool to silence and marginalise women. Her methodology was one of biblical exploration and analysis and in many ways her work anticipated the extensive critical feminist hermeneutics that have been such a shaping and highly visible aspect of the challenging presence of feminism in Christian theology over the last 35 years. For some such feminist informed biblical scholarship constitutes the most challenging if not threatening aspect of feminist Christian encounter. In the two volume work, *The Woman's Bible*, which emerged in 1895 and 1898, Stanton drew on contemporary insights of biblical scholarship and questioned the role of the Bible in supporting and sustaining historical and contemporary gender based oppression facing women. Stanton's project involved the systematic exegesis of biblical texts from a consciously woman identified stance:

> From the inauguration of the movement for women's emancipation the Bible has been used to hold her in the "divinely ordained sphere", prescribed in the Old and New Testaments.
> ...The Bible teaches that woman brought sin and death into the world, that she precipitated the fall of the race, that she was arraigned before the judgement seat of Heaven, tried, condemned and sentenced. Marriage for her was to be a condition of bondage, maternity a period of suffering and anguish, and in silence and subjugation, she was to play the role of a dependent on man's bounty for all her material wants, and for all the information she might desire on the vital questions of the hour, she was commanded to ask her husband at home. Here is the Bible position of woman briefly summed up.[5]

According to Stanton, historically the Bible had been employed to silence, control and blame women for sin and death, and very significantly, marriage and maternity were seen as the outcome or condition of sin. So, the Bible locates blame with women and then prescribes the ensuing outcome of this as marriage.

It is the comprehensive critical attention of works such as *The Woman's Bible* and *Woman, Church and State* that bring descriptions of them as evidence of feminist theologies in their earliest phase. In many ways, the creative radicalism and methodological sophistication that now characterises contemporary feminist theologies is absent, but there is evident a clear anticipation of the key foci and approaches of Christian feminist theologies. Of particular significance in terms of the development of contemporary Christian feminist theological methods and concerns was, first, the insight that characterising this early Christian feminist theological methodology was the recognition of the complicity of Christianity, and especially the Christian Church, in social injustices, and second, the significance of biblical texts and appeals to such texts in sustaining such injustices. Christianity was understood as being part of past and ongoing gender based injustice. The Bible was interpreted as not only prescribing such injustices but was also the basis of authoritative appeals to sustain these injustices. As such, religion, Christianity, the Bible and the Church, were clearly perceived as obstacles, if not actively opposed, to women's liberation or justice concerns.

This first identifiable feminist Christian activity was clearly related to the emergence of the women's movement. Similarly, it was the second wave of feminisms that heralded the emergence of the more recent roots of what have since been identified as feminist theologies. Given the ethos of creativity and radical challenge in North America and Europe in the 1960s it is not surprising that this time is widely taken to mark the emergence of contemporary feminist theologies. And as with earlier developments it is possible to lay down certain textual markers here. One of the most important indicators of the arrival of significant visible feminist presence in theology was an article by Valerie Saiving, "The human situation: a feminine view" which was published in 1960 in *The Journal of Religion*.[6] The significance of this piece is evident in reflections on the text by contemporary feminist writers or critics. It has been described by both Ursula King and Grace Jantzen as a "landmark"[7] and by Daphne Hampson as "the article which is often taken to mark the beginning of the current wave of feminist theological writing".[8] In many ways Saiving's article is celebrated as the beginnings of contemporary feminist theological discourse. After the earlier development of critical concern of the 1890s there were of course further publications that addressed issue of religiosity and gender, but such publications were methodologically discernibly different from Saiving's work. It is the style and content of Saiving's article, along with subsequent theological engagement with the kind of issues she raised that proved to be a definitive breakthrough in feminist theological engagement in terms of subsequent feminist Christian encounter. And this is despite the fact that at the time her article received very little recognition or acclaim.

One of the most important aspects of Saiving's analysis in "The human situation" was her identification of the theological significance of differentiating between male and female experience (which she termed "masculine" and "feminine" experience). She posited as problematic the traditionally accepted generic use of the term "men" by theologians[9] and explored anthropological studies of the cultural influences of differences between male and female experiences such as Margaret Mead's *Male and Female*[10] and Ruth Benedict's *Patterns of Culture*.[11] Drawing on such works Saiving located in the mother-child relationship, exclusive to women, a key formative role in establishing differentiated female and male identity. Reproductive capability was fundamental to Saiving's ideas about differences between male and female. She referred to female identity in terms of "being" and male identity in terms of "becoming".[12] She claimed that contemporary theology "is not adequate to the universal human situation",[13] it does not allow women to be "both women *and* full human beings".[14] From this, she argued for a discernible difference between female and male experiences of sin, and specifically of what she claimed was women's tendency to servitude, and dependency for identity on others. In terms of the development of Christian feminist theologies, of significance here is Saiving's understanding of the theological implications of differentiating between male and female experiences. Saiving's analysis is based on the fundamental insight that it is male experience that informs and shapes our understanding of reality and the human situation. Also evident is the conviction that a very different understanding would emerge if female experience were part of this shaping process. As Carol Christ and Judith Plaskow have argued:

> Saiving's essay, a landmark in feminist theology, was ten years ahead of its time....Saiving set forth what was to become the basic premise of all feminist theology: that the vision of the theologian is affected by the particularities of his or her experience as male or female.[15]

Saiving articulates here a fundamental feminist epistemological concern about the perception and naming of reality and compounds this concern with the insight that traditional namings, theological and doctrinal, are inadequate for both women and men. Unacknowledged gendered perceptions and linguistics lead to a partial theology, and indeed anthropology, of exclusion and privilege. It is important to note here that even at this very early stage of feminist theological analysis there is the crucial recognition that traditional theologies and their underlying assumptions were detrimental and limiting not only for women but for men as well an important factor when considering the claim that feminisms have simply reversed gender hierarchies. The challenge of Saiving's work is to Christian theological formation, as her analysis focused not so much on the historical and biblical traditions of inequality but on the nature and processes of theological reflection and engagement. Specifically, the insight of Saiving's that has proved fundamental to Christian feminist theological methodology ever since, and has in fact become almost foundational to such methodology, is the recognition of the gendered nature of experience and the striking implications that this has for theology.

The period 1960-1979 was a key phase in the development of feminist theologies and is crucial to understanding subsequent patterns of feminist Christian encounter. The publication of texts such as *The Feminist Mystique*[16] (Betty Friedan, 1963), *The Female Eunuch* (Germaine Greer, 1970) and *Sexual Politics*[17] (Kate Millett, 1970), along with the political and social activism that inspired and accompanied these feminist publications, had a substantial effect on many aspects of critical enquiry and practice. And Christian theology was by no means unaffected by this. For some, however, the feminist label and associated implications were clearly problematic. Certain theological studies in the 1960s explicitly resisted the label 'feminist' and yet seem clearly to employ what might be termed by contemporary analysts as 'feminist' approaches and reflect underlying feminist values. An example of this is Margaret Brackenbury Crook's book *Women and Religion*[18] published in (1964). In this work Crook rejected the label 'feminist' in description of the type of theological project with which she was concerned, claiming that, "Women have a heritage in religion to regain, develop, and carry forward. This is not a feminist movement; it concerns men as well as women and offers benefits to both".[19] Yet, despite such disclaimers to engage with the feminist project Crook talks of the "displacement of women"[20] from full participation in the traditions of Judaism, Christianity and Islam. Her aversion or rejection of the term "feminist" in description of her work appears to be grounded in a concern to stress that the kind of revisionary project she was advocating was the concern of both men and women, and not limited just to women. The subtext here is clearly that feminisms, as perceived by Crook, does not extend to, or include, the experiences of men and so are avoided in order to pursue an inclusive agenda. Crook's insights in *Women and Religion*, and the implications of these insights, would be appropriately characterised by many as "feminist" despite her rejection of the term at the time of writing. This is seen, for example, in the way in which she describes women's positioning in Judaism, Christianity and Humanism:

> If a woman born and bred in any of these faiths takes a comprehensive look at the form of theology best known to her, she discovers that it is masculine in administration, in the phrasing of its doctrines, liturgies and hymns. It is man-formulated, man-argued, and man-directed. To bring this charge against the religious leaders is not to display animosity, it is to recognize the actual state of affairs. In the Christian field, for instance, it is taken for granted that all the leading seminaries are almost entirely man-staffed, all the leading pulpits man-filled, that no woman can ever expect to become Archbishop of Canterbury or fill the Papal chair. Only rarely does a woman serve as representative in the great international assemblies of Christendom.[21]

The explicit address to the nature of feminisms and feminist informed theological approaches found in studies like *Women and Religion* evidences a growing consciousness of the implications of engaging in a certain type of scholarship. It also demonstrates an apparent uneasiness or dissatisfaction with the label "feminist" from very early on in the development of an explicit and systematic concern with theology and gender. This is an issue that has persisted in a variety of forms and since the mid 1980s has influenced a very important discourse concerning the limiting and sometimes explicitly exclusivist functioning and implications of feminist theologies, and today may even be said to be challenging the future of these theologies.

After the publication of Saiving's "The human situation", studies in Christianity and gender based injustice began to emerge with force. One concern that was recognised as of particular significance to the whole issue of women and injustice, and was widely addressed in the 1960s in both North America and Europe, was that of women's access to ordained priesthood in a variety of denominations. Rosemary Lauer, for example raised the question of the theological implications of the recognition of gender based equality and the full humanity of women in terms of ordination and Elisabeth Schüssler Fiorenza, then based in Germany, in "Der Vergessene Partner" ("The Forgotten Partner") argued the case for a critical re-examination of the roles of women in the Church. Biblical evidence relating to questions of gender based equality also emerged as an increasingly important focus at this time. C. Parvey in 1969[22] in "Ordain her, ordain her not" examined the relevant biblical evidence in the debate for and against women's right of access to the ordained priesthood. It is significant to note that this issue of priestly roles remains for many at the heart of the gender justice debate. In the late 1960s the gaining of access to such exclusive priestly roles was seen as absolutely fundamental to challenging male privilege and gendered hierarchies. Today, however, it needs to be acknowledged that the reality of many women's experiences since being ordained to full priesthood has not realised the hopes and expectations previously attached to this.

With feminist theological activity evident in North America, Britain, Germany, the Netherlands and Switzerland, by the late 1960s and early 1970s issues of gender, feminism and theology were clearly a growing concern. In Europe, for example, Kari Børresen published *Subordination and Equivalence*[23] in 1968 and Elisabeth Gössman was an influential feminist voice in Germany.[24] In 1970, *Women's Liberation and the Church: The New Demand for Freedom in the Life of the Christian Church*[25] (edited by Sarah Bentley Doely) was published by the Association Press in America. In this collection a number of influential and emerging theologians addressed a fundamental issue underlying the focus on gender and Christian theology, that of authority. Contributors included Norma Ramsey Jones on women and ministry, Rosemary Ruether on male domination, dualism and new humanity, and Sidney Cornelia Callahan in "A Christian perspective on feminism" raised issues of the compatibility of feminism and Christianity. Peggy Ann Way in her contribution to the collection "An authority of possibility for women in the Church" explored the notion of ministerial authority in the light of the traditional exclusion of women from ministerial orders. The importance of this collection is that it represents a significant consciousness among theologians in the 1970s and illustrates the way in which the increasingly important questions of the theological implications of feminist presence in Christianity were being addressed. Callahan's focus on the impact of feminism on Christianity is an important example of this consciousness in that it demonstrates a perceived clash between competing claims of commitment to Christianity and commitment to feminism. Callahan's article opens with the pertinent (and seemingly irresistible) question of "How can you be a feminist and a Christian at the same time?".[26] A question to which she responds by drawing a clear correlation between her own commitment to Christianity and to feminism, "Without taking Christianity seriously I would never have been prepared to accept radical feminism".[27] She draws parallels between the emphasis and demands of Christianity and those of feminism and, most importantly, for her there is a shared critique and vision based in justice. In her understanding both feminisms and Christianity involve critical appraisal, justice through equality, responsibility to affect change and self-empowerment.[28] This advocating of the common convictions of feminism and Christianity is dominated by notions of freedom and independence and is very much concerned with feminism as transformation, and as gaining equality of opportunity and access for women. Yet even with such an analysis of the shared agendas of Christianity and feminism, Callahan still perceives there to be some kind of conflict or at least issue of primary authority claim between feminist and Christian commitment that needs addressing and resolving. She feels the need to prioritise unequivocally her loyalty or commitment as being primarily to Christianity:

> I guess in the end my feminism must be finally subordinated to the demands of Christian faith. Women's liberation is also not an ultimate value or a cause overriding all others. For me, radical feminism must also be put into a larger context and a longer race. But while radical Christianity and radical feminism share the same course they do move each other along. Or so I have found.[29]

Feminisms, in Callahan's understanding, can perhaps be best or most appropriately described as a specific contextual tool of Christian hope and one that essentially shares the visions and values of Christianity. Seen in this way Christianity is not in conflict with feminism. Rather, Christian commitment, in Callahan's understanding, leads to the acceptance of feminist values and analysis. And very importantly, the justice concerns of feminism, as perceived by Callahan, are in accordance with those of Christianity. There is a sense, then, of continuity and tradition. It is writings like Callahan's "A Christian perspective on feminism" that clearly demonstrates the emergence of detailed critical analysis of the theological implications of feminist Christian encounters and most specifically of a Christian appeal to feminisms. This analysis, from very early on, had some level of address to questions of compatibility and authority. Clearly not all writers addressing issues of women and religion at this time adopted an openly feminist stance, or even utilised the term in description of their analysis. Indeed, some explicitly rejected and opposed feminist insights, and yet the theological forum had been broadened, and various issues relating to gender had been forced into the open. In a sense, the concerns had been identified and articulated, and distinct methodological insights and ways forward began to emerge.

Mary Daly and feminist formations

It is with the theology and philosophy of the North American feminist Mary Daly that the first extensive and sustained critique of Christianity from an explicitly committed feminist standpoint is to be found. The impact of the work of Mary Daly in forging the identity of feminist theologies is without comparison, and the issues and questions she dealt with stand as fundamental concerns to the feminist task in Christianity even today. Daly challenged the very symbols and structures of Christianity in fine detail with her analysis of them as patriarchal and oppressive to women, with substantial accumulative effect. Carol Christ, in recognising the impact and significance of Daly's work in 1977 wrote:

A serious Christian response to Daly's criticism of the core symbolism of Christianity will either have to show that the core symbolism of Father and Son do not have the effect of reinforcing and legitimating male power and female submission, or it will have to transform Christian imagery at its very core.[30]

The weight given here in this study of feminist Christian encounters to Daly's feminist critique of Christianity, particularly in the next chapter, in tracing the methodological and conceptual development of Christian feminist theologies, supports Christ's analysis that it was with Daly's work, and especially *Beyond God the Father*, that the fundamental challenge of feminisms to Christianity was laid down. It is inseparably, both the content and form of Daly's analysis of the encounter of feminisms and Christianity that have been so influential. To this end the impetus and coherence of her analysis stands as a critical guardian, and some might argue shadow, over many aspects of subsequent feminist Christian encounter.

Daly's emerging concern with issues of gender and theology can be seen initially in a number of articles she published in the 1960s. For example, after attending Vatican II, she wrote "A built-in Bias" (1965) which was published in *Commonweal* and began to raise pertinent questions about the role of the Christian Church in effecting and sustaining gender based injustice. Whilst Daly has written many articles and books, which have consistently challenged and defied the boundaries of Christian theologies, it is her first two books that were of particular significance for the developing identity of feminist theologies. She began writing *The Church and the Second Sex* in 1965 and it was published in 1968. It was heavily influenced by Simone de Beauvoir's *The Second Sex* and in it Daly makes the important recognition that the Christian Church, and, in particular, the Roman Catholic tradition out of which she was writing at the time, was patriarchal and oppressive to women. Significantly, at this stage, she argues for a reformist approach to the Roman Catholic treatment of women and to the Church as a whole, which essentially advocated both the possibility and the need for review and reform of Christian theology in the light of feminist critique. *The Church and the Second Sex* charts the historical documentation of Christianity's oppression of women and speaks of "a record of contradiction".[31] Daly saw a clear tension apparent in this documentation between theorising and praxis. There was incongruence between the idealisation and the actual treatment of women. She traced Christianity's misogyny through Christian scripture and in particular in the writings of key theologians such as Augustine, Jerome, Tertullian, Thomas of Aquinas and the nineteenth-century and twentieth-century, especially Leo XIII and Pius XII. Within such traditions, Daly also recognised that certain individual women had been able to attain some level of autonomy despite the extensive and systematic misogyny facing them. Daly claims respite from what she understood as a clear tradition of misogyny in the papacy of John XXIII and with the spirit of *aggiornamento*. She cited the 1963 encyclical *Pacem in Terris* as the "first startling breakthrough on the ideological level".[32] And whilst acknowledging the tentative and limited nature of this breakthrough, Daly clearly places groundbreaking significance in terms of issues of gender and justice with both the

Second Vatican Council and in particular with the contribution of Pope John XXIII. Daly's proposals for post-conciliar advancement involved the pressing need to resist stereotypical representations of women. She drew on contemporary psychological studies and referred to the need for "exorcism"[33] of demonic repression through stereotypes. As Daly perceived it, the task facing those concerned with such exorcism was extensive. It included addressing conceptualising and symbolising, god talk, social transformation and the institutional shape and ordering of the Church. Daly's commitment to this transformative task, however, is clear.[34] She talks of the importance of "commitment to radical transformation of the negative, life-destroying elements of the Church as it exists today",[35] and whilst acknowledging the significance of de Beauvoir's contribution to discussions of women, Church and autonomy, she chooses not a "philosophy of despair" but "a theology of hope",[36] a choice which leaves her undoubtedly at this point "within" the traditions of Christianity.

As Daly developed her feminist critique of Christianity, and worked through what she understood as the implications of accepting a radical feminist critique of Christianity, she increasingly moved away from advocating a feminist reformist approach to Christianity. In 1971 she preached a sermon at the Harvard Memorial Church and led a now famous exodus from the Church. Daly, reflecting on the significance of this refers to it as a planned "walkout from patriarchal religion".[37] The sermon preached embodied the spirit of Daly's radicalism of the time, and makes clear her rejection of traditional religion:

> We cannot really talk about belonging to institutional religion as it exists...the women's movement is an exodus community.....we can affirm *now* our promise and our exodus as we walk into a future that will be our *own* future....Our time has come. We will take our own place in the sun. We will leave behind the centuries of silence and darkness. Let us affirm our faith in ourselves and our will to transcendence by rising and walking out together.[38]

Daly, who was influenced considerably by Paul Tillich, talks of this exodus as "a manifestation of the *Courage to Leave*".[39]

In her most influential book, *Beyond God the Father*, first published in 1973, Daly charts her movement to an alternative Postchristian position. This stands as one of the most important feminist theological texts to date and reflects both the radicalisation of Mary Daly and the wider American feminist awakening or consciousness. In *Beyond God the Father* Daly rejected without exception the possibilities of any kind of effective feminist reform for traditional religion and called for recognition and acknowledgement of the death of such religions for women. There are a number of reasons why *Beyond God the Father* was, and remains even today, such an important text (if not the most important text) for locating the development and identity of Christian feminist theologies. One of the key reasons is that Daly's analysis, extensively and with substantial critical detail, argued for the inherently gendered nature of the symbols, theology, practice, language and institutions of Christianity and then unpacked the ensuing implications of these for issues of women and justice. Her analysis formed the basis of her explicit and uncompromising rejection of the possibility and authenticity of Christian feminist theologies. More than this, Daly formulated her critique in such a way as to align the acceptance of feminisms, and all that feminisms stood for, with the rejection of Christianity and other traditional religions. Largely because of this critical positioning of feminisms and traditional religion, and especially Christianity, *Beyond God the Father* marks the beginnings of the sustained debate about the compatibility of Christianity and feminism that has so occupied those engaged with Christian feminist theologies ever since. Further, more detailed consideration is given to Daly's influential rejection of Christianity in chapter two with a particular focus on the dominant discourse of the compatibility/incompatibility of feminism and Christianity that has its contemporary roots in Daly's critical feminist analysis.

Christian feminist voices of revision

Daly's work, in its radicalism, eloquence and promise, has been responded to in a wide variety of ways as Christian feminist theologies have developed. Among those advocating reform at the time *Beyond God the Father* was published was Rosemary Ruether, who was also based in North America and working out of the Roman Catholic tradition. Her contribution to the early feminist theological formations also had a distinctive influence on the shape and direction of this theology, although in a very different way to Mary Daly. She stands as one of the most prolific and widely read feminist theologians to date. Ruether's theology, with all of its diverse concerns and its contextual foci, articulates a fundamental methodology that identifies, elaborates and rejects situations of injustice. Her work has been concerned with the role of theology and religion in relation to the uncovering of systematic injustices, and the promotion of the rights of all to full humanity. In 1971, Ruether wrote:

> The building of a new world has to begin on the grass roots level, in the basic units of human relation, for this is where the history of subjugation and domination first began and where its basic imagery is still vested.[40]

The situations and theoretical bases of oppression that Ruether has consistently addressed in her work since the 1960s, include, the historical development of Christianity in legitimising sexism, racism, Christian anti-Semitism, classism, militarism and the environmental crisis. Her earliest work was concerned specifically with ecclesiology and anti-Semitism and in the late 1960s Ruether developed a critique of the institutional Church and offered proposals for a radical ecclesiology[41] which encapsulated an alternative vision of Church and humanity. A key aspect of this radical ecclesiology as it developed was a critique of the "patriarchal" nature of the Church. By 1971 Ruether was focusing specifically in her critical theological writings on issues of women and liberation, and throughout the 1970s the influence of her distinctive work on the increasing diversity of feminist Christian encounters was considerable. She addressed many different aspects of what she perceived to be the denial of full humanity of women by the Church and Christian theology. Significant writings of Ruether in this early phase of feminist theological development drew particular attention to both the underlying dualism of oppression, and the interdependency of various forms of oppressions and oppressive relationships. Gender based injustice was seen as one form or type of injustice, and one that stands alongside, and was often tied up with other injustices of race, class and sexuality. Also, for Ruether, and many other critical thinkers, injustice was underpinned and arose out of dualistic frameworks, which split and oppose humanity based on perceived difference. Difference, then, was essentially interpreted negatively and ranked accordingly. From such analysis developed the argument that dualisms, and in particular, hierarchical dualisms, needed to be challenged and replaced with a more holistic framework or understanding of humanity and the world. This more holistic, undifferentiated understanding that was advocated was understandable in its origins and intentions, but has proved hugely problematic and arguably ineffective according to its original intention. Blanket descriptions and representations of both women's experiences and of feminisms, it is argued by many, have betrayed the diversity and reality of women's lives.

Fundamental to the reformist feminist approach developed by Ruether in the 1970s was the conviction that the Christian tradition *is* a possible basis from which to develop a liberating feminist theology. By this Ruether seems to mean that Christian theology is not incidental to human justice or can simply be seen as compatible with it on some levels, but actually has justice concerns at its heart. In both actually identifying and overcoming injustice she claimed that Jesus specifically criticised religious and social injustice. Ruether turns to liberation theology and talks about the radicalisation of prophetic critique.[42] She identifies the fundamental task of liberation theology as overcoming alienation that Christianity has legitimised and perpetuated. Importantly, liberation theology for Ruether is not just critique it is essentially constructive as well.[43] In *New Woman, New Earth*[44] published in 1975 Ruether identified and traced the patterns of domination and alienation which she claimed characterised Western societies, focusing especially on the "unholy alliance" of religion and sexism. She traced the shifting patterns of women's oppression, through early tribal culture, urbanisation, and industrialisation and to the contemporary feminist movement. The relationship of feminism to other liberation movements is crucial for Ruether and she examines the interdependent oppressions of racism, sexism, anti-Semitism and the ecological crisis:

> Women must see that there can be no liberation for them and no solution to the ecological crisis within society whose fundamental model of relationship continues to be one of domination.[45]

According to Ruether, the action needed in the face of the extensive and interrelated oppressions that face humanity is wide-ranging and fundamental; it involves a transformation of the underlying worldview. A worldview, which according to her understanding is characterised by patterns of alienation and domination to "an alternative value system".[46] Ruether acknowledges that the specifics of such a view are unclear, but is very clear about the gravity of the current situation. However, from Ruether's writings of the 1970s it is evident that the kind of worldview she is envisaging will be vehemently opposed to dualistic hierarchicalism and that the feminist movement is a site of great hope.[47] This new worldview or commitment to change is also essentially communal and will be characterised by the development of "a new communal social ethic".[48] So, along with Daly, in employing feminist based critique and in appealing to feminist values, Ruether envisages a radical theological departure that will be essentially communal in nature, and cites the women's movement as critical resource for this change. Ruether's feminist informed vision is unambiguously reformist in its approach and intention but nevertheless carries quite radical implications for the organisation, symbols and language of Christianity:

> Perhaps the task of Christians today, as they take stock of this tradition and its defects, is not merely to vilify its inhumanity but rather to cherish the hard-won fruits of transcendence and spiritual personhood, won at a terrible price of the natural affections of men and the natural humanity of women. Without discarding these achievements, we must rather find out how to pour them back into a full-bodied Hebrew senses of creation and incarnation, as male and female, but who can now be fully personalized autonomous selves and also persons in relation to each other, not against the body, but in and through the body.[49]

Developing feminist biblical hermeneutics and historical studies

As the 1970s advanced, identifiable fields of feminist theological engagement began to emerge. Fields of feminist engagement characterised or distinguished by method, discipline area, type of ensuing faith commitment and specifics of denominational grouping. By 1975, in terms of discipline area, the field of biblical feminist hermeneutics in particular was a central concern and feature of feminist theologies, reflecting the concerns and tendencies of the earlier wave of feminist theology. Here, the work of Elisabeth Schüssler Fiorenza contributed an enormous amount, in terms both of the formative explorations of the notion of "feminist theology", and of explorations in biblical feminist hermeneutics with her feminist informed reconstructionist approach to early Christian history. Schüssler Fiorenza's early work stressed that feminism is characterised by a concern with the full humanity of women and with the ensuing demands on the development of full personhood. Like so many others, including Daly and Ruether, she located particular responsibility for women's oppression with Christian theology, and with the underlying value system and with the structures that embody such values.[50] In the face of such analysis she proposed substantive change to the way in which theology was understood and approached. Significantly, along with many subsequent feminist thinkers in theology, Schüssler Fiorenza drew on contemporary critical thinking and rejected the view of theology as objective, value-free scholarship. She argued that theology is very much the product of each individual or group's experiences, and so is determined in form and content by the historical and social context of the theologian. As such, theology can be said to reflect or serve the interests of a particular group or individual.[51] This insight, subsequently refined by feminist theologians and other theologians stressing the contextual nature of theology, centres on the claim that theology is influenced by, and so inevitably reflects, certain interests. Set against this, however, is the claim that the interested nature of theology has largely gone unacknowledged and that instead a myth of theology as objective has perpetuated and dominated understandings of Christian theology. Traditional theology has been represented as universally valid, when in fact it has served the interests of certain groups and individuals. Feminist theologians argue that, generally, theology reflects male interests and ignores or even excludes the interests and experiences of women and other marginalised groups. This exclusion of experiences, other than patriarchal experiences, is hidden and denied by the way in which theological and indeed most traditional scholarship is perceived. For Schüssler Fiorenza, the committed and interested nature of theology must be acknowledged, and the nature of its interests explored and critiqued.

Christian theology is not a politically or socially disinterested endeavour. It not only has the responsibility of acknowledging its partisan nature but, as Schüssler Fiorenza understands it, it has the task specifically of reflecting the interests of the poor and oppressed. This is an insight of fundamental importance to any conceptual survey of the roots of Christian feminist theologies as it moves feminist theologies away from being solely a tool of analysis to one of both critical commitment and specific social concern. Feminist theology, according to Schüssler Fiorenza, is based firmly in a vision and commitment to "an emancipatory ecclesial and theological praxis".[52] This, then, reflects Schüssler Fiorenza's own understanding of theology and of the specific nature of Christian theology as an advocacy theology. According to Schüssler Fiorenza only when theology is on the side of the outcast and oppressed, as she claims Jesus was, can it become fully incarnational and Christian. Christian theology, therefore, has to be rooted in emancipatory praxis and solidarity in order to be authentically Christian. She sees feminist hopes for Christianity as well grounded and locates great significance with a revisionist feminist informed critique of Christianity:

> A comparison between radical feminist spirituality and the Christian spirituality which understands the Spirit, not in a platonic sense but in the biblical sense of the divine power and dynamic enabling us to live as Christians, can show that both are inspired by the same vision, even though radical feminist spirituality is often formulated over and against a patriarchal theology and sexist praxis of the Christian churches.
>
> In my opinion, the Goddess of radical feminist spirituality is not so very different from the God whom Jesus preached and whom he called "Father".[53]

Schüssler Fiorenza's vision of the promise of a feminist informed Christian praxis engaged and further developed the insight regarding the traditional absence of women from explicit theological formation. In her work on biblical feminist hermeneutics and early church history, Schüssler Fiorenza takes forward her vision of the transformatory effects of the inclusion of women's experiences. In "Women in the early Christian movement" which was included in the collection *Womanspirit Rising: A Feminist Reader in Religion*,[54] edited by Carol Christ and Judith Plaskow, Schüssler Fiorenza drew attention to the way in which the Bible has been used both as evidence for, and against, the subordination of women. Citing Galatians 3:28 as evidence, she claimed that the Jesus movement was, in its earliest forms, inclusive:

> The new self-understanding of the early Christian movement is expressed in Galatians 3:28. In the new, Spirit-filled community of equals all distinctions of race, religion, class, and gender are abolished. All are equal and one in Jesus Christ.[55]

She argues that women played key roles as apostles, prophets and leaders in the early Church, and this, especially in her later writings, becomes a focus for Schüssler Fiorenza's feminist reclamation of the liberation nature of Christianity. She proposed a radical reconstructionist approach to the recovery and elaboration of women's Christian history and heritage, which she argues should serve as a lived model of inclusive Christianity, relevant for contemporary Christianity:

> Much of women's "her-story" in early Christianity is lost. The few references which survived in the New Testament records are like the tip of an iceberg indicating what we have lost. Yet at the same time they show how great the influence of women was in the early Christian movement.[56]

Questions of biblical evidence and interpretation in relation to gender based differentials and especially in relation to the Christian Church's attitude to women emerged in this early period as a central concern of Christian feminist theologies. Along with Schüssler Fiorenza, many other writers concerned with feminism and Christianity, in some form or another addressed this issue, of feminism, traditional authority and experience.[57] Among the most influential of the biblical scholars of the 1970s was Phyllis Trible who in *God and the Rhetoric of Sexuality*[58] (1978) explored the ways in which biblical texts have been taken to support sexism. Informed by rhetorical criticism, Trible proposed a hermeneutics of reinterpretation of key biblical texts and language. Other writings of this time focused specifically on the Hebrew Bible (and especially the Genesis creation accounts), the Pauline passages and the gospel narratives.

Coupled with this developing feminist hermeneutics, studies of the past traditions of Christianity also emerged as important at this time. Influential theologians such as Barth and Tillich came under critical feminist scrutiny, as did key periods in Christian history, such as the early Church and the reformation. An important publication in this field that exemplifies the ways in which feminist critical engagement with historical traditions emerges as a pressing concern of feminist theologies was *Women in Christian Tradition* (1973) by George H. Tavard. The work of Eleanor McLaughlin was also important here. In "The

Christian past: does it hold a future for women?" first published in 1975 McLaughlin proposed certain methodological insights which she argued were necessary for a feminist revisionist approach to reclaiming Christian history. She then engaged this method with reference to women's religious lives of the high and late Middle Ages. For McLaughlin, the recognition of the male perspective on church history leads to a problematic resistance to a feminist valuing of Christian history:

> Understandable as this bias is against Christian tradition and the study of the Christian past, I wish to take a methodological stand beyond the antihistoricism of radical Christian feminism while at the same time rejecting the irrelevance, incompleteness, and admittedly often unconscious sexism of much of traditional church history. This alternative or revisionist approach to the Christian past seeks to set forth a history that is at once *responsible* that is, grounded in the historicist rubric of dealing with the past on its own terms and *usable*. I mean by the search for a usable past a phrase recognized by historians who lived through the 1960s an examination of Christian history with a new set of questions that arise out of commitments to wholeness for women and for all humanity. Following from new questions, this is a history that redresses omissions and recasts interpretations.[59]

The revisionist feminist approach to Christian history then was grounded in both the acknowledgement of the patriarchal nature of recorded history, and the belief in the significance of the recovery of women's Christian past.

Post-traditional feminist informed theological engagement

A very important response in the development of feminist theologies in the 1970s was the emergence of feminist theologies based in non-traditional religiosity or spirituality. This development is important here for the nature of its articulated, often uncompromising, rejection of Christianity as a possible resource for feminist spirituality. Following the general direction of Daly's rejection of Christianity, and other traditional religions, on the basis of their irretrievably patriarchal nature, some writers moved on to the constructive task of engaging in the search for alternative bases and language for feminist theologies. One of the most influential of writers here was Carol P. Christ, who in 1975[60] made a self-declared move beyond traditional religion. For Christ, discerning authority was firmly with the diverse and situated experiences of women. The nature and depth of women's alienation from their own experiences, as Christ understands it, is such that the process of authentication and self-realisation will be long and complicated, and yet for Christ the time for such a process is now. Women's experiences, and especially the particular nature of women's experiences, are the proper perspectives of theological feminist claims. The inclusion of experience in theology, and the emphasis on relationship as connection, leads to a methodology, which is critical, constructive, and based in pluralistic awareness.

Having moved beyond the Christian tradition, because of what she experienced as its deeply rooted sexism, Christ explored other sources for the development of a feminist theology or "thealogy" as thinkers such as Christ, Culpepper and Goldenberg named such engagement and reflection. Part of Christ's concern and engagement with non-traditional sources of religiosity for women led her in her earlier work to focus on the stories and poetry of contemporary women writers. Her ideas here are grounded in the conviction that stories are an important part of human existence. They play a significant role in the search for meaningfulness, in understanding, shaping and reflecting experience, "Stories give shape to experience, experience gives rise to stories".[61] Christ locates revolutionary significance with the telling of women's stories by women themselves. Through critical analysis of the work of contemporary selected women writers, especially Doris Lessing, Christ traced a spiritual, liberationist quest myth in feminist writings. Such writings track women's experiences of oppression and exclusion, to awakening into wholeness and autonomy. Women's writings become in Christ's work a key source of women's spirituality. As she herself noted in the first edition of the *Journal of Feminist Studies in Religion*, "Naomi Goldenberg was right when she said that I was treating women's writings as sacred texts".[62] It was the lack of stories and symbols of women in traditional religion that drew Christ to literature at this time and to other resources in later years.

A distinguishing feature of post-traditional feminist theologies is its focus on the language, symbols and traditions of the goddess. Naomi Goldenberg in her 1979 publication *Changing of the Gods: Feminism and the End of Traditional Religion*[63] made clear the radical implications of committed recognition that traditional religion as patriarchal and intrinsically oppressive to women. She argued that feminist analysis and criticism of Christianity and of God is in effect bringing about the downfall of traditional religion. For Goldenberg, feminism and Christianity are irreconcilable. Christianity, with its male saviour, in her view, cannot support the liberation of women. As Mary Jo Weaver has pointed out, 1979 represents an important year in the development of feminist theological or *thea*logical[64] concern with the goddess. In this year two important books were published, Margot Adler's *Drawing Down the Moon*[65] and Starhawk's *The Spiral Dance*.[66] In *Drawing Down the Moon* Adler was concerned generally with neopaganism and feminists often regard Starhawk's *The Spiral Dance* as a handbook of witchcraft. By the 1980's concern with the goddess can be seen to be widespread and manifested in many different ways. As feminist thealogians variously engaged them, the images and symbols of the goddess offered alternative sources and possibilities for understanding and responding to contemporary life. Many feminists turned to the symbols and traditions of the goddess in the face of probing questions of feminist analysis, finding a concern with a connection to nature and the whole of life.

Feminist informed theologies by 1979

By 1979 the depth and scope of feminist theological writings was substantial and although the primary focus here has been on the most visibly influential texts of early Christian feminist theologies, this by no means accounts for the wealth of writings produced at this time. An explicit theological concern with issues of gender and religion, was apparent in a variety of traditions. It is important to stress that the term "feminist theology", even at this early time, did not solely refer feminist critical thinking and practice within Western Christian traditions. Encounters with feminisms were apparent in a range of religious traditions and contexts. Questions of women's status and role had emerged in many different ways and with differing degrees of radicalism, for example, in relation to the traditions and practices of Judaism, Islam, Buddhism, Hinduism and Taoism. Fatima Mernissi's *Beyond the Veil*,[67] published in 1975, signifies the critical consideration of issues of gender and justice in Islam. In Judaism, questions of feminism gained particularly high profile, for example, focusing particularly on issues of god-language and women's inclusions in prayer quorum etc. were addressed.[68] The relationships between different feminist theologies are complex and criticisms of theologies as incorporating into their fundamental analysis criticisms of particular religious traditions has proved problematic in the development of feminist theologies. For example, one major issue that has emerged is that of Christian feminist anti-Semitism. Judith Plaskow has developed as a key critical voice in Jewish feminism, and along with other Jewish feminists, has argued that patterns of domination and exclusion were being enshrined in the conceptual and ethical foundations of Christian feminist theology, despite its professed liberation concerns. The underlying criticism here is that Christian feminists were placing blame for the rise of patriachalism on Judaism, with resultant anti-Semitic tendencies in subsequent Christian feminist theologies. This indicates something of the complexity of injustice, oppression and "patriarchalism".

A further very important differential shaping feminist theologies were particular Christian heritages, denominational affinities and political and social contexts. As early as 1979, Ada Maria Isasi-Diaz, a very influential Hispanic theologian who has been key to the development of mujerista theology, was raising fundamental critical questions about women in Latin American churches[69] and in doing so highlighting issues of racism and exclusion alongside those of gender and exclusion. Within different Christian traditions and within different religious traditions generally, specific issues and areas of concern emerged as important, often related to the specific cultural and historical experiences of the religious tradition in question. From the variety of religious and theological contexts within which questions of feminisms have emerged, there are certain areas of concern that can be seen to be generally important and of concern to feminist theological discourses. These include issues of god-language, ethics, scripture, religious language, ritual and celebration, religious organisation, leadership roles, peace, ecology, motherhood, sexuality, poverty, racism and women's work.

Many of the works referred to so far in this focus on the emerging roots of Christian feminist theologies were written from North American and European perspectives. The proliferation of works in these contexts has inevitably been reflected in the way in which feminist theologies are characterised and understood. However, if the nature and depth of feminist informed theologies are to be fully represented then attention must be paid to crucial diversity of context, form and concern in feminist theologies. This diversity was evident, in embryo at least, as early as 1979. A useful indicator of the dynamics and particulars of this diversity in the late 1970s is available by examining the 1979 collection *Womanspirit Rising*. Edited by Carol Christ and Judith Plaskow, this text brought together writings of women from different traditions, with different concerns and employing a range of feminist theological methods. Plaskow and Christ in the preface wrote:

> Womanspirit Rising brings together the positive and constructive articles on women and religion that our students have been reading in the library over the past several years. We have found that the historical, theological, and ritual pieces collected here provide a clear overview of constructive feminist writing in religion.[70]

Reflecting on the collection in the preface to the 1992 edition, Christ draws attention to the limitations of the diversity of voices represented at this time. Noting particularly the "absence of voices of color, the invisibility of lesbians, and....a failure to discuss class and educational background",[71] all of these have since emerged as central issues in feminist discourse. However, whatever critique is made of the criteria for inclusion, the visible faces of feminist theologies at this time, are evident in *Womanspirit Rising*. Also, the structure of the collection suggests distinct key areas of concern for feminist theologians at this time as being: the theoretical underpinning of feminist theologies, feminist historical reconstruction, revision of tradition and creating new traditions, many of which were explored in relation to Christianity, goddess religion and Judaism.

In review of the period 1960 to 1979, from the seeds of developing feminist consciousness there emerged a range of critical perspectives characterised by feminist informed values and methodologies. From the concerns of the 1960s, the 1970s fashioned a distinctly "feminist" approach to questions of religion, ethics and theology, which can be broadly described as identifying and rejecting gender based oppression. The range of concerns, and the religious and social contexts that gave rise to questions of feminism in the 1970s were vast, and it is on these revolutionary foundations that feminist theologies since the 1980s have built, dismantled, reconfigured and dismantled again the issues, practices and visions of justice of Christian theologies.

The post 1970s diversification of feminist theological discourse

In the 1980s, as feminist theological perspectives rapidly expanded, their diverse forms and settings became increasingly apparent and decisive. Diversities of culture, class, race, ethnicity, sexuality, religious commitment and existential perspective lead to a multi-faceted feminist presence in Christian theology. In Britain, for example, in the early 1980s the feminist theological scene was establishing itself with some force. The influence of writers such as Daly, Ruether,

Schüssler Fiorenza and Christ was apparent but British feminist theologians began to seek and develop their own voices in exploration of the theological implications and determinants of gender based injustice. To date, the emergence and development of feminist Christian encounters in British contexts has not been the focus of much sustained critical study, but as Jenny Daggers stresses, it is important to recognize the distinctness of the British Christian movement and not to subsume it, "...beneath the defining project of dominant North American feminist theology".[72] Daggers' study goes some way in beginning this process with its analysis of the British Christian women's movement of the 1970s and 1980s. What is clear is that many of the earlier works of British feminist informed theology were influenced by, or were in some way related to, issues of Church and ordained priesthood.

Key voices in Britain addressing issues of gender and religion, and drawing on feminist based analysis in the 1980s include Mary Grey, Ursula King, Ann Loades, Sara Maitland, Monica Furlong, Elaine Storkey and Janet Morley. Pointing beyond Britain to the wider European picture, Mary Grey identifies the post-1985 years as distinctive in the development of European feminist theologies, signified in part by a move away from the Church, indeed in some cases, Christianity. She also identifies a significant need for dialogue and pluralism in recognition of diversity:

> The need for a new pluralism is deeply felt, with a consequent need for a decrease in the dominance of Christian feminist theology and an emphasis on dialogue with Jewish and Muslim women scholars, as well as others of the great world faiths.[73]

For some, the unfolding and diversification of feminist theological perspectives was problematic, and for others liberating. So, despite the fact that many of the most public or visible voices of feminist theologies (and some would argue that this remains so today) were often largely those of North American and European women, feminist theological activity was vital and pervasive. Within this critical milieu a number of issues arose which posed difficult questions about the identity, claims, voice and future of feminist informed theologies, issues which all focused on the perceived experiential nature of theology and the implications of such a claim for feminist informed theologies. Recognition of the problematic valuing of women's experiences is crucial not only for an understanding of the development of feminist theologies but is also crucial to any attempt to explore the identity of Christian feminist theologies.

Ever since Saiving's work in the 1960s feminist theological writings have focused in detail, and in many different ways, on the place and understanding of experience in feminist theologies. One of the fundamental insights here has been the recognition of the traditional absence of women's experience from theology. Having made such an assessment different feminist writers address this absence in various ways. Recognition of absence, however, has not translated smoothly into inclusion in feminist theologies. Feminist theologies, like feminisms generally, have struggled with the consequences of what has proved both a vital and problematic insight. For having proposed the importance of recovering and valuing women's experiences, questions then needed to be asked of whose experience is being referred to, and who decides on it value? Mary McClintock Fulkerson points out that "Early criticisms from women of colour, lesbian women, and class-based feminisms noted the false universal in feminist appeals to women".[74] Since the 1980s the claim has been extensively made, that, in fact, feminist theologies have proved as limiting and exclusive in their understanding of experience as traditional theologies. The criticism made is that the experience of a quite narrow, relatively privileged group of women is being set up as normative. So, accusations of exclusion have been made in relation to a fundamental principle of feminist theologies. Audre Lorde in a letter to Mary Daly written in 1980 claims:

> I feel that you do celebrate differences between white women as a creative force toward change, rather than a reason for misunderstanding and separation. But you fail to recognize that, as women, these differences expose all women to various forms and degrees of patriarchal oppressions, some of which we share and some of which we do not
>
> The oppression of women knows no ethnic nor racial boundaries, true, but that does not mean it is identical with these differences.[75]

On one level, this criticism of exclusivism can be said to be a criticism of the failure of feminisms to recognise their particularity, in so far as they are based in a certain group's or individual's experience. Also, it is an issue of the universal and particular relevance of feminisms for women. The problem has proved pressing because despite the fact that feminisms (and feminist theologies specifically) are concerned with gender inequality, they are determined in form and interests by particular contexts. So, some of the difficulties inherent in feminist theologies are linked to their identity as being fundamentally bound up with experience. Ellen Leonard has argued that the shift in theology, which has come to recognise and use experience as a foundation for theology, has led feminist thinkers to the realisation of the need for "a new epistemology".[76]

The voices of women outside the mainline Christian traditions have emerged with strength and depth, as key critical forces in feminist theologies to challenge the understanding of what constitutes women's experience. Asian feminist theologies, mujerista theologies and womanist theologies, for example, have stressed that no one group of women's experience is normative, and that feminist theologians, like all theologians, should be aware of their own commitments and influences. Some white Christian feminist theologians, recognising the difficulties surrounding the way in which women's experience has so far been understood in feminist theologies, have attempted to address the issues of the functioning of women's experiences here. Anne Carr in her editorial reflections in *Women, Work and Poverty*[77] (1987) acknowledged that feminist theologies did indeed emerge out of the experiences of middle-class women, but argued that through self-criticism they have subjected themselves to challenging and transformative questions. Judith Plaskow and Carol Christ argued that the realisation of the failure of feminism to reflect adequately the diversity of experiences found among women brings the obligation to recognise and pursue its important implications for feminist theologising, "To continue using the concept of women's experience under these circumstances obligates us to uncover and describe the diversity it encompasses".[78]

The critical recognition being made by theologians concerning the limiting and unreflective way in which feminist theologies have understood experience necessitates change. For many it has become strikingly apparent that feminist theologies in order to fulfil their liberation theological agenda for women must remain open to transformation through self-criticism, if indeed this liberation theological agenda is their concern today. Such openness is seen as necessary to deal with the fundamental but very challenging contention that being a woman is bound up closely with the kind of woman one is. Increasingly within feminist theologies there is evident a committed concern to remain consistently aware of diversity. Emily Culpepper argues that, "If we are genuinely committed to hearing the voices of women of color, this commitment will interrupt and change that basic academic enterprise the search for sources".[79] This will involve celebration of diversity as a significant, distinctive quality. Unity that forsakes the reality of the diversity of experience is of no real value in terms of the vision and effectiveness of feminist theologies.

As will be examined in chapters five and six, since the late 1990s some of the most challenging and insightful of feminist informed theological engagement has emerged from a diversity of contexts and heritages, which leads Kwok Pui-lan to claim that "Feminist theology has become a global movement".[80] Here, the voices of Asian, Asian American, African, African American and Hispanic/Latina women are important. From these, for example, there have emerged distinct mujerista and womanist theological perspectives, to name but two. Since Alice Walker's proposal of the term "womanist" the term has been variously developed and elaborated by black women to locate their work and concerns as within a certain tradition. The term articulates the ambiguity of black feminist informed positions in powerful and convincing terms. It draws attention to the gender aware critical perspectives of the womanist whilst at the same time stresses the particular and grounded nature of black, and indeed all, women's experiences. Delores Williams and Katie Cannon are two womanist writers who have developed very influential womanist theological and ethical perspectives. Cannon describes well the ambiguity of womanism to both feminist theologies and black male theologies:

> Intrigued by the largely unexamined questions that have fallen through the cracks between feminist ethics and Black male theology, the womanist scholar insists on studying the distinctive consciousness of Black women within Black women's institutions, clubs, organizations, magazines and literature. Appropriating the human condition in their own contexts, Black women collectively engage in revealing the hidden power relations inherent in the present social structures. A central conviction is that theo-ethical structures are not universal, colorblind, apolitical, or otherwise neutral. Thus, the womanist ethicist tries to comprehend how Black women create their own lives, influence others, and understand

themselves as a force in their own right. The womanist voice is one of deliverance from the deafening discursive silence which the society at large has used to deny the basis of shared humanity.[81]

Ada Isasi-Diaz in *Mujerista Theology: A Theology for the Twenty-First Century* describes mujerista theology as "liberative praxis" which arises from the situation of Latina/Hispanic women[82] that works with a keen awareness of the limitations of European and American feminist theologies.[83] She distinguishes between the different stages in her own development, talking of when she was "born a feminist"[84] and when she was a "born a mujerista".[85] She argues that the preferential option of mujerista theology is for Latina women[86] and that this theology has a communal nature. However, despite this, she does not attempt to incorporate all Latina/Hispanic women into a unity. She reflects the diversity of locations or "locus theologicus"[87] that mujerista theologians work from and stresses the need for sensitivity to pluralism of women. It has a very strong liberation theological base, where liberation is seen as "the criterion by which we judge what is right or wrong, what is good or bad, what is salvic or condemnatory".[88] For her, mujerista theology is grass-roots liberation theology, which is concerned with community and with embracing diversity in which "epistemological vigilance refers to the need to avoid avoidance".[89]

There is now a wide acceptance that if feminist theologies are to stand as liberating theologies for women, then they must more fully reflect the experiences of women in their great diversity. Feminist theologians are stressing that experience of class; race, religion and culture are important differences among women, as are their experiences of oppression. Maura O'Neill in identifying the importance of recognising difference in interreligious dialogue between women argues that:

> The meaning of concepts such as oppression, liberation, and feminism cannot be assumed...the women who come together to dialogue must forsake a preconceived notion of specific unifying factor to launch this discussion. One cannot assume that all of the women have either been oppressed or have seen their religion as excluding them in any way.[90]

Studies of method have also begun to impact the overall picture of feminist informed theologies. Pamela Dickey Young's *Feminist Theology/Christian Theology*,[91] which was published in 1990, was a significant study of the methods of feminist informed theologies and it gave particular attention to the methodological significance of women's experiences. Studies such as Chopp, R.S., and Davaney, S.G., (eds.), (1997), *Horizons in Feminist Theology: Identity, Tradition and Norms*[92] mark a new kind of interrogation of the bases and informants of these theologies. *Horizons in Feminist Theology* includes contributions from theologians such as Rebecca Chopp, Sheila Greeve Davaney, Paula Cooey, Serene Jones, Thandeka and Mary McClintock Fulkerson. It carries forward their previous work[93] in relation to questions of the theoretical underpinnings of feminist informed theologies, subjectivity, gender and feminist theory, and proposes a new kind of study of the methodological workings of such theologies. Chopp and Davaney argue that *Horizons in Feminist Theology*, among other things, "is one example of the coming of age of a new generation of feminist theologians".[94]

Feminist informed Christian theologies in the early 2000s

In the early 2000s the range of feminist informed Christian theologies is vast and constantly shifting, and the justice concerns and expressions of these theologies diverse. Feminist theological concerns are transdisciplinary and specific, and are found in varieties of cultural, sexual and social contexts. The issues addressed and explored in such theologies are numerous, and studies in theory and feminist theologies are emerging as an essential part of this landscape. There is lengthy debate of the linguistic restrictions and possibilities of feminist theologies and issues of exclusion and priority must be addressed as part of the inherent justice centred perspective of Christian feminist theologies. The picture that has been outlined here is partial and interpreted, but what has been stressed is that more than ever, the theory, practice and theological workings of Christian feminist theological discourse must be subject to detailed scrutiny. The appearance of diversity, based on experience, is profoundly challenging to the notion of Christian feminist identity. And within such a diverse landscape the question of the identity of Christian feminist theologies is difficult but illuminating. Critical study of these theologies is necessarily accompanied by informed, explicit reservations. It not only must acknowledge the situated and particular experiences of women both of oppression and of visions of justice, but also actually place these at the heart of critical evaluation.

The fact that today it is increasingly difficult to pin down dominant feminist theological voices, bears witness to the diverse level of activity that is actually taking place in feminist informed theologies. At the same time, however, the intense contextual stress found in many feminist informed theologies does mean that many theologies remain most recognisable through particular theologians' work rather in than generic categories. In Britain and Ireland feminist informed theological publications are claiming both increasing visibility and reflecting a range of theological and cultural contexts. The British and Ireland School of Feminist Theology, the journal *Feminist Theology* and the Introductions in Feminist Theology book series are important contributors to the field of contemporary feminist informed theologies here. The work and involvement of theologians such as Elizabeth Stuart, Lisa Isherwood and Mary Grey is encouraging an impressive amount of activity in this area. For example, recent publications in the Introductions in Feminist Theology series include, Musimbi Kanyoro's *Introducing Feminist Cultural Hermeneutics*[95] (2002) Mary Grey's *Introducing Feminist Images of God*[96] (2001) and Kwok Pui-lan's *Introducing Asian Feminist Theology*[97] (2000). The work of Ursula King continues to challenge and question the categories and boundaries of feminist theological activity. Since her earlier works *Women in the World's Religions, Past and*

Present[98] (1988) and *Women and Spirituality: Voices of Protest and Promise*[99] (1988) she has succeeded in both offering her own reflections on the field of religion and gender, and to edit collections which bring together a range of perspectives and approaches. And Mary Grey's feminist informed theology continues to explore the theological implications and outworkings of the presence of feminisms in Christian theology with publications such as *Introducing Feminist Images of God* (2001) and *Sacred longings: Ecofeminist Theology and Globalisation*[100] (2003).

Over the last few years Susan Parsons is an important voice in contemporary feminist informed theology in Britain. Publications such as *Feminism and Christian Ethics*[101] (1998) and *The Ethics of Gender*[102] (2002) give serious critical attention to the ethical implications of feminisms and gender awareness. And her editorial work in *Challenging Women's Orthodoxies in the Context of Faith*[103] (2000) and *The Cambridge Companion to Feminist Theology*[104] (2002) has contributed towards significant collections of contemporary feminist informed reflections on issues of gender, culture, orthodoxy, doctrine and practice. Womanist theologies in British contexts are also influencing the range of feminist informed theologies, and among those whose reflections are claiming visibility here, especially through the journal *Black Theology: An International Journal*, are Kate Coleman and Lorraine Dixon. Today, the list of those involved with feminist informed Christian theologies and producing written texts in Britain and Ireland is ever expanding, and includes new and more established scholars such as Elaine Graham, Marcella Althaus-Reid, Janet Soskice, Sarah Coakely, Ann Loades, Beverley Clack, Linda Hogan, Pamela Anderson, Nicola Slee, Celia Deane-Drummond, Grace Jantzen and Ruth Mantin.

Beyond Britain and Ireland the picture is equally diverse and evolving. Feminist informed Christian theological activity is evident in Africa, Europe, Pacific region, North America, Latin America and Asia. A brief snapshot here demonstrates something of the range of perspectives, concerns and approaches involved. European theologians such as Catharina Halkes, Kari Børresen, Ina Praetorius and Elisabeth Gössman are contributing towards an ever-developing picture of feminist informed activity in Europe. Latin American feminist informed theologies now incorporate a great diversity of perspectives, contexts and outlooks, which María Pilar Aquino has described as including indigenous theology, black feminist theology, holistic, and ecofeminist theology.[105] As noted earlier, womanist theologies have developed with huge impact among African American women in North America and influential theologians writing in this field include Katie Cannon, Emile Townes and Jacquelyn Grant. African feminist informed and womanist theologies are equally important within the global picture of feminisms and Christian theology and key theologians here include Mercy Oduyoye who stresses the challengingly prophetic aspect of feminist informed African Christian theology[106] and Musimbi Kanyoro who is exploring and developing a feminist cultural hermeneutics. Lisa Meo describes feminist informed theologies in the Pacific region as addressing the multi religious contexts of people's lives with a strong liberation theological concern, which, "...takes the message of Jesus to heart and applies it, through advocacy and empowerment, to rid women of all forms of oppression".[107] The mujerista theology of Latina women based in North America is developing with a strong liberation theological base, and praxis driven concerns and questions about nationalism, globalisation and displacement are concerning scholars such as Ada María Isasi-Díaz. From Asian contexts a great diversity of voices, including those of Kwok Pui-lan, Hyun Kyung Chung, Virginia Fabella, Sun Ai Park and Rita Nakashima Brock, are challenging both traditional and feminist informed Christian theologies.

The level of feminist informed activity in religious contexts other than Christianity is also significant. A very important debate that has always been present since the 1970s about recognising the importance of the diversity of religious contexts in which issues of gender and religion are being considered is still challenging feminist informed Christian theologies to examine their presuppositions and exclusionary practices and to recognise the full range of feminist informed activity in religions. Rita Gross has argued very strongly that feminist theology as it has widely been understood does not fully recognise the religious pluralism of the world in which it lives and argues that it is not paying heed to the true diversity of the world:

> One of the great discoveries of the past century and a half has been that of religious pluralism and of the fact that non-Christian religions cannot simply be labeled "errors" but are just as sophisticated and cogent as Christianity. No reputable theology that ignores religious diversity and continues the tradition of Christian hegemony is possible in this religiously diverse world. Yet as the world becomes more aware of and sensitive to diversity of all kinds, the feminist theology movement, like much mainstream (or malestream, as some feminists would say) theological writing and education, is oblivious to the reality of religious diversity and acts as if all theology were Christian theology.[108]

She calls on those working in the area to challenge such limitations, and argues that true diversity will only be achieved when feminists from Muslim, pagan, Buddhist, Hindu, Jewish, Confucian, Taoist and indigenous perspectives are genuinely included in discussions and seen as authentic partners by Christian feminists.[109]

It is very interesting to note that types and contextual descriptions which themselves only a few years ago were seen to constitute diversification and to be challenging mainstream Christian theology seem themselves to becoming constraining categories which are beginning to break down because of contextual needs and diversity. So, just as the term "feminist theology" has been challenged as an adequate way of describing all feminist informed Christian theology so terms such as "mujerista" and "womanist" are also beginning to be disputed.

This small scale exercise in mapping out a perspective on the origins and developing picture of Christian feminist theologies leads to a view of feminist Christian encounter as diverse, vital and often problematic. Having established something of the key patterns and concerns that have characterised the critical encountering of feminisms and Christianity questions now arise about the inherently contextual and specific nature of theologies which employ the tools and insights of feminisms to investigate, challenge and interpret the relationship between gender and Christianity. Christian feminist theologies are diverse in terms of context, radicalism and political and social setting, and from the emergence of clear patterns of Christian feminist theological engagement it is apparent that issues of subjectivity and exclusion are key concerns. Dialogues between Jewish feminists and Christian feminists, for example, have highlighted these problems, as have dialogues between Postchristian feminists and feminists working out of traditional religious contexts. Similarly, gaps in understanding and communication exist as black women, Asian women, women from developing countries, lesbian and bisexual women and other marginalised or excluded groups of women are articulating visions of justice and methodologies that are challenging some of the mainline Christian feminist voices. And this will be explored in more depth in chapter six. Stress here has to be with the contextual nature of feminisms and feminist theologies as the whole feminist enterprise is increasingly subject to intense critique with the deconstruction of universal notions of "feminism", "women", "women's experience" and "liberation". Given such problems that are increasingly arising in relation to "feminist theology" it seems appropriate not only to speak of feminist theologies in the plural but also to move beyond the clear cut and limiting identification of particular theologies as "feminist". It actually seems more helpful now to speak of "feminist informed theologies" rather than "feminist theologies". This recognises that theologies may well be informed by particular feminist insights and methodologies, or influenced in part by feminisms alongside other critical perspectives, whilst at the same time be critical of other aspects of feminisms and even reject the validity of such feminisms.

In the next chapter one particular and highly significant aspect of the development of feminist theological encounters as they have been outlined in this first chapter will be explored in depth, that of the feminist rejection of Christianity and traditional religion as a possible context or framework for feminist theologising. This will be explored for the ways in which it has had a determinate, and often limiting, impact on both feminist Christian encounter and on detailed critical analysis of this encounter. This will then complete the mapping out exercise of the development of feminist informed theologies of part one of this study. It will stress that due to the ways in which early encounters were approached, by both those who reject and those who accept the possibilities of feminist informed theologies, many such theologies since have been preoccupied with establishing the validity or truth of "feminist theology" or the compatibility of feminisms and Christianity.

Notes

[1] Hirsch, P., (1998), *Barbara Leigh Smith Bodichon*, London: Random House, p.ix.
[2] Gage, M.J., (1980), [1893], *Woman, Church and State*, Watertown, Massachusetts: Persephone Press.
[3] Cady Stanton, E., (1999), *The Woman's Bible*, U.S.: Prometheus Books.
[4] Gage, 1980:237.

[5] Cady Stanton, 1999:7.
[6] Saiving, V., (1960), "The human situation: a feminine view", *Journal of Religion*, 40(2), pp.100-112.
[7] King, U., (1993), *Women and Spirituality: Voices of Protest and Promise*, 2nd Edition, Macmillan Press, p.158; Jantzen, G.M., (1998), Becoming *Divine: Towards a Feminist Philosophy of Religion*, Manchester: Manchester University Press, p.159.
[8] Hampson, D., (1990), *Theology and Feminism*, Oxford: Basil Blackwell, p.122.
[9] Saiving, V., in Mackinnon, H. and McIntyre, M., (eds), (1980), *Readings in Ecology & Feminist Theology*, Kansas City: Sheed & Ward, p.3.
[10] Mead, M., *Male and Female: A Study of the Sexes in a Changing World*, William Morrow.
[11] Benedict, R., (1935), *Patterns of Culture*, London: Routledge and Kegan Paul.
[12] Saiving, in MacKinnon and McIntyre, (eds.), 1980:9.
[13] Saiving, in MacKinnon and McIntyre, (eds.), 1980:12.
[14] Saiving, in MacKinnon and McIntyre, (eds.), 1980:12.
[15] Christ and Plaskow in Christ, C. and Plaskow, J., (eds.), (1992) *Womanspirit Rising: A Feminist Reader in Religion*, San Francisco: Harper SanFrancisco, p.29.
[16] Friedan, B., (1963), *The Feminine Mystique*, WW Norton and Co.
[17] Millett, K., (1977), [1970], *Sexual Politics*, London: Virago.
[18] Crook, M.B., (1964) *Women and Religion*, Boston: Beacon Press.
[19] Crook, 1964:1.
[20] Crook, 1964:1.
[21] Crook, 1964:5.
[22] Parvey, C., (1969), "Ordain her, ordain her not", *Dialog*, 8(3), pp.203-208.
[23] Børresen, K., (1968), *Subordination and Equivalence*, Oslo: Oslo University Press.
[24] Grey, M., (1996), in Russell, L., and Shannon, J., (ed.), *Dictionary of Feminist Theologies*, London: Mowbray, p.103.
[25] Doely, S.B., (ed.), (1970), *Women's Liberation and the Church: The New Demand for Freedom in the Life of the Christian Church*, Association Press.
[26] Callahan, S.C., in Doely, S.B., (ed.), (1970), *Women's Liberation and the Church: The New Demand for Freedom in the Life of the Christian Church*, Association Press, p.37.
[27] Callahan, in Doely, S.B., (ed.), 1970:37.
[28] Callahan, in Doely, S.B., (ed.), 1970:37-38.
[29] Callahan, in Doely, S.B., (ed.), 1970:45.
[30] Christ, C., (1977), "The new feminist theology: a review of the literature", *Religious Studies Review*, 3(4), p.205.
[31] Daly, M., (1985), [1968], *The Church and the Second Sex*, Boston: Beacon Press.
[32] Daly, 1985:118.
[33] Daly, 1985:176.
[34] Daly, 1985:184-185.
[35] Daly, 1985:221.
[36] Daly, 1985:223.
[37] Daly, M., (1993), *Outercourse: The Be-Dazzling Voyage*, London: The Women's Press, p.137.
[38] Daly, 1993:138.
[39] Daly, 1993:139.
[40] Ruether, R.R., (1971), "Male chauvinist theology and the anger of women", *Cross Currents*, p.183.

[41] Ruether, R., (1969), "New wine, maybe new wine-skins, for the church", *Christian Century*, 86(14), pp.445-449.
[42] Ruether, R.R., (1976), "What is the task of theology?" *Christianity and Crisis*, 36, p.122.
[43] Ruether, 1976:125.
[44] Ruether, R.R., (1975), New Woman New Earth: Sexist Ideologies and Human Liberation, New York: The Seabury Press.
[45] Ruether, 1975:204.
[46] Ruether, 1975:204.
[47] Ruether, in Christ, C.P., and Plaskow, J., (eds.), 1992:51.
[48] Ruether, in Christ, C.P., and Plaskow, J., (eds.), 1992:52.
[49] Ruether, in Ruether, R.R., (ed.) 1974:179.
[50] Schüssler Fiorenza, E, (1975), "Feminist theology as a critical theology of liberation", *Theological Studies*, 36(4), p.611.
[51] Schüssler Fiorenza, 1975:616.
[52] Schüssler Fiorenza, 1975:612.
[53] Schüssler Fiorenza, in Christ and Plaskow, (eds.), 1992:137-138.
[54] Christ, C., and Plaskow, J., (eds.), (1992) *Womanspirit Rising: A Feminist Reader in Religion*, San Francisco: Harper SanFrancisco.
[55] Schüssler Fiorenza, in Christ and Plaskow, (eds.), 1992:88.
[56] Schüssler Fiorenza, in Christ and Plaskow, (eds.), 1992:92.
[57] See for example, Scanzoni, L., and Hardesty, N., (1974) *All We're Meant to Be: A Biblical Approach to Women's Liberation*, Word Books.
[58] Trible, P., (1978), *God and the Rhetoric of Sexuality*, Fortress Press.
[59] McLaughlin, E., in Christ, C.P., and Plaskow, J., (eds.), 1992:94-95
[60] Christ, C.P., "Spiritual quest and women's experience", *Anima*, 1975, 1(2), pp.4-15.
[61] Christ, C.P., (1980), *Diving Deep and Surfacing: Women Writers on Spiritual Quest*, Beacon Press, pp.4-5.
[62] Christ, 1985:120.
[63] Goldenberg, N., (1979) *Changing of the Gods: Feminism and the End of Traditional Religion*, Boston: Beacon Press.
[64] Concern with the goddess came to be termed *thealogy*, distinguishing it from *theology*.
[65] Adler, M., (1986), *Drawing Down the Moon: Witches, Druids, Goddess-Worshippers, and Other Pagans in America Today*, Beacon.
[66] Starhawk, (1979), *The Spiral Dance: The Rebirth of the Ancient Religion of the Goddess*, San Francisco: Harper and Row.
[67] Mernissi, F., (1975), *Beyond the Veil: Male-Female Dynamics in a Modern Muslim Society*, Cambridge, Mass.: Schenkman.
[68] Sigal, P., (1974), "Women in a prayer quorum", *Judaism*, 23(2), pp.174-182.
[69] Isasi-Diaz, A.M., (1979), "Silent women will never be heard", *Missiology*, 7(3), pp.295-301.
[70] Christ and Plaskow in Christ, C.P., and Plaskow, J., (eds.), 1992:xiii.
[71] Christ and Plaskow in Christ, C.P., and Plaskow, J., (eds.), 1992:viii.
[72] Daggers, J., (2002), *The British Christian Women's Movement: A Rehabilitation of Eve*, Aldershot: Ashgate, p.xviii.
[73] Grey, M., in Russell, L., and Shannon, J., (ed.), (1996), *Dictionary of Feminist Theologies*, London: Mowbray, p.104.
[74] Fulkerson, M.C., in Chopp, R.S., and Davaney, S.G., (eds.), (1997), *Horizons in Feminist Theology: Identity, Tradition and Norms*, Minneapolis: Fortress Press, p.99.
[75] Lorde, A., in Humm, M., (ed.), (1992), *Feminisms: A Reader*, London: Harvester Wheatsheaf, p.139

[76] Leonard, E., (1990), "Experience as a source for theology: a Canadian and feminist perspective", *Studies in Religion/Sciences religieuses*, 19(2), p.147.
[77] Carr, A., and Schussler Fiorenza, E., (eds.), (1987), *Women, Work and Poverty ("Concillium")*, Edinburgh, T & T Clark.
[78] Plaskow, J., and Christ, C.P., (1989), *Weaving the Visions: New Patterns in Feminist Spirituality*, San Francisco: Harper and Row, p.3.
[79] Culpepper, E., (1988), "New tools for theology: writings by women of color", *Journal of Feminist Studies in Religion*, 4, p.40.
[80] Pui-lan, K., (2002), in Parsons, S., (ed.), *The Cambridge Companion to Feminist Theology*, Cambridge: Cambridge University Press, p. 23.
[81] Cannon, K.G., (1987), "Hitting a straight lick with a crooked stick: the womanist dilemma in the development of a Black liberation ethic", *Annual of the Society of Christian Ethics*, pp.171.
[82] Isasi-Diaz, A.M., (1997), *Mujerista Theology: A Theology for the Twenty-First Century*, New York: Maryknoll, p.3.
[83] Isasi-Diaz, 1997:16.
[84] Isasi-Diaz, 1997:16.
[85] Isasi-Diaz, 1997:40.
[86] Isasi-Diaz, 1997:61.
[87] Isasi-Diaz, 1997 64.
[88] Isasi-Diaz, 1997:69-70.
[89] Isasi-Diaz, 1997:76.
[90] O'Neill, M., (1990), *Women Speaking, Women Listening: Women in Interreligious Dialogue*, Maryknoll, NY: Orbis Books, p.103.
[91] Young, P.D., (1990), *Feminist Theology/Christian Theology: In Search of Method*, Eugene, OR: Wipf and Stock Publishers.
[92] Chopp, R.S., and Davaney, S.G., (eds.), (1997), *Horizons in Feminist Theology: Identity, Tradition and Norms*, Minneapolis: Fortress Press.
[93] See for example, Chopp, R., (1995), *Saving Work: Practices of Theological Education*, Westminster John Knox Press and Davaney, S.G., (1991), "Directions in historicism", *Zygon*, 26(2), pp.201-220.
[94] Chopp, R.S., and Davaney, S.G., in Chopp, R.S., and Davaney, S.G., (eds.), (1997), *Horizons in Feminist Theology: Identity, Tradition and Norms*, Minneapolis: Fortress Press, p.16.
[95] Kanyoro, M.R.A., (2002), *Introducing Feminist Cultural Hermeneutics*, Sheffield: Sheffield Academic Press.
[96] Grey, M., (2001), *Introducing Feminist Images of God*, Cleveland, Ohio: The Pilgrim's Press.
[97] Pui-lan, K., (2000), *Introducing Asian Feminist Theology*, Continuum International Publishing Group.
[98] King, U., (ed.), (1987), *Women in the World's Religions, Past and Present*, New York: Paragon House.
[99] King, U., (1993), *Women and Spirituality: Voices of Protest and Promise*, 2nd Edition, Macmillan Press.
[100] Grey, M., (2003), *Sacred Longings: Ecofeminist Theology and Globalisation*, London: SCM Press.
[101] Parsons, S., (1998), *Feminism and Christian Ethics*. Cambridge University Press.
[102] Parsons, S., (2002), *The Ethics of Gender*, Oxford: Blackwell.
[103] Parsons, S., (ed.), (2000), *Challenging Women's Orthodoxies in the Context of Faith*, Aldershot: Ashgate.

[104] Parsons, S., (ed.), (2002), *The Cambridge Companion to Feminist Theology*, Cambridge: Cambridge University Press.
[105] Aquino, M.P., in Russell, L., and Shannon, J., (eds.), 1996:116.
[106] Oduyoye, M.A., in Russell, L., and Shannon, J., (ed.), (1996), *Dictionary of Feminist Theologies*, London: Mowbray, p.112.
[107] Meo, L., in Russell, L., and Shannon, J., (eds.), 1996:110.
[108] Gross, R.M., (2000), "Feminist theology: religiously diverse neighborhood or Christian ghetto?", *Journal of Feminist Studies in Religion*, 16(2), p.73.
[109] Gross, R.M., 2000:77.

Chapter Two

Feminist Rejections of Christianity

Introduction

A defining feature of the development and critical understanding of feminist informed Christian theologies since their emergence in the late 1960s and early 1970s has been a persistent focus on the question of the compatibility of Christianity and feminisms. This has been influenced particularly by the variously made feminist claim that Christianity is not a viable site for feminist theologies or spirituality and that the justice concerns and aims of feminisms can not be accommodated or supported by Christianity. The case has been made both forcefully and convincingly by a number of key feminist thinkers that "Christian feminism" is quite simply unfeasible. Equally persistent, however, has been the Christian feminist response to such claims, which have often been concerned to demonstrate the compatibility of feminism and Christianity. In recognition of the impact of the compatibility/incompatibility discourse, and of the critical interaction between the Christian and Postchristian feminist perspectives, in the development of feminist informed Christian theologies, this chapter explores in detail the form and substance of the feminist rejection of the viability and even possibility of Christian feminist theologies. It will identify key feminist claims and interpretations that lead to this rejection and will explore the evidence offered by those advocating a feminist based rejection of Christianity and identify the problems that this has posed for those working from a feminist informed theological perspective. In so doing it will argue that the very powerful, and for some very convincing alignment of feminisms with the rejection of Christianity by key feminist thinkers, particularly in the early stages of the development of feminist theological discourse, has shaped the theological agenda and critical focus of many feminist informed Christian theologies. To the extent that responding to the implicit and sometimes explicit challenge laid down by the feminist rejection of Christianity has preoccupied both feminist informed Christian theologies and critical explorations of these theologies.

The Second Sex

Feminist analysis has consistently viewed religion, and in particular, Christianity with suspicion and sometimes outright hostility. Feminist critique has often focused on the claim that stereotypical and derogatory understandings of women shape and determine a variety of traditional religious perspectives and as such these perspectives and associated religious traditions legitimise views of women that are demeaning, limiting and ultimately, damaging. One particular text that heavily influenced the clarification of the feminist rejection of the legitimacy or possibility of Christian feminisms is Simone de Beauvoir's *The Second Sex*, which was first published in 1949. Now a classic in early feminist analysis, de Beauvoir's study was an Existentialist exploration of woman as 'Other'. She developed the argument that the secondary status of 'woman' is universally supported by the category of 'Other'[1] and is dependent on a binary system that differentiates between what is deemed to be normative ('the One'), male, and that which is not ('the Other'[2]), female, "Thus humanity is male and man defines woman not in herself but as relative to him; she is not regarded as an autonomous being".[3] De Beauvoir argued that women, "...have no past, no history, no religion of their own"[4] and that the otherness and inferiority of 'woman' is supported, indeed sustained by an extensive system in which religion and associated authority have key roles to play, "Legislators, priests, philosophers, writers and scientists have striven to show that the subordinate position of women is willed in heaven and advantageous on earth."[5]

De Beauvoir, at some length, addressed the nature of woman as "Other", and detailed the changes needed if women were to be autonomous, and "aspire to full membership in the human race".[6] *The Second Sex* is important not least in terms of the extensive and detailed ways in which de Beauvoir attempts to do this. In exploring understandings of the physiological and psychological differences between men and women she raised important questions about the role of biology, reproduction, economics, social development and reality in defining woman as "Other". In her analysis there are some presuppositions and ideas that contemporary feminisms and linguistics might well be uneasy with, but her work, nevertheless, is very significant. For example, fundamental to her argument is a conflictual reading of history in which male and female, "each aspires to impose its sovereignty upon the other".[7] Patriachalism, a concept now hotly debated and critiqued by contemporary theorists for its simplicity of categorisation, is understood by de Beauvoir to be the stable force behind woman's otherness. She understands it as playing upon women's biological possibilities, and secured by societal development and exclusion and the "male will to power".[8] Her analysis is also important for its clarification of the ambivalence of men's understanding and approach to women, as one of fear and yet benevolence.[9] She partly located responsibility for women's oppression with dependency on men, and with the associated laws, beliefs and customs that are effective in maintaining such dependency. Like many feminist analysts since, she pointed to the importance of creation stories, particularly the Genesis stories, as confirming and enforcing dependency and the "Other" nature of women in Western societies.[10] Men as "Subject" shape and determine religion and invest their own, male, subjectivity with religious significance, given the "Otherness" ascribed to women, "...the Woman-Mother has a face in the shadows: she is the chaos whence all have come and whither all must one day return; she is Nothingness".[11] Women are feared by men, in part, because of their association with birth and death, "it is the horror of his own carnal contingence, which he projects upon her".[12] De Beauvoir argued that this dualism was fundamental to Christianity:

> It is Christianity which invests woman anew with frightening prestige: fear of the other sex is one of the forms assumed by the anguish of man's conscience. The Christian is divided within himself, the separation of body and soul, of life and spirit, is complete, original sin makes the body the enemy of the soul, all ties of the flesh seem evil...
> And of course, since woman remains always the Other, it is not held that reciprocally male and female are both flesh: the flesh that is for the Christian the hostile *Other* is precisely woman. In her the Christian finds incarnated the temptations of the world, the flesh, and the devil.[13]

In contrast to her reading of Christianity's understanding and valuing of women, de Beauvoir advocated an independent woman, and located hope with the possibilities of societal development with her words, "One is not born, but rather becomes a woman".[14] So in this early feminist text there is evidence of a juxtapositioning of feminisms and Christianity, in which Christianity is an obstacle to, and not a tool of, feminisms. De Beauvoir argued that society traditionally has not allowed for the "subjective freedom"[15] of women, and that religious myth and belief reflect a limited, dependent view of women.[16] She located the possibility for change with "social evolution"[17] and argued that the "free woman is just being born".[18] For de Beauvoir, religion, and particularly Christianity, is part of the sustained repressive otherness of women.

This association of religion, and particularly Christianity, with the limiting of women's potential and autonomy was further developed in the late 1960s and early 1970s as the feminist movement strengthened. Christianity was increasingly posited as part of the challenge to be negotiated by women in their quest for justice. Cynthia Eller in her study of the North American Goddess movement, *Living in the Lap of the Goddess*,[19] placed the rise of feminisms and the questioning and rejection of traditional religions alongside each other. She argued that:

> It is surely true that some women began a process of questioning in CR (consciousness raising) whose end result was a denunciation of established religions and an attempt to create a religion for women.[20]
> The attack on Christianity is the natural extension of what was a real impetus for the birth of feminist spirituality in the first place: an analysis of traditional religions that argues that they are the central cultural legitimators of the oppression of women. In the light of this, what is curious is not that spiritual feminists should despise traditional religions (as some do), but that they should be so relatively tolerant of them (as most are).[21]

Such an interpretation claims a direct correlation between the emergence of feminist consciousness and the questioning and rejection of traditional religions, and Eller's analysis places traditional religions at the heart of the problems facing women, and so at the heart of the solution.

Mary Daly

From these beginnings emerged feminist theological perspectives that very firmly, and with great influence, rejected the possibility of feminist informed Christian theologies. Mary Daly, whose significance in the development of feminist theologies was outlined briefly in Chapter One, is one theologian/philosopher who was very clearly influenced by the feminist unease with traditional religions, and particularly as this was presented in the critique of Simone de Beauvoir. In one of her more recent publications, *Outercourse*[22] (1992), Daly acknowledges the significance of de Beauvoir's thought to the development of her own critical perspective, "...my gratitude to her was enormous".[23] Daly, more than any other feminist theologian or philosopher has coherently formulated a feminist based critique of the complicity of Christianity in the subjugation of women, with the uncompromising conclusion that feminisms and Christianity are simply not compatible.

Ann Loades gives recognition to the significance of Mary Daly's work in critical dialogues surrounding the compatibility/incompatibility of Christianity and feminisms:

> ...it is important to recognize that although many Protestant women have contributed to the discussion of the relationship between Christianity and feminism...it is the North American Roman Catholic tradition which has produced the most prolific and distinguished women theologians, including Mary Daly, the most formidable and uncompromising critic of them all. Her argument with her tradition, begun in *The Church and the Second Sex*, precipitated her out of it in the course of writing *Beyond God the Father*....[24]
>
> Her polemic is so lively, her ability to communicate and stimulate people to think is so lively.[25]

The development of Daly's Postchristian feminist theological/philosophical perspective as documented in her writings is very revealing of her alignment of feminisms and the rejection of traditional religions, especially when seen alongside her own retrospective reflections. In the preface to the 1975 edition of *The Church and the Second Sex* Daly describes her move from a Catholic to a Postchristian feminist position in such a way that suggests an uneasy regard for her former position:

> ...I moved on to other things, including a dramatic/traumatic change of consciousness from "radical Catholic" to postchristian feminist. My graduation from the Catholic church was formalized by a self-conferred diploma, my second feminist book, *Beyond God the Father: Toward a Philosophy of Women's Liberation* which appeared in 1973. The journey in time/space that took place between the publication dates of the two books could not be described adequately by terrestrial calendars and maps. Experientially it was hardly even a mere trip to the moon but more like leap-frogging galaxies in a mind voyage to further and further stars. Several woman-light years had separated me from *The Church and the Second Sex* whose author I sometimes have trouble recalling.[26]

Daly's dismissal of her earlier position, a position which proposed reform instead of rejection, combined with the sheer force of her radicalism in *Beyond God the Father*, impacted hugely on the perception of the differential between Christian and Postchristian feminist theologies as problematic. The development between the two positions in Daly's understanding can clearly be read as progression, informed by feminist consciousness. Rejection is part of the process of awakening. Language is always so important for Daly, and her choice of terminology, of "graduation" and "mind voyage" reinforces this notion of advancement. Daly's recognition of the importance of language and naming anticipates a persistent concern of contemporary feminisms. The power of naming, the ability and opportunity for women to name and describe their own experiences is a central issue of contemporary feminist theological discourse, and of feminist discourse in general. For example, various scholars have explored and challenged the gendered nature of language, and the work of the French women philosophers, and especially Irigaray, is of particular importance here. According to Daly's understanding, the phallocentric nature of language requires radical attention and what is required is nothing less than a "*castrating* of language and images that reflect and perpetuate the structures of a sexist world".[27] Indeed, her use of the term "Postchristian", in itself is an important and radical relocation away from the sites, influences and authority of traditional religions. Daly uses the term "Postchristian feminist" with clear intention:

> "Postchristian" to me, did not merely mean "atheist". I longed passionately for the transcendence that was held prisoner and choked by religion and theology and for the emergence of *Feminist* philosophy/theology.[28]

Daphne Hampson in *The Dictionary of Feminist Theology*[29] notes the significance of the term as used by Daly and many others since:

> It designates someone standing within the western theological tradition who is not a Christian...The term might well refer equally to a man who holds this position and is used by men of themselves. But it is mostly women, who are feminists, who have left Christianity behind them at least in part on account of a feminist critique who so employ it.
> The term is good in that it expresses that one has come out of the Christian (and not any other) tradition and that one may have taken much with one; while also acknowledging that one no longer adheres to Christian faith. It is problematic if it becomes confused with the term post-Christian (as in post-Christian society) meaning simply secular.[30]

Daly herself, in Webster's' *First New Intergalactic Wickedary of the English Language*,[31] describes "Postchristian" as, "...occurring after definitive departure from christianity in all its religious and secular forms and simultaneously with entry into New Time/Space".[32] Radical and new uses of language are distinctive and challenging features of Daly's work. In a deliberate subversion of conceptual and linguistic accusations traditionally directed at women Daly demonstrates the interdependent responsibilities of imagery, language and practice for women's oppression. Fundamental to the feminist philosophical vision that she articulates for women is the move beyond the symbolism and institutions of Christianity, and indeed all traditional religions, with a renaming of ultimate reality.

An examination of Daly's theological/philosophical explorations in Christianity's encountering of feminisms needs to acknowledge the ways in which Daly's specific formulation helped to influence the pattern of subsequent engagement with this issue. It might well be argued that Daly not only rejected Christianity as a viable setting for women's becoming, but also, through the substance and style of her approach, influenced an antagonistic, defensive encountering of feminisms by many Christians. For Daly, the decisive challenge of feminisms to Christianity, and to all patriarchal religions, is constituted not so much in its critique, as in its advancement beyond such religions. In 1979, she claimed "The women's movement will present a growing threat to patriarchal religions less by attacking it than by simply leaving it behind".[33] Daly offered no possibility for accommodating commitment to Christianity within her feminist vision.

A legacy of this early feminist theology is still evident today in feminist Christian encounters. The methodological significance of this is that the passion and anger, or "creative rage"[34] of Daly's self-voyage translates into language and imagery of rejection and progression. So, not only was she "moving on", or indeed "forward", but she sees the committed feminist as following a similar path toward self-actualisation and liberation. However conscious or intentional, the effect of this kind of experiential awareness and explicit articulating of the personal roots of any theological/religious position, needs to be taken into account when assessing the antagonism between Christian and Postchristian feminists and Jewish and Christian feminists. In the 1970s and 1980s the assertion of one feminist theological/philosophical position often entailed the named rejection of another, in such a way as to place blame and accusations of lack of critical feminist awakening and even the complicity of those women who remained within these traditions. The assertion of one committed position entailing the named rejection of other positions, has led to an almost apologetic approach to feminist informed Christian theologies. This is compounded by the fact that most critics seeking to engage with the impact of feminisms on Christian theology are working from a particular committed religious perspective.

The theological influence or content of Daly's feminist rejection of Christianity plays a very significant role in the impact of her critique. Her vision of the challenge of feminisms and inevitable rejection of Christianity begins with the claim that the patriarchal god is redundant for women:

> The biblical and popular image of God as a great patriarch in heaven, rewarding and punishing according to his mysterious and seemingly arbitrary will, has dominated the imagination of millions over thousands of years. The symbol of the Father God, spawned in the human imagination and sustained as plausible by patriarchy, has in turn rendered service to this type of society by making its mechanisms for the oppression of women appear right and fitting.[35]

She outlines a definitive correlation between patriarchal symbolism and language and the oppression of women, "If God in 'his' heaven is a father ruling 'his' people, then it is in the 'nature' of things and according to divine plan and the order of the universe that society be male-dominated".[36] This recognition of the importance of symbols and symbolic representation has come to feature consistently in feminist critical analysis. Daly's feminist analysis of the implications of the gendered Christian representations of God is radical, and she articulates the ensuing challenge to Christianity in uncompromising language.[37] The challenge is to symbolism and the terminology used for god, to understandings and representations of history, to christology and to method. Her vision in terms of its depth and extent is demanding and the claims that she makes for the emergence of this second wave of feminism are immense, arguing that the women's movement is potentially, "the greatest single challenge to the major religions of the world".[38]

A significant and seemingly deliberately antagonistic or confrontational element of Daly's vision of women's liberation is her articulation of sisterhood as "Antichurch",[39] and this is a fundamental notion in Daly's rejection of Christianity:

> Sisterhood, then, by being the unique bonding of women against our reduction to low caste is Antichurch. It is the evolution of a social reality that undercuts the credibility of sexist religion to the degree that it undermines sexism itself. Even without conscious attention to the church, sisterhood is in conflict with it.[40]

> Male religion entombs women in sepulchres of silence in order to chant its own eternal and dreary dirge to a past that never was. The silence *imposed* upon women echoes the structures of male hierarchies. It is important to listen to the structures of this imposed silence in order to hear the flow of the new sounds of free silence that are the source of sisterhood as Antichurch.[41]

Daly stresses that ontological hope is central to the women's movement and that this is not individualistic, but is essentially communal in nature. This emphasis gives to Daly's vision and understanding of feminisms a basis for community, because hope is communal, cosmic and spiritual. Daly's understanding of the women's movement places it in direct opposition to the Church, and given this, the possibilities for constructive and liberative dialogue between feminisms and Christianity seem far removed. Within Daly's critique it would seem that the values, symbols and practices of Christianity, and not only its organisational forms, are open to the same level of criticism. So, the revealing and enabling distinction found in other feminist informed theologies between the institutional, historical forms of Christianity, and the essential Christian vision or "core", is absent from Daly's work, which is consistent with her rejection of the possibility of feminist revisions of Christianity. From the point of view of feminist informed Christian theologies, in the face of feminist critique of Christianity, there has to be some scope for reinterpretation or location of some aspect that has not been affected or tainted by gender based discrimination if a feminist informed Christian theology is to be developed.

Daly's assessment of the vision of feminisms and their implications for Christianity does not remain with its objections and conflictual relationship with traditional patriarchal religions. Part of the implications of sisterhood as Antichurch is the emergence of new symbols and the death of old, patriarchal ones. She speaks of the women's movement as both Antichurch and as "Antichrist".[42] This constructive element is crucial for the critique of religion, as an alternative is offered replacing and fulfilling the needs left by that which has been rejected. False religion is served and perpetuated by sexist ritual "Antichurch says 'No' to these 'reminders'".[43] The women's movement, for Daly, is intrinsically concerned to reach "toward something *beyond* opposition"[44] and she talks of "an *exodus community*" and of sisterhood as "Cosmic Covenant".[45] Despite the very negative assessment of the role of religion in historical and continuing gender based oppression religion or spirituality remain key elements of Daly's feminist vision. Her hope for radical transformation is based in ontological hope, of new being or consciousness, which is for her the promise of feminisms:

> ...the women's revolution, insofar as it is true to its own essential dynamics, is an ontological, spiritual revolution, pointing beyond the idolatries of sexist society and sparking creative action in and through transcendence.[46]

In her works produced since laying down the initial challenge of feminisms to Christianity in *Beyond God the Father*, Daly has concerned herself with the development and expansion of this vision of feminist spiritual revolution. But this development in no way diminishes the significance of her earlier analysis. In many ways the basis of Daly's critique of Christianity – its symbols, practices and structures – stands even today as of fundamental importance to the Christian task of responding to feminist critique. Daly's conviction that feminisms is necessarily aligned with the rejection of Christianity has not diminished over the last 30 years. In 1985, in "New Archaic Afterwords" in *The Church and the Second Sex*, Daly's commitment not just to the possibilities beyond Christianity but to the real need and pressing ethical choice for women to leave is evident, "The Courage to Leave springs from deep knowledge of the nucleus of nothingness which is at the core of the fallacious faith that freezes/fixes its victims".[47] Critique and construction are core to Daly's approach here. Critique of past traditions in itself is not enough; new ways and possibilities are part of the feminist movement.

This implicit ethical imperative is paradoxically one of the most striking indicators of her radical feminist commitment whilst at the same time being also one of the key problematics of Daly's work. In *Beyond God the Father* there are clear indications that Daly is prescribing what can be interpreted as amounting to an ethical imperative for women to leave the Christian tradition. The influence of this on the shape and ethos of feminist informed Christian theologies is substantial. Daly's visibility, particularly in the early stages of the second wave feminist movement, which was perhaps largely tied up with the radicalism of both method and content she employed, meant that Daly's feminist voice established and maintains even today, a strong presence in feminist informed Christian theological discourse. For Daly, there is quite simply no choice, the feminist informed woman seeking autonomy and justice will inevitably choose to leave because the movement towards self-actualisation necessarily involves moving beyond traditional religions. Daly acknowledges that glimpses of hope, of potential may be evident, but these glimpses are simply not enough:

> It can be legitimately pointed out that the Judeo-Christian tradition is not entirely bereft of elements that can foster intimations of transcendence. Yet the liberating potential of these elements is choked off in the surrounding atmosphere of the images, ideas, values and structures of patriarchy.[48]

This then is a clear dismissal of the feminist informed Christian claim that liberative aspects can be located and recovered from the Christian tradition. Daly is aware of the strength, commitment and courage that such a move beyond Christianity requires but sees the courage to take such a risk as being incorporated into and so an indication, and part of, the feminist liberative process. For Daly, courage is essential, "existential courage to confront the experience of nothingness".[49] Faced with nothingness the temptations to return to the familiar are obvious but she argues that great danger faces women who may choose "premature reconciliation",[50] but in the face of danger, the possibilities are vast, "what is at stake is a real leap in human evolution, initiated by women.[51] Revision and reformation are illusory, "The appearance of change is basically only separation and return – cyclic movement",[52] to "stay in patriarchal space is to remain in time past".[53] Daly speaks the language of revolution, conceptually juxtaposed to reformation,[54] and the revolutionary nature of the women's movement means that the women's movement as "exodus community",[55] moves beyond traditional religions:

> The adequate exodus requires communication, community and creation. The truly moving space will not be merely unorthodox or reformist, but will be on its way beyond unorthodoxy as well as orthodoxy, discovering and bringing forth the really new.[56]

Daly continued to develop this vision of spiritual liberation/revolution and in *Gyn/Ecology: The Metaethics of Radical Feminism*[57] she outlined a three-stage journey of becoming in the spiritual revolution for women. This, then, continued to flesh out the vision of feminist liberative spirituality that Daly proposed as the successor to traditional religions. The first stage identified by Daly in this journey beyond traditional religion is the analysis of the myths of patriarchal religions as deceptive and oppressive. Secondly, there is the analysis of misogynist practices as the murdering of women's self. Third, there is a movement away from patriarchy to being, to communal religion. Daly restates in *Gyn/Ecology* her basic conviction that women must reject patriarchal religions as part of this revolution because it is inherently male-dominated. Daly envisages this process of becoming, and this throwing off of the old, as a metapatriarchal journey. It is an uncovering of the self, recognising the powers of the self alongside the realisation of connection to the earth as a voyage into danger. For Marjori Suchocki, it is with

Gyn/Ecology that we get Daly's unequivocal rejection of the feminist Christian possibility:

> ...it is Daly's work in *Beyond God the Father* which has inspired many women to find new ways of being as Christian who are also feminists. In *Gyn/Ecology*, however, the possibility of being both Christian and feminist is radically denied.[58]

Such is the extent of Daly's influence through her critical articulation of the rejection of Christianity as a possible feminist context or base, that many have come not only to recognise the significance of her analysis but to understand also that she has influenced a dominant dialogue about whether it is possible to be a Christian and a feminist. Ann Loades makes very clear the importance of Daly's argument and the need for feminist informed Christian theologies to address the claims she makes relating to the incompatibility of Christianity and feminisms. Loades, then, places the need to respond to Daly at the centre of the feminist informed Christian theological task. The radicalism and veracity of Daly's critique and methodology are not grounds for dismissing her analysis without adequate and detailed response:

> We may think some parts of her picture overdone.....Yet her work is indispensable reading none the less for those who want to begin to feel and so to think about the contribution Christian institutions and their theology have made to the distress that fails the feminist agenda, assuming that we all have something to gain by attending to that stress.[59]

A very powerful and potentially exclusivist aspect of Daly's claims for the development of feminist consciousness relate to her positioning of knowledge and feminisms. She argues in *Gyn/Ecology* that "The Otherworld Journey begins with a loss of ignorance",[60] making clear and unequivocal, the contrasting of the feminist-liberated-enlightened state for women with any other. Daly's claims and positioning of feminisms in her critique and philosophy amount to a very specific, if not fixed, understanding of what feminisms are and should be. Such an interpretation of Daly's reading of feminisms is supported by her own response to contemporary gender studies and critical theory. She has shown herself to be being highly critical of developments in feminist theory:

> Postmodernism is the ultimate in patriarchal scholarship. Therefore it is perfectly dead. It has produced a monster, "postmodern feminism", which, like itself, is a dead thing and can be legitimated only by postmodernism.[61]

At some length Daly critiques feminist theory and the shape and presence of feminisms in academia or "academentia",[62] with the accusation that focus on gender (as opposed to feminisms) and postmodern theoretical constructs are negative "...we did not foresee the invasion of Feminist Theory by minions of post-modern masters".[63] She is almost contemptuous of women who promote and engage such theory in their analysis:

> So what else is new? Women under patriarchy have always been assigned to be carriers of woman-negating ideologies...But recently there has been a serious escalation...How did it get this bad?[64]

Daly has an almost prescriptive view of what feminist informed leaving of traditional religions should actually be in terms of the shape it takes. So she is also critical of women who appear in one sense to have left the Christian tradition, but who have not, according to her understanding, moved decisively away from its associated patriachalism, "In order to escape the tyranny of Christianity, some have turned to other forms of institutionalised spirituality....All patriarchal religions sap female energy".[65] In *Quintessence* Daly's adversarial language and imagery is further developed adding even more weight to the unequivocal alignment of feminisms with the rejection of Christianity. She describes *Quintessence* as "..a Desperate Act performed in a time of ultimate battles between principalities and powers".[66] The late twentieth century, for Daly, was a time of great danger,[67] a time in which women needed to be both vigilant and creative:

> Ignoring phony promises of a "better future", Wayward Women *will* to find and create a Real Future. We Time-Space travel beyond archetypal deadtime and reach deep into our own Memories, our Deep Past, to Dis-cover the roots of an Archaic Future, beyond the limits of patriarchal time.[68]

This unrelenting vision of the inevitability of the rejection of Christianity and traditional religions aligned clearly by Daly with the realisation of feminist goals, impacts as a hugely committed and powerful vision. At the same time, however, there is the potentially hegemonous implication of the apparent refusal to acknowledge or allow for individual creativity and movement. Daly's understanding of feminist possibility seems firmly determined, and so perhaps limited, by her own experiences. The effect of this on her ensuing philosophy for many is fundamentally problematic. Committed and unwavering creative rage appears compromised by the imposed vision of the fixed nature and form of feminist liberation and justice.

As well as this problematic emphasis and determination of women's liberation in relation to traditional religions, Daly's unwavering and uncompromising prescriptive vision has also attracted critical attention in other areas of her work. It has been claimed that Daly throughout her work offers idealised understandings of "woman", gives clear priority and value to the experiences of women, and sees women as clearly conflictually differentiated from men. Lynne Segal in *Is the Future Female? Troubled Thoughts on Contemporary Feminism*[69] argues that in Daly's work there is a "consignment of men, and all things male, to universal execration now and forever"[70] and relates this to a further limiting of her vision:

> ...there is a snag. Mary Daly's writing is also A-mazingly anti-woman as well as anti-political...Not only all men, but most women, are excluded from any possible creative being or salvation.[71]

In effect, epistemological claims and privilege are being made for women and feminisms that places the ability to discern, create and participate in possibilities for new ways of living very firmly and perhaps exclusively with women, and particular types of women. As Daly claims:

> Memory-Bearing Women are Here and Now charged with the responsibility of blasting open the walls that have been installed in our minds/souls and opening the way to participate in the Biophilic Elemental Integrity of the Universe, which is Quintessence.[72]

The possibility of knowledge and participation here is linked to rage, and Daly reasserts the importance of radicalism and focus. Rage is not a barrier to development but a catalyst or a tool, "Our Rage enables us to recognize the reality which is hidden by the foreground. It triggers our Breakthrough to seemingly esoteric, yet utterly available knowledge".[73] Rage is key to knowledge, and women, as Daly puts it, who are "In Touch with Quintessence",[74] "...become more than ever like trees and like angels. Extending our roots deeper, we are free to expand and participate in the creation of the universe".[75]

Sheila Greeve Davaney in "Problems with Feminist Theory: Historicity and the Search for Sure Foundations",[76] a key article in the development of feminist theological analysis published in 1987, was very critical of the particular significance attributed to women and feminisms in Daly's work. Davaney places Daly alongside other feminist theologians in terms of the claims that she implicitly, and indeed often explicitly, makes for feminist values and perspectives:

> Despite her insistence upon the constructive/creative character of these symbols and visions, Daly, no less than Schussler Fiorenza and Ruether, refuses to understand such feminist perspectives as merely alternatives to male-construed interpretations of reality...Daly argues for the validity of feminist visioning on the grounds that it participates in and corresponds to ultimate reality.[77]

Davaney's criticism here relates to a concern with the authoritative valuing of women's experiences in feminist informed theologies. She argues that feminist informed theologies generally make unacceptable truth claims for women's experiences. For Davaney, it is a problem concerning the assertion of the perspectival nature of knowledge and truth alongside the quest for norms or truths and the feminist assertion of vision. Many critics have come to recognise that for a number of reasons, not least of all the development and effectiveness of feminist informed theologies, that truth claims must be assessed carefully and critically by feminists, "...each thinker has refused to sever the connection between knowledge and ontological reality".[78]

More recently, Marsha Aileen Hewitt *Critical Theory of Religion: A Feminist Analysis*[79] has argued that the feminist philosophy articulated by Mary Daly depends upon an understanding of woman as idealised and reified:

> The core structure of her feminist philosophy conceptualizes an authentic female Being to which all women ultimately correspond, but from which they have become alienated through the dominating and repressive practices of patriarchy.[80]
>
> Gynocentric feminism, as represented by Daly and as a general theory of women's liberation, is self-defeating in that it rests on an identitary logic that generates a regulatory fiction of what true femaleness is by imposing a compulsory correspondence between a transcendental female subject and individual women.[81]
>
> Most disturbing of all, the political implications of Daly's theorizing are authoritarian and hierarchical; not only are males excluded from her unifying vision of reconciliation of existence and essence, but so, it appears, are those women who do not conform to her view of real womanhood, the criteria of which are defined by Daly alone.[82]

Hewitt is quite clear about the implications of Daly's philosophy as prescriptive, authoritarian, and essentially limiting. She also envisages that Daly's understanding is hugely problematic for women, particularly in terms of negotiating and valuing difference, "Daly's feminist philosophy at best is capable of providing only an abstract unity *among* women at the expense of the concrete differences that exist *between* women".[83] This, then, ties in with the very insightful and influential critique of Daly's work and presumptions by Audre Lorde, in *Sister Outsider* already mentioned in Chapter One:[84]

> What you excluded from Gyn/Ecology dismissed my heritage and the heritage of all other non-European women, and denied the real connections that exist between all of us...
>
> The oppression of women knows no ethical nor racial boundaries, true, but that does not mean it is identical within those differences. Nor do the reservoirs of our ancient powers know these boundaries. To deal with one without even alluding to the other is to distort our commonality as well as our difference.
>
> For then beyond sisterhood is still racism.

Amber Katherine has described Lorde's criticisms here as "the paradigmatic example of challenges to white feminist theory by feminists of color".[85]

The significance of Mary Daly's thought, especially her earlier work, for the development of feminist informed Christian theologies is clearly outstanding. Daly's challenge is alluring and enticing, and Marjorie Suchocki, along with many others, interprets the challenge of Mary Daly's thought as an essential focus for feminist informed Christian theologies, asking, "Can Christianity afford to ignore it? Let us dare to accept the challenge of Mary Daly".[86] The strength and weakness of Daly's philosophy relate to the force of conviction and uncompromising assertion of her rejection of Christianity as a focus of feminist possibilities. Whatever the perspective taken on the approach and argument of Daly, clear acknowledgement must be given to the groundbreaking and quite decisive departure in feminist informed theological engagement heralded by Daly's work. Carol Christ's recognition of the pivotal significance of Daly's challenge, already noted in Chapter One, is an appropriate note to conclude in assessing the impact of Daly's thought on the development of feminist informed Christian theologies:

> A serious Christian response to Daly's criticism of the core symbolism of Christianity will either have to show that the core symbolism of Father and Son do not have the effect of reinforcing and legitimating male power and female submission, or it will have to transform Christian imagery at its very core.[87]

Naomi Goldenberg

Although Mary Daly's feminist critique is clearly of key, and some would claim unrivalled, significance to the development of Christian feminist theologies, she was by no means the only feminist critic articulating a clear feminist based rejection of the possibilities of feminist informed Christian theologies as tools or contexts of justice in the 1970s and 1980s. Naomi Goldenberg, a feminist psychologist of religion, outlined in her 1979 publication *Changing of the Gods: Feminism and the End of Traditional Religion* the radical implications of the feminist assessment of traditional religions as fundamentally patriarchal and oppressive to women. She argued that feminist analysis and criticism of Christianity were, in effect, bringing about the downfall of traditional religions. In Goldenberg's assessment, feminisms and Christianity are fundamentally irreconcilable and she cited a key reason for this as Christianity, with its male saviour, can not support the liberation of women. As will be seen later, the focus on the perceived male symbolism of Christianity, and the implications of Christ's maleness, have been a particular concern of a number of feminist informed Christian theologies.

Like Mary Daly, Goldenberg, who was also based in North America, argued that it was within the setting of feminist activity of the 1970s, such as consciousness-raising groups, that the question of "what will happen to God?"[88] arose. She not only placed the critique of religions as within the field of feminist critical concern but also argued that religion should in fact receive particular attention for its apparent role in the oppression of women. Goldenberg was particularly critical of Judaism and Christianity for their role in the oppression of women and one specific reason that she gave for this is that both "involved accepting God as the ultimate in male authority figures".[89] This focus on authority as particularly problematic for women is a feature of feminist informed theological analysis and has proved particularly troublesome for those who are concerned to incorporate the insights and values of feminisms into a Christian perspective. Such a focus then leads to related questions of the representation and embodiment of authority in priestly roles, issues that Goldenberg also highlighted as problematic for Christian women. She asks how can women effectively represent this authority in ascribed priestly roles? Like many other feminists at this time, she argued that the changes of society brought about by feminisms, would lead to "an end to God",[90] "The feminist movement in Western culture is engaged in the slow execution of Christ and Yahweh".[91]

Goldenberg firmly rejected the possibility of feminist religious reformism, with the claim that changes necessary for Christianity and Judaism to support and accommodate feminist goals, would be "major departures from tradition".[92] Such an interpretation of the implications of feminist Christian encounter clearly has a definite, if not always explicitly detailed, understanding of what constitutes Christianity. Reflecting on the 1977 papal declaration reasserting the denial of access to ordained catholic priesthood for women, Goldenberg pointed to the significance of the denial of priesthood because of the representative, symbolic role of the priest. She predicted major changes in the number of women in positions of authority in Christianity and from this went on to pose the very important question of whether if the changes feminisms calls for are realised would this not so change Christianity as to "radically alter the religion".[93] For Goldenberg, then, a key part of her approach is the claim that a feminist transformed Christianity, a Christianity of justice, would not, in effect, be Christian. This is a very contentious but important part of the debate surrounding feminist Christian encounters. Given such an assessment by Goldenberg the religious feminist reformers are "engaged in a hopeless effort",[94] an effort, which given the nature and strength of feminist aims and values is not enough. The need is to move forward with creative imagination, "Some of us must have the nerve to go beyond mere research and imagine new possibilities"[95] and, reminiscent of Mary Daly, she talks of "a philosophical leap entirely out of patriarchal structures".[96]

As a psychologist of religion, Goldenberg focused specifically on the significance and function of symbols in human life:

> The nature of a religion lies in the nature of the symbols and images it exalts in ritual and doctrine. It is the psychic picture of Christ and Yahweh that inspires the loves, the hates and the behaviour patterns of Christians and Jews.[97]

Reflecting particularly on the significance of the symbol of Christ, Goldenberg like other feminist critics made a direct link between this central Christian symbol and the oppression of women:

> Jesus Christ cannot symbolize the liberation of women. A culture that maintains a masculine image for its highest divinity cannot allow its women to experience themselves as the equals of its men. In order to develop a theology of women's liberation, feminists have to leave Christ and the Bible behind them.[98]

For Goldenberg, feminist critique was uncovering the dualistic hierarchies of Christian symbolism and beliefs. She argued that a fundamental and essentially destructive implication of Christian symbolism and belief is the resulting dependency of women on men. Women need to move away from such dependency to a valuing of their own experiences. Goldenberg has paid tribute to the significance of Christian theologians working from a feminist informed perspective, and noted particularly the contribution of theologians such as Sallie McFague. Nevertheless she has remained very critical of the reformist enterprise as a whole. Drawing on a Freudian critique Goldenberg noted that the way in which all religion asserts male authority figures leads to dependency and damage,[99] and argued specifically that Christian imagery prevents women leaving their "Oedipal prisons".[100] The movement away from dependency on these symbols and authority lead women to constructive liberative possibilities, "...we can certainly gain direction from construction of our own personal religious consciousness".[101]

Jungian analysis of the significance of myth has also featured in Goldenberg's approach and she pointed particularly to Jung's stress on the significance of myth for human living, and the importance of religion and discovering "a religious process within the self".[102] This is where Goldenberg located the significance of psychoanalysis. Following the feminist fuelled demise of traditional religions and traditional religious symbols Goldenberg located great significance and possibilities with psychoanalysis. She talked of the need for a "living religion";[103] a religion that fulfils individuals needs through its myths and meaningfulness. Goldenberg has developed this concern with the interplay and possibilities of feminisms and psychoanalytic theory in *Returning Words to Flesh: Feminism, Psychoanalysis, and the Resurrection of the Body*[104] published in 1990. In an attempt not only to advocate the importance of psychoanalysis for feminisms but also to stress the essential compatibility of them she claimed that there were four features shared by both feminisms and psychoanalytic theory, which promise fruitful dialogue:

1. A concern and focus on the past as of particular significance and source of meaning,
2. a focus on female symbols and images, particularly with a view to deconstructing patriarchal images,
3. a stress on the importance of community to the formation of the individual,
4. a recognition of the significance of fantasy in human thinking.

So, a very significant feature of Goldenberg's feminist critique, following her rejection of traditional religions, and especially Christianity, was her insistence on the central importance of symbols for human meaning. Like Daly, she recognised the importance of symbol and community for human living, central aspects of many traditional religions, and was concerned to incorporate these as core elements of the feminist based living that will replace such religions. Traditional religions incorporate elements that are a part of meaningful and imaginative living but these can be addressed by feminisms in dialogue with psychoanalytic theory.

Carol Christ

Like Mary Daly and Naomi Goldenberg, Carol Christ rejected the possibility of feminist reform of the Christian tradition. In terms of her own commitment and theological scholarship she has moved, and documented this move, from a Christian to a Postchristian position. The particular significance of Christ's critique and constructive theologising here is twofold; first in her search beyond traditional religious symbols and second in the inclusive approach that she adopts to this.

In the early to mid 1970s Christ was influenced by the emerging feminist informed theological discourse and particularly by Daly's innovative thinking. The insights that she developed, about God, patriarchy, scripture and language, led eventually to a rejection of biblical and traditional religions. This rejection was based on her belief that the core symbolism of these traditions was not capable of supporting a positive and liberating image for women. In her 1997 publication *Rebirth of the Goddess: Finding Meaning in Feminist Spirituality*,[105] Christ detailed her feminist awakening, arguing that, "Gradually, it began to dawn on me that the image of God as Father, Son, and Spirit was at the root of the problem".[106] So, one of the underlying problematics for Christ of Christian theology was its understanding of, and imagery used for, God. For Christ, the Christian God is a judgmental God, a God of war and military force, "Feminists view the judgmental, dominating ethos as an integral part of the image of God as a patriarchal male".[107] The feminist driven explicit inclusion of experience in theology, alongside the emphasis on relationship as connection, has lead Christ to a methodology, which is critical, constructive, and based in pluralistic awareness. She has demonstrated throughout her theological writings an openness to different potential sources of religiosity. As a result some of the most challenging and transformative insights, particularly of early feminist informed theologies, are found in the theology of Christ. Her work is characterised by two distinctive and persistent concerns that effectively shape the ethos of both her feminist based rejection of Christianity and of her search for alternative forms and sources of religiosity. First, a pluralistic feminist understanding of the wide range of potential sources for religiosity, and second, the critical awareness of the particular and yet diverse nature of women's experiences. At all levels, the authoritative inclusion and functioning of women's experiences gives identity and coherence to Christ's work. Collectively these two features distinguish Christ's very clear and powerful rejection of traditional religions, and especially Christianity, in such a way as to make explicit her own position without encroaching on or making critical judgements of the feminist awareness or sophistication of women working with different approaches. So, having moved beyond the Christian tradition, because of what she experienced as its deeply rooted sexism, Christ has gone on to explore other potential resources and traditions for the development of a feminist thealogy. Part of Christ's concern and engagement with non-traditional sources of religiosity for women led her in her earlier work to focus on the stories and poetry of contemporary women writers. Her approach and ideas here are grounded in the conviction that stories are an important part of human existence. In her view, they play a significant role in the search for meaningfulness and in understanding, shaping and reflecting experience.

This search for meaning has also taken Christ to the symbols and traditions of the goddess, and she notes the attraction of such traditions for many women who themselves have a heritage of traditional religions but who are looking elsewhere in the search for meaning:

In America, Europe, Australia, and New Zealand, hundreds of thousands of women and increasing numbers of men brought up in the biblical religions are rediscovering the language, symbols, and rituals of the Goddess.[108]

Christ links this post-traditional feminist search specifically to the second wave feminist movement.[109] One of the most interesting and significant features of her approach to the grounding of her thealogy in the traditions of the ancient goddesses is the claim that this does not bring her to an exclusivist approach to religiosity. Christ claims that the images and symbols of the Goddess here are *one* source of her thealogy and not the only possible source. She claims that she has not simply replaced the Christian sources of authority (which she identifies as scripture and tradition) with the goddesses. This then leaves open the possibility both for Christ's own movement or development and very importantly, communicating an ethos of openness and non-judgement towards other feminist informed theologies. The criterion for assessing the value and validity of what she learns about the goddess is pragmatic, and based firmly in experience. In an article published in 1985 "What are the sources of my thealogy"[110] she claims that, "I judge everything I learn from the past on the basis of my own experience as shaped, named and confirmed by the voices of my sisters".[111] This, then, moves away from an external locating of authority and leaves open the possibility for change. For her the attraction and suitability of Goddess spirituality and symbolism is that they reflect her own concerns and experiences. These include a strong ecological concern, and belief in nature as holy. For Christ, there is a direct link between the imaging of God as female and women's liberation; the Goddess is a transformative image for women and society. Ritual and celebration also have an important role here, "While images and metaphors inspire the rebirth of the Goddess, rituals bring her power into our lives".[112] Christ does not take her own experiences, her rejection of Christianity and focus on goddess symbols and traditions, as normative in her work. She sees herself as remaining in conversation with, and reflecting upon the Christian traditions. Writing in *Rebirth of the Goddess*, for example, she claims that, "...this book is very much in conversation with Christian and Jewish understandings of God...".[113]

The Postchristian engagement with goddess symbols and traditions has been subject to extensive criticism, particularly in terms of historical accuracy, the claims made for ancient religions in relation to the status of women, and charges of inverse sexism. For Christ, however, the goddesses have been both sources of power and symbols of power. Within her own life they have uncovered her experience of powerlessness in the face of male imagery for the divine, and have revealed her own power and existence within the world. Like many feminist thealogians engaging with such traditions, the importance of the goddess as a symbol of contemporary women is to do with the affirmation of autonomous female power. The goddesses are seen to have an important role to play in the need to recognise and celebrate our connections to each other, to our bodies and to the earth. Christ has argued that even if goddess religion in the past functioned to support patriarchal power, this is not necessarily the case today. Christ's own approach and involvement in goddess thealogy has a firm grounding in practice, in ritual celebration. She has been particularly influenced here by the Greek goddesses, especially Gaia and Demeter, Persephone and Aphrodite. Now each year through the Ariadne Institute for the Study of Myth and Ritual Christ organises and takes part in Goddess pilgrimages to Crete and sacred journeys in Greece.

Christ's methodological approach to goddess symbols and traditions has also involved analysis of historical and prehistorical records for resources and evidence for female power to support her developing thealogy. In *Laughter of Aphrodite: Reflections on a Journey to the Goddess*, published in 1987, Christ outlined a feminist reconstructionist approach to goddess history in which she focused on images and records of the goddesses and traces their development and transformation. She examined the way in which the prehistoric goddess was transformed to meet patriarchal needs. The feminist development of Christ's thealogy, particularly in her connections with the goddess, incorporates alongside this a strong ecological concern. She proposes a move away from an understanding of god or divine reality as transcendent to a more immanental understanding.

It is important to stress that Christ's rejection of Christianity is very clear, but alongside this is her consistent awareness of diversity and her methodological commitment to empathy and this distinguishes her approach. She is very open to difference and especially to transformative possibilities. In line with this, Christ has proposed a model of feminist scholarship that attempts to overcome separation and is based in experiences of connection. As she understands it, theological scholarship, as well as imaginative and constructive theologising, if such distinctions are possible, need to be informed and transformed by values and insights of feminisms. So, important changes are needed in the ways in which theology, and scholarship in general, are understood. The failure of traditional scholarship to recognise and incorporate the distinctive experiences of women must be challenged; a "paradigm shift"[114] is necessary for the functioning of feminist scholarship. Feminist scholarship, as noted earlier, is concerned with the deconstruction of the myth of objectivity and with the development of a different model. The model of scholarship that Christ has proposed integrates the personal and the political and is determined by her openness to possibility. It begins in its "first moment"[115] with the ethos or desire, that which informs or motivates the work of the scholar, "to understand, to connect, to preserve or to change the world".[116] From this, the scholar must then concern herself or himself with expansion of perspective through the experiences of others. Christ names this "the second moment of scholarship",[117] and here the insights and methods of critical scholarship are important. The aim remains with the ethos of empathy. Christ names the "third moment" of scholarship as judgement. The scholar is able to incorporate, through judgement, that which has been discovered, into an informed or expanded standpoint. Such judgements that may be made are acknowledged to be finite and limited, but scholarly. Christ argues that the valuing of women's experiences in feminist informed theologies and thealogies avoids a fully relativist position being adopted:

> We acknowledge the perspectival nature of all truth claims, but we are not thoroughgoing relativists, because our feminist experiences contradicts that. We are not nihilists, because we believe that feminism has the potential to better the world.
>
> We seek to speak a truth rooted in our experience, our time and place, our bodies. We can affirm the relativity of all universal truth claims, because we know that all truth claims are rooted in time and space, in our experience and body. And there is no experience or body that is not perspectival.[118]

Christ stresses commitment along with awareness of the relativity of personal circumstances and thought. For her it is important to remain open to diversity of perspective and to criticism that such diversity brings, "We should think of our 'truth claims' as the product of embodied thinking not as eternally or universally valid thought".[119] For Christ, then, universalism, relativism and claims for objectivity are avoided by the integration of personal experience with theological reflection. The fact that Christ understands her own experiences and women's experiences in general, to be diverse and yet particular, means that her understanding of the possibilities of feminist informed theologies and thealogies are flexible and fluid, whilst at the same time still asserting her own rejection of Christianity. This brings Christ to a post-traditional feminist thealogical position that whilst clearly rejecting the reformist possibilities of Christianity for herself, does not impose the same kind of alignment of feminisms and rejection of Christianity that the approach of Daly seems to bring. This difference seems to rest largely with their respective understandings of and visions of feminisms.

Daphne Hampson

The focus so far in this chapter has been on feminist informed theological criticism and rejection of traditional religions that have emerged out of North American contexts, which is indicative of the location and direction of the development of early feminist theologies. However, the final key feminist thinker to be examined here, whose rejection of Christian feminist theology has impacted substantially on the whole question of the possibility of Christian feminist theologies is the Scottish-based feminist theologian Daphne Hampson. Hampson is Professor of Post-Christian Thought in the School of Divinity at the University of St Andrews in Scotland. The significance of Hampson's critique here is that her work in this area continues this critical debate with renewed vigour and is a highly visible aspect of contemporary feminist informed theologies in Britain. Her publications in 1990 (*Theology and Feminism* which was revised in 2002) and 1996 (*After Christianity* and *Swallowing a Fishbone*) and numerous articles demonstrate the continued focus in feminist informed theological discourse on questions of incompatibility/compatibility and the significance of this dialogue for contemporary feminist theologies.

Hampson's theology gives significant currency to the claim that Christianity is fundamentally oppressive and can not support or incorporate feminist based visions of justice. She has argued that, "...feminism represents the death-knell of Christianity as a viable religious option".[120] In her publications she gives clear, and for some, convincing reasons, as to why feminisms and Christianity are incompatible. Hampson not only presents a feminist informed theological position which moves beyond Christianity, but she also levels a forceful criticism against those who *do* advocate a feminist informed Christian position, in some ways comparable to the force and logic of Mary Daly's criticism, "I am contending that it is intrinsic to the nature of the Christian religion that it is sexist: that Christianity cannot continue to be itself and allow for the equality of women".[121] Like Goldenberg, Hampson talks of Christianity in crisis, and this is a crisis distinguished by the depth of the challenge it faces from feminist criticism. Hampson's own criticism of feminist informed Christian theologies, and especially her assessment of the incompatibility of feminisms and Christianity, has brought strong objections from Christian theologians working from a feminist informed perspective. An important, and now very well-known, discussion on the possibilities of Christian feminist theology, took place in 1986 at Westminster Cathedral Hall. This was an event coordinated by two key organisations involved with women, Christianity and feminisms the *Catholic Women's Network* and *Women in Theology*. The debate was between Hampson and Rosemary Radford Ruether, and in this Hampson outlines her rejection of a feminist informed Christian position at some length.[122] The paper published from this debate details a very revealing and engaging discussion of the key factors, which have influenced two of the most influential feminist theologians to date in their feminist theological journeys. It is not only the content of the exchange between Ruether and Hampson that is of interest but also the different methodological emphases and fundamental assumptions about both Christianity and feminisms that have shaped their respective arguments.

Hampson identifies what for her are the essentially problematic aspects of the Christian faith for a feminist. She describes how painful the break with Christianity was for her, and poses the fundamental question of whether it is possible to be a Christian and a feminist. For her, the answer lies in her own experiences of leaving Christianity, and her conclusion that Christianity is "intrinsically sexist". It is based on an historical event, the incarnation of God. It is the nature of Christianity as bound up with the historical event of the incarnation of God in Christ that is so problematic. Hampson argues that as God is known through Christ, the teachings and actions of Christ carry great significance for Christians:

> Because Christianity believes that God was in a particular way bound up with one particular thread of human history, in particular what Jesus Christ did and said, becomes in some way normative or authoritative for what is truth for how we should understand God, or how to relate to one another. Let me repeat this. Christianity believes that God is especially known though a particular history. Moreover, Jesus Christ is not just seen as a good man, a human like the rest of us, one who lived close to God. Christianity proclaims God to have made God's self

known through revelation in history. Therefore that revelation and the events surrounding it become a kind of benchmark for the religion.[123]

So, for Hampson it is the nature of Christianity as an historical religion that is the source of problems for feminists such as herself. She describes her movement to a post-traditional position and describes the problematic nature of traditional religions as an ethical issue for feminists. She argues that feminisms incorporate a rejection of external authority; women are claiming the right to be their own authority. In facing the fundamental issue of whether feminisms and Christianity are compatible she replies:

> I think that the feminist must go further than Christianity will allow. And, in any case, I do not believe Christianity to be true. That does not however mean that I do not want to be a religious person. I do. But I must be religious in a way which is commensurate with all else which I believe about the world and my feminism. I hold it to be the case that in feminism Christianity has met with a challenge to which it cannot accommodate itself. That challenge is not going to go away, for feminism has raised a profound ethical issue concerning human equality.[124]

In response, Ruether challenges Hampson's understanding of the nature of Christianity as a historical religion. For Ruether, Christianity as an historical religion, is not bound to the past, but is ever changing and developing. Feminist critique has a key role to play in this development. Ruether argues that God *is* experienced in history, but in a very different way from Hampson's understanding:

> We do not need to take literally anthropomorphic expressions such as "God acts'" or "God intervenes" in history, as though these were events taking place apart from human action. Rather, I would say that God is experienced in the midst of human action in conflicts over social justice and injustice. God is experienced as "breaking into" existing social reality as judgement upon human claims to righteousness. This "shattering" of present reality does not mean shattering the goodness of human nature, an Augustinian-Calvinist distortion of this idea based on a quasi-Manichaan anthropology. Rather, what are shattered are the ideological pretensions of dominant systems of power.[125]

Ruether accepts that, historically, women have experienced Christianity as unjust and oppressive. This recognition, for Ruether, however, does not inevitably lead to the rejection of this tradition on the grounds that it is incompatible with feminisms. She argues for the need for a cultural base for feminisms and for the importance of memory. For her, Christianity *is* compatible with feminisms, and so Christian feminist justice is viable.

Hampson argues that feminist informed theologies have the important task of reconceptualising God in such ways that are not shaped by patriarchal influences and interests. This needs to be done in such a way that both reflects, and is relevant to, contemporary experiences, "the locus of authority as to what we think true and what we want to say, remains with us".[126] She argues that Christianity is "neither true nor moral",[127] and sets out to re-vision ways of talking about and conceptualising God. She notes that feminisms are one aspect of contemporary challenges to the credibility and viability of Christianity, but argues that distinctively:

> ...the feminist challenge makes it difficult to make the sideways move of saying that Christianity is symbolically true. For precisely the feminist contention is that symbols are powerful and may damage relationships.[128]

Accordingly, Hampson is critical of those feminists concerned with reforming the Christian tradition. She remains firm in her understanding of interpretation and transformation, and criticises Christian feminists for their attempts to remain with Christianity and reform it, claiming they "twist Christianity to mean whatever they will"[129] and argues that, "...there is a certain dishonesty in this".[130] This has inevitably brought accusations against Hampson of a fundamentalist reading of Christianity, a charge that she strongly denies. For some, Hampson is very inflexible in her understanding and interpretation of the transformative possibilities of Christianity. For Hampson, the claim of revelation of God in Christ, a historical and particular revelation is as the heart of Christianity. Christian development is possible according to Hampson, but it can not move away from the Christ event, "Christianity is sexist because the past histories to which Christians necessarily make reference was a patriarchal history".[131] This, she claims, is not a fundamentalist reading of Christianity,[132] but argues instead that the values and criteria linked to this historical time and event are patriarchal. Her critique of Christianity, or rejection of Christianity, is based on two key, interrelated ideas, those of truth and ethics. She rejects the possibility of a unique revelation that she claims is absolutely central to the Christian faith, "I do not think that there can be one-off examples in nature or interruptions in the causal nexus of history (such as a bodily resurrection *par excellence* would imply)".[133]

Hampson has gone to some lengths to carefully define what she means with the description that Christianity is an historical religion, based on the particularity of "the Christ event".[134] For her the problem is this claim to particularity. Faith in particularity that is untenable and in her terms "Christian claims cannot stand".[135] The Christological claims which the Christian faith rests on demand this particularity. The second part of Hampson's argument is ethical, and concentrates on feminist understanding of the self,[136] an understanding that is intrinsically incompatible with Christian theological understandings, doctrines and implications. The corresponding symbols and discourses of this theology have determined and perpetuated the subjugation of women. According to Hampson, a shift[137] in understanding and imagination is needed.

Hampson minimally defines Christianity and feminisms, and finds them to be mutually exclusive. In *After Christianity* (1996) Hampson further develops what she terms the twofold crisis facing Christianity, of ethics and truth[138] and points towards new possibilities in the face of such crisis:

> Christianity has become untenable. But that does not necessarily entail a void. It may be that, free of the Christian myth, a new spirituality will flourish. Indeed,

the very paradigms of relationality with which we are beginning to feel comfortable may allow us to capture something of that which is God. A religion based in human experience and in the will to conceive the world as having, at some profound level, sense and purpose, will precisely require for its conceptualisation the kind of thinking in which feminists are engaged. It is with such a theological task that we must make a start.[139]

There are fundamental clashes in Hampson's understanding between feminist values and Christian values, first between autonomy as opposed to heteronomy, and second in terms of the particular nature of Christianity, normative appeal made to this both in terms of the nature of claims made for this and the patriarchal setting.

> For a feminist to be a Christian is indeed for her to swallow a fishbone. It must stick in her throat. To be a Christian is to be placed in a heteronomous position. Feminists believe in autonomy.[140]

Christianity involves authority, and submitting to the authority of another, this blocks equality and "maturity",[141] and leads Hampson to the following, hard-line conclusion, "But for a feminist to be a Christian and also to be true to herself and to her feminist beliefs is, I am suggesting, not possible".[142] Christians, argues Hampson, are "centred"[143] on Christ, God, the Church or the Bible, in other words, looking to and gaining meaning from external authority. Feminisms value autonomy and stand in direct opposition to Christianity.

> What women should do is to have the courage to claim equal rights and be fully adult members of our society. May it not be much more politically effective that I should confront men with my equality with them, denying that any model for relations between men and women is to be found in the past?[144]

An indication of the continued significance, if not dominance, of the debate over the compatibility of feminisms and Christianity, is the collection of essays edited by Hampson, *Swallowing a Fishbone*[145], published in 1996. This text emerged from a discussion that took place in 1990 between Daphne Hampson, Sarah Coakley, Julie Hopkins, Janet Soskice and Nicola Slee focusing on Christian feminist possibilities. Here, again, Hampson makes absolutely clear the incompatibility of Christianity and feminisms, seen in her definition of feminisms:

> I think we must have some *minimal* definition of ...the equality of women and men with all that that implies. I am contending that a religion based on this past, patriarchal history and these patriarchal symbols ...cannot actually promote equality as long as it is based on this history and retain the symbols for God which arise out of this context.[146]

Conclusion

It is of course very difficult to quantify the impact of such rejections on the development of feminist informed Christian theologies, but given the amount of concern with the issue of compatibility/incompatibility to be found in the work of Christian theologians working from a feminist informed perspective, the powerful articulation of this rejection has clearly shaped, and continues to shape, feminist informed Christian theological engagement. All four of the feminist critics whose writings have been explored in this chapter cite feminist insights and claims as contributory in their decision to "leave" Christianity and to reject the possibility of a feminist based reform of traditional religions. In this sense, then, there is a shared acceptance of the findings of feminist critical analysis that traditional religions have been complicit in, if not responsible for, gender based injustice and oppression. This realisation has lead each of them to reject the viability of the feminist informed Christian enterprise, claiming that Christianity cannot be reformed. And, as Goldenberg argues, if the necessary transformation was attempted, that which would emerge would not be Christianity. This rejection of reformist possibilities is a fundamental feature of all four writers' feminist work. Significant differences in approach emerge, however, in the ways in which this conviction is expressed and in the implications drawn out.

Mary Daly unequivocally, and with extensive reasoning, rejects the possibility that Christianity can be reformed by feminist values and critique to the extent that it will support, accommodate and share liberationist feminist aspirations with all of their implications. The language and imagery employed by Daly in her detailed and eloquent rejection of Christianity and other traditional religions leaves the reader in no doubt that in the unfolding or progression of feminisms there is no room for Christianity. The terminology used by Daly, of progression into consciousness, of ontological and spiritual revolution, linked to feminist awareness makes a qualitative distinction between those who have the courage to create a new future, away from patriarchal time, and those who do not. Daly's unwavering identification of feminist informed liberation as involving the rejection of traditional religions, and all associated with it, presents a very clear path for women to follow. The strength of Daly's commitment is derived from her own experiences and valuing of those experiences. So that women must, with rage, create a new future. The way forward is clearly laid down by Daly, from ignorance to knowledge, and even to participation in creation, in being. Naomi Goldenberg and Carol Christ are no less committed in their rejection of traditional religions, and particularly Christianity, than Mary Daly, but are significantly different to Daly, and indeed to some extent to each other, in the ethos and presentation of their rejection. Carol Christ, in particular, offers a pluralistic approach to her feminist based critique.

As well as the clear rejection of traditional religions, post-traditional feminist informed theologies are also distinguished by their continued concern for symbols and traditions that will meet women's needs and desires. Carol Christ, for example, with her focus on the traditions and symbols of the Greek goddesses has explored at some length potential resources for her own pragmatic feminist informed theology. Naomi Goldenberg's exploration of psychoanalysis as an important point of connection with feminisms, also offers many exciting possibilities. This consideration of new or previously marginalised symbols and traditions has also impacted on feminist informed Christian theologies, with many contemporary feminist informed Christian theologians widening their search for useable Christian traditions beyond the canonical limits. One of the most challenging developments of the Post-traditional rejection of Christianity is the challenge that it has laid down specifically to women in their acceptance of authority. Traditional sources of Christian authority are stripped away by feminist critics such as Daly and Hampson, and are indeed cited as sources of injustice. Feminist critique is increasingly calling on women themselves to determine and be their own authority, and to use their experiences, and the experiences of other women, informed by critical thinking, to determine what is and what is not acceptable and just.

A key argument here is that the form and content of the Postchristian feminist rejection of Christianity amounts to a feminist ethical imperative for women to leave traditional religions. Addressing and refuting this alignment of feminisms with the rejection of Christianity has preoccupied many feminist informed Christian theologies. Whilst acknowledging the diversity of perspectives of Postchristian theologies, at the heart of the feminist rejection of the possibilities or viability of feminist informed Christian theologies is an understanding that a feminist informed vision of justice can not be supported or accommodated by Christian based theologies.

Notes

[1] De Beauvoir, S., (1981), *The Second Sex*, Penguin Books p.16.
[2] De Beauvoir, 1981:16.
[3] De Beauvoir, 1981:16.
[4] De Beauvoir, 1981:22.
[5] De Beauvoir, 1981:22.
[6] De Beauvoir, 1981:29.
[7] De Beauvoir, 1981:93.
[8] De Beauvoir, 1981:110.
[9] De Beauvoir, 1981:112.
[10] De Beauvoir, 1981:173.
[11] De Beauvoir, 1981:179.
[12] De Beauvoir, 1981:180.
[13] De Beauvoir, 1981:199.
[14] De Beauvoir, 1981:295.
[15] De Beauvoir, 1981:307.
[16] De Beauvoir, 1981:317.
[17] De Beauvoir, 1981:740.
[18] De Beauvoir, 1981:728.
[19] Eller, C., (1993), *Living in the Lap of the Goddess: The Feminist Spirituality Movement in America*, New York: Crossroad.
[20] Eller, C., (1993), *Living in the Lap of the Goddess: The Feminist Spirituality Movement in America*, New York: Crossroad, p.44.
[21] Eller, 1993:225.

[22] Daly, M., (1993), *Outercourse: The Be-Dazzling Voyage,* London: The Women's Press.
[23] Daly, 1993:55.
[24] Loades, A., in Andrew Linzey and Peter Wexley, (eds.), (1991), *Fundamentalism and Tolerance: An Agenda for Theology and Society,* London: Bellew Publishing, p.114.
[25] Loades in Linzey and Wexley, 1991:114.
[26] Daly, M., (1985), *The Church and the Second Sex,* Boston: Beacon Press, p.5.
[27] Daly, 1985:9.
[28] Daly, 1993:174.
[29] Russell, L., and Shannon, J., (eds.), (1996), *Dictionary of Feminist Theologies,* London: Mowbray.
[30] Hampson, D., in Russell, L., and Shannon, J., (eds.), (1996), *Dictionary of Feminist Theologies,* London: Mowbray, p.219.
[31] Daly, M., (1988), *Websters First New Intergalactic Wickedary of the English Language,* London: The Women's Press.
[32] Daly, 1988:88.
[33] Daly in Christ and Plaskow (eds.), 1992:57.
[34] Daly in Christ and Plaskow (eds.), 1992:62.
[35] Daly, M., (1986), *Beyond God the Father: Towards a Philosophy of Women's Liberation,* London: The Women's Press, p.13.
[36] Daly, 1986:13.
[37] Daly, 1986:19.
[38] Daly, 1986:13-14.
[39] Daly, 1986:138.
[40] Daly, 1985:133.
[41] Daly, 1985:156.
[42] Daly, 1985:140.
[43] Daly, 1985:142.
[44] Daly, 1986:154.
[45] Daly, 1986:157.
[46] Daly, 1985:6.
[47] Daly, 1985:XIII.
[48] Daly, 1985:18.
[49] Daly, 1985:23.
[50] Daly, 1985:25.
[51] Daly, 1985:35-36.
[52] Daly, 1985:43.
[53] Daly, 1985:35-36.
[54] Daly, 1985:158.
[55] Daly, 1985:157.
[56] Daly, 1985:158.
[57] Daly, M., (1984), *Gyn/Ecology: The Metaethics of Radical Feminism,* London: The Women's Press.
[58] Suchocki, M., (1980), "The Challenge of Mary Daly", *Encounter,* 41, p.307.
[59] Loades in Linzey and Wexley, (eds.), 1991:122.
[60] Daly, 1984:413.
[61] Daly, M., (1988), *Webster's First New Intergalactic Wickedary of the English Language,* London: The Women's Press, p.144.
[62] Daly, 1998:132.
[63] Daly, 1998:135.
[64] Daly, 1998:136.

[65] Daly, 1998:147.
[66] Daly, 1998:1.
[67] Daly, 1998:3.
[68] Daly, 1998:3.
[69] Segal, L., (1987), *Is the Future Female? Troubled Thoughts on Contemporary Feminism*, London: Virago.
[70] Segal, 1987:17-18.
[71] Segal, 1987:20.
[72] Daly, 1998:6.
[73] Daly, 1998:180.
[74] Daly, 1998:230.
[75] Daly, 1998:230.
[76] Davaney, S.G., (1987) "Problems with feminist theory: historicity and the search for sure foundations" in Cooey, P.M., Farmer, S.A., and Ross, M.E., (eds.), *Embodied Love: Sensuality and Relationship as Feminist Values*, San Francisco: Harper and Row,
[77] Davaney in Cooey, Farmer and Ross, (eds.), 1987:90
[78] Davaney, 1987:62.
[79] Hewitt, M.A., (1995), *Critical Theory of Religion: A Feminist Analysis*, Minneapolis: Fortress Press.
[80] Hewitt, 1995:133-4.
[81] Hewitt, 1995:140.
[82] Hewitt, 1995:141.
[83] Hewitt, 1995:140.
[84] Lorde in Humm, (ed.), 138-139.
[85] Katherine, A., in Hoagland, S.L. and Frye, M., (eds.), *Feminist Interpretations of Mary Daly* Pennsylvania: The Pennsylvanian State University Press.
[86] Suchocki, 1980:317.
[87] Christ, C., (1977), "The new feminist theology: a review of the literature", *Religious Studies Review*, 3(4), p.205.
[88] Goldenberg, N., (1979) *Changing of the Gods: Feminism and the End of Traditional Religion*, Boston: Beacon Press, p.1.
[89] Goldenberg, 1979:3.
[90] Goldenberg, 1979:3.
[91] Goldenberg, 1979:4.
[92] Goldenberg, 1979:4.
[93] Goldenberg, 1979:7.
[94] Goldenberg, 1979:12.
[95] Goldenberg, 1979:17.
[96] Goldenberg, 1979:18.
[97] Goldenberg, 1979:5.
[98] Goldenberg, 1979:22.
[99] Goldenberg, 1979:35.
[100] Goldenberg, 1979:35.
[101] Goldenberg, 1979:45.
[102] Goldenberg, 1979:49.
[103] Goldenberg, 1979:51.
[104] Goldenberg, N., (1990), *Returning Words to Flesh: Feminism, Psychoanalysis, and the Resurrection of the Body*, Boston: Beacon Press.
[105] Christ, C.P., (1997), *Rebirth of the Goddess: Finding Meaning in Feminist Spirituality*, New York: Routledge.

[106] Christ, 1997:2.
[107] Christ, 1997:23.
[108] Christ, 1997:XIII.
[109] Christ, 1997:3.
[110] Christ, C., (1985) "What are the sources of my theology?", *Journal of Feminist Studies in Religion*, 1(1), pp.120-122.
[111] Christ, 1985:122.
[112] Christ, 1997:25.
[113] Christ, 1997:45.
[114] Christ, C.P, "Toward a paradigm shift in the academy and in religious studies" in Farnham, C., (1987), *The Impact of Feminist Research in the Academy*, Bloomington: Indiana University Press, p.53.
[115] Christ in Farnham, (ed.), 1987:60.
[116] Christ in Farnham, (ed.), 1987:60.
[117] Christ in Farnham, (ed.), 1987:60.
[118] Christ, C.P., (1989) "Embodied thinking: reflections on feminist thealogical method" *Journal of Feminist Studies in Religion*, 5, p.14.
[119] Christ, 1989:15.
[120] Hampson, 1990:1.
[121] Hampson in Hampson and Ruether, 1987:8.
[122] An account of this debate was published in *New Blackfriars* in 1987 (Vol.68, No.801, January, 1987, pp.7-24) entitled "Is there a Place for Feminists in a Christian Church?".
[123] Hampson in Hampson and Ruether, 1987:10.
[124] Hampson in Hampson and Ruether, 1987:14.
[125] Ruether in Hampson and Ruether, 1987:16.
[126] Hampson in Hampson and Ruether 1987:11.
[127] Hampson, 1990:1.
[128] Hampson, 1990:3.
[129] Hampson in Hampson, (ed.), 1996:3.
[130] Hampson in Hampson, (ed.), 1996:3.
[131] Hampson in Hampson, (ed.), 1996:7.
[132] Hampson in Hampson, (ed.), 1996:7.
[133] Hampson in Hampson, (ed.), 1996:112.
[134] Hampson 1996:12.
[135] Hampson 1996:12.
[136] Hampson 1996:84.
[137] Hampson 1996:105.
[138] Hampson, 1996:V-VI.
[139] Hampson, 1996:11.
[140] Hampson in Hampson, (ed.), 1996:1.
[141] Hampson in Hampson, (ed.), 1996:2.
[142] Hampson in Hampson, (ed.), 1996:2.
[143] Hampson in Hampson, (ed.), 1996:2.
[144] Hampson, D., (1996), *After Christianity*, London: SCM Press Ltd, p.73.
[145] Hampson, D., (ed.), (1996), *Swallowing a Fishbone?: Feminist Theologians Debate Christianity*, London: SPCK.
[146] Hampson, D., (ed.), (1996), *Swallowing a Fishbone? Feminist Theologians Debate Christianity*, London: SPCK, p.117.

Chapter Three

Christology and Passionate Mutuality: The Feminist Theology of Carter Heyward

Introduction

The focus of the first detailed consideration of feminist Christian encounters in this study will be the strategy of feminist informed radical reinterpretation of christology that has been developed by Carter Heyward and employed by her in the development of a theology of mutuality. The Christ symbol, and in particular, the perceived possibilities for mutuality that she understands to be enshrined in the life and work of Christ, lie at the heart of Christianity for Heyward, and at the heart of her proposed feminist informed theology of mutuality. Carter Heyward is a theologian whose writings over the last 25 years chart a solid and passionate engagement of feminisms and Christianity. Her theological writings are characterised by a persistent focus on injustice, and with the development of theological responses and challenges to injustice. To facilitate this critical theological engagement Heyward has explored and drawn on a range of different critical and social theories. She has also been influenced in her approach and ideas, in some cases quite explicitly, by a number of thinkers with diverse concerns and working out of a range of different contexts, including for example, Gustavo Gutierrez, Martin Buber, Paul Tillich, Elie Wiesel, Mary Daly, Beverly Harrison and Dorothee Solle.

For Heyward, the historical manifestations of human alienation through social, political and religious injustice are diverse. And the task facing those concerned to address injustice is enormous and the problems involved should not be underestimated. Like certain other theologians who draw on feminist insights and analysis, she has a broad and quite inclusive understanding of the forms and types of injustice. This is an understanding that includes gender based injustice, but by no means is limited only to this. Given the extensive and often debilitating criticisms levelled at the presumptions and understandings of justice and injustice by feminisms so far, as highlighted in Chapter One, such an insight is important. It indicates something of Heyward's perception of the multilayered and sometimes competing types of injustice facing humanity. In *Our Passion for Justice*[1] published in 1984, Heyward's detailed explication of injustice illustrates the depth and diversity of her concern; she highlighted a spectrum of injustices that are of particular concern to her and in so doing articulated an understanding of the complexity of injustice as a multilayered and interlocking system. She named the varieties of injustice as:

1. White supremacy (racism), by which persons of darker colors have been denied social power to shape their own lives in this and many other societies;
2. Male gender superiority (sexism) and its twin, the oppressive assumption in sexist society that the male-over-female relation is sexually normative (heterosexism);
3. The accumulation of profit at the expense of human wellbeing (the effect of advanced capitalism in practice) and its structural corollaries: the mystified wounds of class (classism) and the business of war-making as profitable (militarism);
4. National, cultural, and/or religious arrogance (imperialism), which, among Christians, has taken the form of a virulent antagonism toward Jewish people (anti-Semitism) and which is manifest also in the unholy alliance between the current governments of the United States and Israel in their treatment of Palestinian people;
5. Public policies that dictate the isolation of elderly, sick, and differently-abled persons from full participation in society.[2]

Heyward, who is now Howard Chandler Professor of Theology at Episcopal Divinity School, Cambridge, Massachusetts has set herself the daunting task of uncovering, opposing and articulating theologies in the face of such injustices. And the commitment and enthusiasm that she brings to this task is characteristic of her approach, and one of the most compelling features of her methodology.

Despite the diversity of influences on Heyward's theology, and the range of her concern with the varieties of injustices as indicated above, she consistently gives particular weight to the insights and values of feminist criticism and feminist based visions of justice. So that despite the important recognition that she gives to both the diversity of injustices and the different significant critical discourses for challenging such injustices she nevertheless still seems to place particular significance, if not priority, with feminisms as effective tools of critical analysis and as tools for overcoming such injustices. This recognition of the possible variety of valid and effective critical tools for uncovering and opposing injustices juxtaposed against the apparent prioritising of feminisms as the chosen critical tool is for some an uncomfortable tension in need of detailed critical investigation in relation to the field of feminisms and feminist theologies generally. This tension relates to the fact that many feminist informed theologians are increasingly recognising both the particularity and contextual nature of feminisms as critical tools and yet still seem to prioritise them as having some kind of overriding significance. As will be examined later in this chapter it was the encountering and consideration of the insights and methods of feminisms in the early stages of the emergence of contemporary feminist informed theologies that really set a very clear precedent in Heyward's patterns of theological engagement and in particular a precedent in terms of the ways in which she has consistently employed the critical base and categories of feminisms.

This chapter focuses primarily on Heyward's awareness of injustice, particularly gender based injustice, and on the values and categories of feminisms that she employs to challenge such injustices. Her approach is one which brings to bear the critiques and values of feminisms on Christian theology both in the development and clarification of a justice seeking theology. In doing this she has developed a theology, in her words, *a theology of mutuality*, that attempts to hold in tension the traditions of Christianity and the often demanding and challenging insights of feminisms through a radical reinterpretation of some of the core symbols and traditions of Christianity. In particular, her theology has been concerned with a radical reading or reinterpretation of christology. Heyward's direct address and feminist rereading of christology, of what has proved to be one of the most problematic aspects of Christianity for many feminist informed theologians, is very revealing of the problems and challenges posed by feminist Christian encounter. In order to explore key aspects of Carter Heyward's theology, and in particular, the strategies that she has developed and employed in her radical reinterpretation of the Christ symbol this chapter begins with a brief overview of her own journey towards Theological Seminary and ordained priesthood. Heyward's life events and personal encounters are bound up very closely with her theological reflections and so any study of the feminist informed theological methods employed by Heyward needs an appropriate contextualisation in her own life experiences. Her journey towards ordained priesthood marks her radical involvement with feminist inspired direct action and demonstrates the way in which her theology of mutuality emerged out of her earlier ecclesial and feminist experiences. Having established something of the background to Carter Heyward's feminist informed Christian theology, the main section of this chapter focuses on the ways in which Carter Heyward has placed christology at the very centre of the theology of mutual relation and explores her concern to develop and advocate this as consistent with and appropriate to both Christianity and feminisms.

The development of Carter Heyward's early theology

Heyward's theological and educational backgrounds are very revealing in the attempt to identify and critically assess the strategies that she has developed and applied in her theological encountering of Christianity and feminisms. She was born in North Carolina and grew up in an Episcopalian environment. Whilst at college in Virginia[3] she developed an academic interest in religion and became aware of a strong sense of vocation to being ordained a priest, a vocation that through denial and challenge had a determinate influence on the development of her own feminist informed theological perspective. After graduation from college Heyward was accepted at Union Theological Seminary at a time when women could not be ordained to the full priesthood in the Episcopal Church. This in itself was a somewhat ambiguous and indeterminate position for Heyward at this time. Given such an ambiguity and the perceived gendered differential regarding theological training, Heyward and those around her began to consider seriously, and eventually employ, the tools of the emerging feminisms and feminist informed theologies in analysis of their situation. This involved the challenging of both theological justification and reasoning and also of institutional authority that denied the possibility of women's sense of vocation to ordained priesthood or other "off limit" areas:

> In a society and a Church in which woman has been put into a place out of which she cannot move, and effort on her part to burst out of this place will be considered strange or abnormal. Those invested with institutional authority are likely to get their backs up and balk defensively at her efforts. For such a woman is a threat to both men and women who have heavy investments in maintaining the present order.[4]

Faced with such institutional resistance and brick-walling Heyward entered a very difficult time personally as her own sense of injustice at the situation she faced developed. She was convinced that there was no sound theological reason for the exclusion of women from ordained priesthood and so withdrew from Union Theological seminary for a while. In pursuit of a clear understanding of her situation and of the possibilities for change, she began attending both a women's consciousness-raising group and psychotherapy, where she explored her own feelings of anger and denial. This intense addressing and engagement with often-painful issues, in this instance the denial of her vocation to be ordained into priesthood, has come to characterise the passionate approach of Carter Heyward and marks her theology as one of personal contextualisation. Heyward's radical commitment is founded on her own experiences and upon empathetic reflections on the experiences of those around her.

The strength of Heyward's commitment and belief in her vocation was evidenced in 1971 when she put herself forward for ordination in North Carolina. This however was rejected at the time but she was accepted for ordination in 1972 in New York. She was ordained a deacon in 1972 with the hope and belief that the Episcopal Church would soon admit women to the full priesthood. However, in 1973 in Louisville, Kentucky the General Convention of the Church rejected a motion that which would have allowed women to enter the priesthood. This perceived rejection fuelled Heyward's sense of injustice. Justice for her was intrinsic to her understanding of Christianity and God, and she began to differentiate very firmly between the traditions and doctrines of Christianity and the possibilities and intentions of Christian commitment, a key element of her feminist informed theological approach to Christianity. She has consistently refused to be bound by claimed tradition or apparent orthodoxy if they are unjust, according to her understanding. Authority, then, within such an approach, does not lie unconditionally with proclaimed authorities or traditions but rather with the core interpretation of the values and meaning of Christianity, in this case the interpretation of Carter Heyward. This highlights a number of very important questions to do with Heyward's approach of radical reinterpretation. First of all, in relation to what authority she engages in this radical reinterpretation of the Christian tradition or of a key symbol of the Christian tradition? Second, how does she present her own subjective interpretation within her rereading? And how does she guard against, if she does at all, the dangers of setting up her own interpretation as a truthful reading or interpretation of the tradition? Third, is her methodology one or reinterpretation or rewriting, and who decides or makes such a distinction? These questions are relevant not only to Heyward's approach but to many strategies of feminist Christian encounter.

Heyward's ordination to priesthood

Heyward became active in campaigning for admission to the ordained priesthood and the direct action of those hoping for ordination culminated in 1974 with their ordination as Episcopal Priests in 1974 in North Philadelphia's Church of the Advocate. In recognition of the radical and challenging implications of this Heyward has referred to it as an "unauthorized ordination of eleven women priests".[5] The ordination was made possible by the willingness of three bishops who had resigned or retired from their posts to carry out the ordination without the "official" backing of the Church. This event inevitably attracted a mixture of resentment and anger, as well as support from many different sources. The Episcopal Church eventually voted in 1976 to allow the ordination of women as both priests and bishops, an event that Heyward believes was influenced and actually made possible by their own ordination.[6] So, only two years after the unlicensed ordination, the Episcopal Church sanctioned the official ordination of women to priesthood. Heyward believes that the committed action and unwavering vision of the women who pushed for ordination had a direct impact on the Church and so was a significant factor in its decision to allow women to be ordained. That her subversive action, and that of those around her, had a transformative impact on church practice and Christian theology. Which is a clear claim to authority for her own experience.

The ordination was not only one of entry into priesthood, but according to Heyward's retrospective reflections on the event, had much wider implications and consequences for the Episcopal Church and beyond. She claimed that those who were ordained were active as Christian feminist liberation theologians and through their critical awareness and employment of feminist critique were effective in analysing and challenging the injustice[7] they faced. The ordination, in Heyward's understanding, was a deliberate act of subversion in challenging a hierarchical system that was shaped by the subjugation of women and depended on this subjugation to support and perpetuate its existence. Her assessment of the gender based inequalities characterising Christianity and Christian theology that arose out of this situation were substantial. She claimed that misogyny lies at the very heart of Christian tradition and theology, and that this necessarily requires radical challenge and confrontation. The implications of such an analysis are sweeping. Writing in 1998 she argued that:

> Women's spiritual and intellectual power historically has been vilified by the church – feared as unclean, denounced as evil, named as un-Christlike, and

> perhaps most commonly in the modern West simply disregarded as "emotional", "lightweight," and derivative of men's more fully human ("rational") status. In this context, Christian women of whatever sectarian or denominational tradition are called, always and forever called, by a woman-loving Spirit, to step out of patriarchal line by stepping into our full stature as people of God.[8]

As well as the practical and direct implications of the ordination for the Episcopal Church Heyward claims unequivocally that it also carried substantial theological implications, involving the symbolic rejection of the sin against women. What she is claiming, then, is that her action, and that of the other women ordained at this time, had a determinate impact on Christian theology and practice.

Very importantly, when analysing Heyward's reflections, it is clear that she did not perceive herself as breaking with tradition through her actions, but actually as being faithful to the traditions of Christianity and Jesus. Committed practical action, with its often radical consequences, and not just verbal affiliation, is needed, according to Heyward's understanding, in order to challenge injustice. Similarly, tradition, or perceived tradition, can not be allowed to stand in the way of justice. This perception of standing within a liberative tradition, despite its departure from the dominant tradition, is a feature of many different liberation and critical theologies, including Latin American liberation theologies, black theologies, feminist theologies, body theologies, queer theologies and sexual theologies. In some ways it can be interpreted as a non-traditional claim to orthodoxy and tradition, and a rejection of orthodoxy through power or dominance.

The key tools and critical base motivation for Heyward, and those other women who were seeking ordination at the same time, were those of feminisms. At this early stage, both of her writing and engagement with committed action in the face of perceived injustice, Heyward very consciously drew on the values and critical insights of her own situation and the situation of these around her. Reflecting in later writings, Heyward claims to stand within a tradition of direct, participatory action:

> God has acted and acts now. So we are told by those who have left us a legacy of faith – Moses, Miriam, Hagar, Mary, Jesus, Paul, Martin Luther King, Jr., Archbishop Oscar Romero, Chief Albert Luthuli, Victoria Mxenge, Isaac Muofhe. Our question is not when or how *God* will act to save women, men, and the earth itself, but rather when and how *we* will act.[9]

The here and now imperative of liberation theologies, to engage in direct social and political action, places responsibility and authority with the individual or the community seeking to oppose injustice or determine its own interpretation and engagement with the Christian faith. Part of Heyward's approach to Christian theology and the Christian Church is her need to record autobiographically her theological struggles and experiences. She has consistently demonstrated her willingness to share her own experiences of injustice and the ways in which she has attempted to challenge these injustices by publishing accounts of her experiences. In 1976 she published *A Priest Forever*[10], in which she recounts the events and emotions surrounding her own ordination into priesthood. She records that the writing of the book was an attempt to uncover and challenge the silences of the Christian Church over its treatment of women. There is in Heyward's approach almost a sense of obligation to speak out as an act of integrity to demonstrate both injustice and the overcoming of injustice as she has experienced it.

The issue of priesthood, and more specifically, of women gaining access to the procedures of selection and admission to ordained roles within the various Christian denominations is a highly contentious and interesting aspect of feminist Christian encounter. A considerable amount of early feminist informed Christian theological writings focused extensively on this issue as a kind of determinate measure of women's equality within the churches. Gaining the right to go forward for ordained priesthood became almost a figurehead of the Christian feminist movement, and in retrospect, the gaining of such a right is perhaps not all it was thought to be. In the Church of England, for example, a considerable amount of feminist energy over the last 30 years prior to the admission of women into the priesthood focused almost solely on this issue, often to the detriment of other issues and areas of concern. As Jenny Daggers has argued in *The British Christian Women's Movement: A Rehabilitation of Eve* published in 2002. It is interesting to reflect that the elusive and seemingly exalted, but essentially exclusionary role of the male priest, was somehow isolated and depicted, particularly in the earlier days of the development of feminist informed Christian theologies, as all that women faced and needed to breakdown in their feminist driven search for justice. Almost as the sum and definitive expression of gender based injustice. A number of important studies recently have reflected on the outcomes and experiences of ordained women priests in the Church of England since 1992 and the findings of these studies raise key questions about what gaining the right to admission to ordained priesthood has actually meant for women in the Anglican Church. Helen Thorne, for example, in *Journey to Priesthood: An in-depth study of the first women priests in the Church of England*[11] focused on the experiences of women priested 1994 to 1995. Her findings recorded mixed experiences of those first women to be ordained to priesthood following the General Synod's "yes" vote but made clear that discrimination, the infamous glass ceiling, and the inflexibility of traditional priestly roles and expectations were limiting to women:

> These women have experienced considerable success in their ministry which has brought them great personal fulfillment of the priesthood because of these wilderness years. Yet these are also women who have experienced great darkness, some have known, and some still experience the pain of rejection, abuse and bullying. Their stories are bitter sweet and weave together strands of light and shadow in ways which enable the tellers to demonstrate and affirm the success of their ministry, whilst speaking out about their unjust and painful treatment in the Church.[12]

A further significant study in this area is Jean Cornell's recent analysis of the experiences of women priested in the Gloucester Diocese, *Women Priests, Assimilation and Transformation.*[13] Cornell's conclusions bear out these mixed experiences and stress the betrayal felt by many women since admission to priesthood. In both studies it is clear that gaining admission to structures by itself is not enough and there is need for radical reconsideration of what the priestly role is and should be, and how women should or can determine this. As Thorne points out:

> My research has clearly shown that women are unlikely to be agents of transformation in the Church through their presence alone....Even if the proportion of women priests in the Church of England increases to make these numbers comparable with men, there is no guarantee, or indication, that their presence will radically reshape the ordained ministry in the Church of England.[14]

Feminisms

Not all of Carter Heyward's work has an explicit feminist address or element but the methodologies and values that she has described and discerned as feminist are fundamental to her theologising. The attraction of feminisms for Heyward seems to be an understanding of the possibilities or alternative visions they offer for change. For example, immersed in a situation in which ordination to priesthood was being denied her, seemingly on the basis of gender, Heyward employed critical insights and theories that might illuminate this denial and also offer a critical and theological basis from which to challenge the validity and authority of such exclusions. The early feminist informed theologies that Heyward encountered whilst at Seminary came to influence her thinking and methods and also offered a theological framework from which she could work out and articulate a critique of Christianity, whilst at the same time, according to her understanding, maintain allegiance to that tradition. From this emerged Heyward's lasting concern to incorporate the insights and challenges of feminisms into an often radically reinterpreted understanding of Christianity. For Heyward feminisms are to do with the self-respect of women, and involve a clear praxis based commitment to justice. She claims an important point of connection between feminisms and Christian theology in their shared experiential grounding. Feminisms, for her, are not just about the rights and justice for women, but have a much wider frame of reference and critical concern.[15] This is a claim often made by many but perhaps often not really evidenced effectively. For Heyward, feminisms include an appeal for men to stand alongside women to challenge injustice. Christianity, in Heyward's understanding, shares and supports feminist concerns, "For women, the Christian message is a feminist challenge to take ourselves as subjects of our own lives".[16] There is no sense of disjuncture between feminisms and Christianity, but rather an understanding of a shared basis of values and commitment to justice.

Despite Heyward's agreement with, and acceptance of, some of the very radical feminist based critiques of Christianity, and of traditional religion in general, she retained a firm commitment to the possibilities of a very positive and liberative feminist Christian encounter. In an influential article first published in 1979 entitled "Ruether and Daly: Speaking and Sparking / Building and Burning"[17] Heyward detailed why for her the feminist informed theological way of reformation, as articulated by Rosemary Ruether, appealed to her own commitments and concerns rather than the rejectionist voice of post-Christian feminist informed theology articulated by Mary Daly.

> I understand our work as feminist theologians to be that of explorers, diggers, artists, reformers. We do not work to tear down symbols and structures that have been, and continue to be, meaningful to Christians throughout the world.[18]

Such words, of reformation and exploration, place Heyward with a very firm commitment to Christianity, because of its meaningfulness to Christians both historically and today. A motivation, or at least an articulation of motivation, that is at best simplistic, if not problematic. Leaving the Christian tradition because of its apparent gender based oppression is, for Heyward, not an option. Instead, what is important, and one of the key focal points of her approach, is the ability to discern injustice and analyse it. With this comes not just the possibilities but also the obligation to challenge it. Just as Daly's analysis, as argued earlier, leads to an apparent feminist ethical imperative for women to leave the Christian tradition, so Heyward's analysis leads to a commitment to challenge injustice. The culmination or outworking of Heyward's position is challenge and reform, whilst Daly's is rejection. As mentioned above, the question of why, in the face of such associated gender based injustice, Heyward remains committed to Christianity seems to be one ultimately of authority. Put perhaps most simplistically, the authoritative or guiding base of Heyward's feminist informed Christian position is her commitment to Christianity, which in this context is not the point of analysis, whilst for Daly it is feminisms and women's experiences.

The strategy that Heyward has developed and employs to effect her acceptance of the feminist based recognition of the complicity of Christianity in the oppression of women, whilst at the same time maintaining a very clear commitment to Christianity (or rather to her understanding of Christianity), is to place what she has interpreted as the oppressive element or developments of Christianity in a discernible location that can be in someway separated from other experiences or elements of Christianity. She is careful to locate the problematic element of Christianity as being not with faith or commitment but as being with the Christian tradition, that she refers to as a "stumbling block",[19] a stumbling block to her own real Christian faith or experience of Christianity. This is further developed in Heyward's description of her relationship to Christianity. Reflecting on the process of her admission to priesthood Heyward very interestingly sees herself as a "traditionalist",[20] referring to her relationship to the heritage or roots of Christianity. She is concerned to stress the points of contact between her own faith and commitment and the Christian heritage or tradition. Tradition seems to be the connection with continuity. Tradition can not stand in the way of justice, "I cannot accept Church tradition, canon law, collegiality among bishops, polls, priority of other issues, timing, misogyny or fear as excuses".[21] The writing of *A Priest Forever* was intended to show this sense of continuity and the connections between contemporary women and Jesus, she writes that it "reflected my own effort to show continuity between the life and teachings of Jesus and contemporary events among women in the church".[22]

> History, continuity, and sacramental connections between all points of time and space...I find much joy in remembering our ancestors – like Sarah and Abraham. I'm grateful to them for what they have given us: our roots.[23]

So, she seems to be making a distinction between the roots of Christianity and Christian tradition, emphasising or prioritising the former, rather than the latter. The legitimacy of this, according to her own interpretation, is informed by her understanding of the illegitimacy of the processes by which understandings of orthodoxy or the determining of what actually constitutes the Christian tradition and symbols have been established. These processes are understood as illegitimate because of their gendered, oppressive implications and motivations. The claim to what might be referred to as authenticity or even orthodoxy is absolutely crucial here to Heyward's approach. For Heyward, Christian tradition, as she understands or interprets it, is problematic because of the way in which certain groups have been treated but also because of the ways in which the Christian tradition has marginalised the experiences and contribution of such people. As a result, as a woman, one of those marginalised by the Christian tradition, according to her feminist informed understanding, Heyward has to reconsider and recover the tradition in such a way that it restores or emphasises the liberative element. The problem then becomes, given that tradition is so rife with such gender based oppressions and injustices, how can Christianity be reinterpreted in the liberative, positive light that Heyward is arguing for. Or, to put it differently, where is this liberative aspect of Christianity that she seems to be arguing for? To the sceptic, the question might also be – why bother? For if Christianity is so problematic why bother trying to reclaim and reinterpret, especially when the problematic elements are not limited to the peripherals. In some ways this is a question of faith, but given the focus of this study, the question here is one of justification and method or strategy. How does Heyward, given this acceptance of the oppressive nature of Christianity as it has been uncovered by feminist critique and feminist based reflections on women's experiences, articulate and justify a committed Christian position from a feminist informed position?

In developing the strategy by which she can respond to this central dilemma facing those who both accept the feminist critique of Christianity and advocate a reformist approach to Christianity, Heyward has placed what might be considered as perhaps the central Christian symbol, the Christ symbol, at the very centre of her theology. Then, in a sense, she has worked outwards from this in her attempt to develop a feminist based theology of mutuality. And at least a part of the reason for such an approach, seems to be heritage:

> With my sisters-in-Christ, I have had to go back again and look again and feel and think and explore again, to find out whether or not in fact our humanness *is* fully affirmed in Christ Jesus.[24]

The description of her work as "feminist" is in part, perhaps inevitable and self-determined, given the terminology that she employs and the explicit address to feminist based critique and reformation that she makes. In addition to this, her work can be described as feminist informed in that it is marked by an emphasis on connection and on a radical feminist informed rereading of traditional symbolism, all of which leads to her theology of mutual relation.

Feminisms, in so far as they claim to be based in a concern with justice and with a passionate commitment to justice, promise much. But Heyward is always concerned to stress the interconnectedness of different forms of justice and justice seeking movements. Connection and relationship have long been affirmed as concerns and characteristics of feminisms, and are usually seen to be in opposition to separation and division. These characteristics of connection and relationship lie at the heart of Heyward's Christian theology, although clearly these features are not limited to feminist informed theologies. For example, the body theology of James Nelson has a very strong emphasis on connection.

Carter Heyward has variously described herself as a feminist, humanist, lesbian, and liberation theologian and this varied and often fluid positioning of her own political, social and theological identity is significant to her theological approach. She is clearly aware of the limitations and indeed possible dangers, of identity politics and of over-stressing one particular element of her life at the expense of other aspects, dangers, which could lead to separation and fragmentation. Also, this stress on identity might be seen to stand in conflict with her appeal to postmodern emphases on fluidity of identity. However, methodologically, the stress on bearing witness through personal identification and participation in oppressive struggles are important for her. For example, in explaining the reason for subtitling her 1989 text *Speaking of Christ As A Lesbian Feminist Voice* she argues that this is to do with her "primary accountability"[25] and to give voice to those silenced and marginalised. It also stresses and gives recognition to the ways in which her own experiences shape her theology, "The words I speak – whether about grocery shopping, Anglican spirituality, sex, or Christ – are lesbian feminist words because I speak them".[26] There is a stress, then, on making visible that which has been hidden:

> We are theological deviants and spiritual resisters less because we are gay and lesbian than because we are out. We celebrate, make visible, bear public witness to the connection between power relationships and abuse...[27]

Clearly, she perceives her sexuality as a significant shaper and determinant of her theology, and perhaps especially so because of the historical and continued oppression of lesbian and gay people. She seems to perceive some level of responsibility to use her voice to oppose such injustice and articulate alternative theological visions or interpretations. However, this does not remain the sole determining pivotal point of her theology. It is certainly part of it but not the sum of it. Heyward does place human experiences of sexuality at the center of experiences of the divine, "I believe that the sexual flow within us is sacred, a manifestation of spiritual movement".[28] Lisa Isherwood has recognized the centrality of her sexuality to her theology, "It is, however, her lesbianism that plays a large part in her christological explorations, as it is the ground of her experience of mutuality and her most embodied reality".[29] Reflecting on the traditional taboo subject of the relationship between God and human sexuality and also on the need to celebrate and incorporate sexuality into awareness of God she argues that connection necessarily involves taking into account all human experiences, and Heyward here talks of "an epistemology of embodiment".[30] James Nelson has expressed something similar with his description of the methodology of body theology, "…it is doing theology in such a way that we take our body experiences seriously as occasions of revelation".[31]

Heyward's theology of mutual relation

Heyward's theology has been characterised by a focus on what she is proposing as mutual relation, which, in brief, amounts to a strong emphasis on relationship and the interaction of all forms of life. The prominence given to this emphasis in her theological reflection at all stages of her work, suggests that "mutual relation" must be a serious focus for any critical investigation hoping to establish something of the strategies employed by Heyward to maintain the creative and very production tension between feminisms and the Christian tradition found in her theology. The determinate role that her vision of mutual relationship has in her theology justifies it in being identified as the theological underpinning of Heyward's theology. Whilst there has certainly been some development of the concept and theological vision of mutual relationship over the last twenty years, even today it remains central to her theological reflections. According to her own articulation and subsequent explanations of mutual relation, it is the key point at which feminisms and Christianity can be seen most clearly to come together in her theology and so is an important point of access for exploring the dynamic relationship between feminisms and Christianity. Given the task here of the critical intention of discerning and unpacking the strategies and mechanisms employed by different theologians to perpetuate a creative dialogue from feminist Christian encounter, Carter Heyward's theology of mutual relation and its emphasis on the radical reinterpretation of the Christ symbol is crucial.

Heyward's vision of a theology of mutual relation is at times quite elusive. But one of the clearest and certainly most comprehensive accounts by Heyward of what she actually means and intends when she speaks of a theology of mutual relation can be found in her 1982 publication *The Redemption of God: A Theology of Mutual Relation*.[32] This text was her unrevised doctoral thesis and provides a passionate and poetic introduction to Heyward's theology. Heyward's style and method in this text are inspired and shaped by issues of injustice, Christian theological need and passion. As in so many of her writings she places her own experiences and reflections on these experiences as central to her own theological explorations, and in a consciously self-reflexive way remains open to criticism of this. This kind of valuing and incorporation of women's experiences as theological resources is found in the work of many different theologians working from a feminist informed perspective and has in its time drawn substantial critical attention. Her mode of recounting and incorporating these experiences into her theological perspective is one which acknowledges the kinds of criticisms that might be made of her especially in terms of her radicalism but she rejects such criticisms outright, and claims a clear and uncompromised relationship with Christianity.

Reflecting on her methods and the key ideas to be found in *The Redemption of God* she notes that her style and content might bring accusations of "...a faulty hermeneutic given zealous voice by one confused woman",[33] she rejects this, and claims consistency and indeed orthodoxy for her ideas, claiming that it to be "...a recurrent voice of orthodox Christians".[34] Heyward's claims for the continuation of tradition, and in this case, orthodoxy, in her proposed theology of mutual relation are articulated strongly throughout her work. What is interesting, however, is that this issue of the relationship of Heyward's feminist informed theological work and action to the traditions of Christianity and to current church practice is a source of concern for Heyward and something that she returns to again and again in her writings. As will be seen later in this chapter, Heyward in the face of the apparent radicalism of her theology and concern about how it might be interpreted often addresses head on such criticisms or potential criticisms, which nearly always relate to tradition and authority. The underlying criticism or concern, however, inevitably still remains.

Heyward's theology of mutual relation is a theology that has emerged out of her experiences and seems shaped strongly by her own early negative experiences of the Christian Church and her own awareness and eventual involvement with the emerging feminist criticism in theology in the late 1970s. Underlying Heyward's work is the commitment to identify, challenge and offer theological alternatives to such injustices. So from perceived situations of injustice comes the theological obligation to address and challenge these issues. It seems that part of Heyward's approach is to develop or put together effectively a theological and social process that would collectively allow theological responses and the development of alternative theologies. Mutuality and relationality are by no mean unique features of Heyward's work and are found as key themes or characteristics of a number of theologians engaged with feminist Christian encounter. Mary Grey, for example, acknowledges the influence of Heyward here to the development of feminist informed theologies and argues that:

> "Relational power" is part of feminist theology's re-imagining of God's power as alternative to the patriarchal power of the 'God of power and might'. I have tried to see this as the power of sensitivity, of compassion, of empathy, of affiliation and bonding...[35]

Heyward's vision of a theology of mutual relation seems to be a vision of a socially just theology that is characterised fundamentally by connection and relationality. Theology and politics are almost indistinguishable in Heyward's theology and her theology here seems to be grounded in the conviction that to make connection is good and to deny the possibility of connection is sinful.

Some indication of the apparent intention of Heyward's theology is to be found in her approach and criticisms of traditional Christian theologies. In fact, extensive criticism of traditional theologies is often incorporated into the theological writings of Heyward. Her approach involves a very explicit criticism of traditional Christian theologies, claiming that such theologies have so often articulated separation and distinction, incorporating an ontology of distinction between God and humanity, which has ultimately resulted in estrangement and loneliness.[36] She challenges the validity of such theologies with her fundamental conviction that God and humanity are relational, and should be seen as in redemptive cooperation with each other. This then, rejects dualistic frameworks which depict a stark separation and distinction between human historical existence, the here and now, and some future, other existence. Here, then, Heyward stands alongside other contemporary theologians who have identified dualism as a fundamental problematic of Christian theology. As Sarah Maitland has articulated so clearly, "Dualism, for all the different ways it is structured and all the different names it is given, means splitting the wholeness of God's creation into divisions labelled 'good' and 'bad'".[37] Like many liberation theologies, Heyward stresses the redemptive action of God in history, with clear ensuing implications for human participation in such activity.

A very pressing question for Heyward and one which lies behind many of her investigations is the question of human responsibility for human redemption. Human responsibility, for Heyward, is paramount. In her understanding God is known through action in history, and very importantly, through human relational activity with God in redemptive action.[38] This is the source, or theological justification, offered by Heyward for her stress on participative action for justice. Which raises the now well established questions of the possibilities of human participation in human salvation. She consistently rejects an emphasis that focuses on future liberative possibilities and hope, and calls instead for an emphasis on the here and now, and on the liberative possibilities open to humanity. This is exemplified in her fight for ordination. In that despite claims from many around her that the Episcopal Church would soon ordain women and for the specific appeals made to Heyward and the others considering ordination that their action could have a divisive affect on the Church, Heyward chose the path of direct and confrontational action. She is fuelled by a concern with the nature and depth of our responsibility, asking, ".....to what extent are we responsible for our own redemption in history?"[39]

This reading of the relationship between God and humanity as "co-creative"[40] seems to lie at the very heart of Heyward's Christian theology, and particularly her understanding of the Christian God as a God of righteousness. It is an understanding or experience that she sees as having being distorted and essentially lost through the historical process and specifically the development of Christianity. Similar to the thought of other liberation theologians, Heyward argues that a crucial theological shift has taken place in human understanding of God, redemption and humanity, a shift that she traces specifically to developments in christology, and particularly to Chalcedon.[41] The shift was one from an understanding of redemptive historical cooperation to a spiritualised emphasis on redemption:

> ...a critical shift in the understanding of how justice is established and by whom: a shift from work in history to faith in that which lies beyond history; a shift from humanitys' responsibility for creating justice to God's gift of a 'natural' justice; a shift from the love of ones' neighbour in the world to the love of one's God above the world.[42]

This shift is fundamentally problematic given Heyward's understanding of epistemology. Knowledge of God and of humanity, begins with one's own experiences and so is grounded not in distinction or separation but actually in connection and relationality. The connection between people, fuelled by justice, seems to be the location of God, or the action of God, for Heyward. This connection or relation is the "creative power, that which effects justice-right-relation-in history".[43] Heyward recognises that for some her ideas here will be challenging and might even be questioned for consistency or in terms of the identification of the God portrayed by Heyward with the Christian God. Such an acknowledgement, however, does not bring any recognition of the validity of such accusations, and she argues for "...a qualified identification between the God of whom I speak and the god of Jewish and Christian traditions".[44] As part of her concern to establish a clear link with the traditions of Christianity she claims a scriptural basis to support her notion of the Christian God as a God of relation and justice. Citing for example, Exodus 3, John 159-15, Psalms 4, 16, Matt 25:31-46.[45] The underlying criticism that Heyward is responding to is that reflected in the words of Naomi Goldenberg, mentioned earlier, who when considering the possibilities for a feminist based reform of Christianity argued that the level and depth of reformation necessary would result in a religion that was essentially no longer recognisably Christian as it would involve "major departures from tradition".[46]

Set in opposition to mutual relation is disconnection, and this, for Heyward, in effect constitutes sin. At the heart of humanness and creatureliness is connection, and that which links us is the Spirit.[47] To deny connection is to deny that which brings humanity together, that which she refers to as "the Sacred Source of our being",[48] in disconnection, in separation, for Heyward are the roots of evil, and is manifested clearly in fear of otherness.[49] The denial or betrayal of others, out of fear of their otherness, is for Heyward sin, and is echoed in the Jesus story. In denying our connection we deny the power of God:

> Evil is the betrayal of our ourselves and one another, one day at a time, in our failures to realize, name, and celebrate the power of God that moves among us constantly, an energy that is sacred *because* it belongs to us all – all creatures, not simply to you, me, those like us, or those we like.[50]

Rejection of the other, based on difference and hierarchical separation, is not only socially and ethically problematic, but actually denies a central Christian belief, that of connection as fundamental to both God's intention and creative activity. Her clear identification with the Christian biblical tradition comes with her emphasis on rationality and justice centred social responsibility, which she understands as love:

> The theological norm is the primary hermeneutical principle...the theological norm operative for me is right-relation or the love of one's neighbor as oneself. In the Old and New Testaments this is referred to as the 'second commandment'...[51]

So, the origins or justification for Heyward's stress on connection and her theology of mutuality do not lie solely with social and political outrage. Rather, she forces an identification of core Christian values and purpose as being with connection, the denial of which is socially manifested as injustice, whether based in poverty, race, gender, class or sexuality, but the implications of which are intrinsically theological, a denial of core Christian principles and understandings. In this sense, then, there is no real or possible distinction between social justice and Christian theological commitment:

> Injustice is the breaking apart of the One Body. Injustice is our alienation from the possibility of living in common-wealth. Injustice is the breeding ground of hatred. It keeps us cut off from one another and from our own spiritual depth. It alienates us from God. Actions or attitudes that disrupt the enjoyment of mutually empowering relations between and among us are sinful. Unjust structures, such as heterosexism, racism, and class elitism, in which our attitudes and actions are shaped, are evil.[52]

Radical reinterpretation and christology

One of the interesting features of the development of feminist informed theologies was that until quite recently many theologians concerned with bringing the discourses of feminisms into conversation with Christianity have not given any kind of sustained critical focus on Jesus as a central theological component and symbol of the Christian faith. This is despite the often made criticism by those rejecting the viability of a feminist reformed Christianity that the Christ symbol has not only participated in the historical oppression of women and other injustices, but may in part be identified as a root cause of such injustices. Those who draw particular attention to the problematic role of this symbol have argued extensively for Christ as a barrier and not a solution to feminist informed gender based justice.

There are clearly many different kinds of criticisms of the way in which the Christ symbol has participated in gender based oppression. For some, the very fact of the maleness of Christ is inherently problematic. As Naomi Goldenberg has put it most bluntly, "Jesus Christ cannot symbolize the liberation of women. A culture that maintains a masculine image for its highest divinity cannot allow its women to experience themselves as the equals of its men".[53] From such a perspective it is the maleness in and of itself of Christ that is so difficult. With a different emphasis, Daphne Hampson has argued that: "...through the very nature of Christology, there can be no Christology which is compatible with feminism".[54] For her, as outlined earlier, it is the claimed uniqueness of Jesus within the Christian tradition that is so problematic:

> If one holds, of Christ, that he was, in whatever way, unique, then one is clearly a Christian. There arises the problem of reconciling a religion which has a unique Christ (who in his human nature is male) with feminism. But if Jesus of Nazareth is not thought to be unique, and the Christian story is just a myth, why, one must ask, should one who is a feminist choose to take up this particular myth, why, one must ask, should one who is female choose to take up this particular myth when it is so male, and has central to it a male person who is held to be unique?[55]

Elizabeth Johnson argues that it is not so much the maleness of Jesus that is problematic as the theological interpretation given to this maleness:

> The difficulty arises, rather, from the way this one particularity of sex, unlike the other historical particularities, is interpreted in sexist theology and practice. Consciously or unconsciously, Jesus' maleness is lifted up and made essential for his christic function and identity, thus blocking women precisely because of their female sex from participating in the fullness of their Christian identity as images of Christ.[56]

Also, critiques of the symbolic functioning of christology are not limited to gender. Many different kinds of criticism of the functioning of the symbol of Jesus have been developed, including from cultural, post-colonial and queer perspectives. Jacquelyn Grant has argued comprehensively that:

> In the white church tradition, Jesus Christ has functioned as a status quo figure. Because historically Christology was constructed in the context of white supremacist ideology and domination. Christ has functioned to legitimate these social and political realities. Essentially, Christ has been white.[57]

Of course, since the development of feminist informed Christian and womanist theologies, questions about Jesus and feminisms have always been raised and most notable here among early feminist informed Christian theology were Leonard Swidler's 1971 article "Jesus Was a Feminist"[58] and Rosemary Ruether's study in 1981 *To Change the World*.[59] However, increasingly, this is an issue which is emerging with significant force in womanist and a range of feminist informed Christian theologies. There are now a number of significant theological studies which mark a sustained and often systematic feminist critical focus on Jesus and address the possibility of the development of feminist christologies. These include, Julie Hopkins' 1995 study *Towards a Feminist Christology*[60] which explored the problems facing feminist concerned with the reconstructive task and attempted such a feminist christology, the various works of Elizabeth Johnson, Jacquelyn

Grant's 1989 womanist critique and response to the development of feminist christologies *White Women's Christ and Black Women's Jesus*,[61] Kelly Brown Douglas's 1994 study *The Black Christ*,[62] Elisabeth Schussler Fiorenza's *Jesus: Miriam's Child, Sophia's Prophet*[63] (1995) and Lisa Isherwood's 2001 publication *Introducing Feminist Christologies*.[64] Susan Ross recognises the centrality of this issue for feminist informed theology: "For feminist theology, developing an adequate christology has been one of its most serious challenges".[65] Similarly, Isherwood argues that:

> Christology, and the reality of incarnation that it claims to expound, is at the heart of Christianity. The "person and significance" of Jesus, as we are told the word signified as undergraduates, is of course, what Christianity is about.[66]

For Chung Hyun Kyung in *Struggle to be the Sun Again* the task of Asian women in relation to Jesus involves both the reclamation of traditional images and the development of new images:

> ...there are *traditional* images of Jesus, which are being interpreted in fresh, creative ways by Asian women, largely based on their experiences of survival in the midst of oppression and on their efforts to liberate themselves. We have also observed *new* images of Jesus that offer a direct challenge to traditional Christologies. These new images of Jesus are also based on Asian women's experiences of survival and liberation.[67]

Each of the studies detailed above is dealing with or addressing the central issue that has been raised by many critics such as Daly and Goldenberg, namely, that Jesus as a saviour, and as a central and defining symbol of Christianity is fundamentally problematic for feminist analysis. Julie Hopkins holds out hope whilst at the same time recognising the problems faced:

> The thoughts expressed in these essays are my personal response to the challenge posed by the feminist critique of traditional and contemporary christology. It is not an attempt to defend Christianity against these criticisms, I share these and have elsewhere offered my deconstruction of christology. This book is therefore a second stage in the debate around the religious significance of Jesus of Nazareth for modern faith. The feminist critique has systematically exposed the layers of mystification and ideological abuse which has brought christology into disrepute in the eyes of many women. I have come to feel that this negative approach is surely emotionally and existentially unsatisfactory.[68]

Similarly, for Carter Heyward the very fact of the way in which the Christ symbol has been used in the justification and detailing of gender based and other oppressions, far from being a reason for avoiding this symbol, is a compelling reason for giving serious and sustained focus, "...Jesus matters for me, a woman, because his name has been wielded as a bludgeon against my sisters and me".[69] She will not be deterred from her task of feminist based re-imaging and reinterpreting because of the way in which christology has been incorporated into gender based oppression:

> The doctrines of the trinity and the incarnation, together with the atonement, provide the grist for the christological mill and constitute a particular scandal for christian feminists. I believe we must study these doctrines long and well.
> We must study these doctrines and we must study our lives if we do not want to relinquish either our senses of self or our roots in a religious tradition that we experience both as shamefully misogynist and as a place of friendship and solidarity in our search for meaning and value as women.[70]

In Heyward's theology of relationality and justice, christology claims a central place with a very clear emphasis on the significance of Jesus as an image for understanding relationality, and in particular, the relationality of humanity and God. Jesus' nature and the significance of this nature for Christians centres on the relationship or possibilities for relationality as examplified by him, she argues that, "...relational theology is incarnational".[71] Heyward proposes a move here away from a stress on a divine Christ which she argues has often been emphasised at the expense of the humanity of Christ. Instead, she is more concerned to focus on what might be described as a functional christology,[72] a christology that asks questions about Jesus' actions, rather than postulate about his nature. Such a functional christology includes an analysis of what can be known of Jesus' actions but also moves on to more constructive proposals for the implications of these actions for contemporary and particular situations in which people find themselves. This, then, inevitably involves some kind of reimaging of Jesus according to contemporary means and needs. Reimaging for Heyward seems to involve taking text and recasting the meaning, so in effect reinterpreting using different terms and images, for example, using such as the parent-child image for Jesus and God. In *The Redemption of God* Heyward focuses on the Jesus that can be known from St Mark's Gospel. What she seems to be calling for or engaging in methodologically, is a shift in the christological concern or focus of Christians. This shift, as she understands it, is one that moves away from an emphasis on the debate between the historically located Jesus and the divine Jesus, a debate which she claims has simply served as a "distraction".[73] She employs the metaphor of "pruning away"[74] that which obscures christology. She wants to challenge the assumption that christology is study that focuses on the various ways in which Christians approach or negotiate the relationship between the humanity and divinity of Jesus. This for Heyward is not life-enhancing but rather obscuring. The focus on such debates, and involvement in such enquiry, should not, according to Heyward's understanding, be the concern of Christians:

> ...classical christology, as an arena of constructive work, is dead. Its symbolic universe belongs to the history of Christian thought which, when studied honestly, reveals the history of Christian power relations.[75]

What she is arguing then is that the patterns of social and ecclesial domination have been influenced by classical christology and that by rejecting such theological engagement, such distracting engagement, what Heyward is calling for in replacement is a redefinition of the theological discipline of christology.[76] Heyward's criticisms of the problems associated with the way in which christology and studies of christology have been approached do not end here. She argues that there is also a need to move away from the projection of human experiences and understandings of self onto Christ. For if human experience is taken as normative, and closed, then what in effect happens is that humanity posits and universalises its own experiences. This is clearly what Heyward understands as happening and she interprets as problematic, as it is not an effective or dynamic theological activity. According to her argument, humanity has to stay open to different possibilities:

> The christological task of Christian feminism is to move the foundations of christology from the ontology of dualistic opposition toward the ethics of justice-making. This happens only in a praxis of relational particularity and cooperation.[77]

A recent text published by Heyward illustrates just how central to her thinking a revision of christology actually is. Published in 1999 *Saving Jesus From Those Who Are Right: Rethinking What it Means to be Christian*[78] gives a coherent and detailed presentation of Heyward's thinking on christology. She does stress in this book that she is not attempting to write a systematic christology, which would really go against the methodological grain of her approach to christology, but rather to offer new interpretations and understandings of the Jesus story. The conviction that belief in Christ is essential to the Christian faith pervades this text at many levels. However, deciphering what this actually means or what actually such belief constitutes, is not so clear. Heyward argues that:

> It has always mattered what Christians believe and pass on to others about JESUS CHRIST. It has mattered to women and children of different races, classes, and Christian cultures, because as the centrepiece of one of the world's foremost patriarchal religions, "JESUS CHRIST" has been used consistently and naturally to put women and children under the authority of fathers and husbands who have learned to assume that they themselves reflect most fully the image of God the Father.[79]

What Christians believe about Jesus matters, she is arguing, to all people who have been and continue to be affected by christological images and authority, and especially people not deemed to be in the majority or the norm, or people who have not occupied the theological and political positions necessary to determine and shape christologies. This, then, recognises the symbolic significance of the Christ figure in Christianity and wider culture, and really places responsibility with those concerned with justice to decipher, deconstruct and eventually reimage this central Christian symbol.

Heyward begins her recent exploration of christology in *Saving Jesus From Those Who Are Right* by posing the question of "Jesus – what does this name mean to me?",[80] in this she is acknowledging, and indeed stressing from the outset, the committed and subjective nature of her interpretations and visions. She intends or hopes that her reflections will have direct transformative implications, seeing and describing her approach as "...an alternative way of thinking about what it means to be Christian.[81] Her explicit detailing of what "Jesus" means to her is very revealing and helpful when attempting an analysis of her feminist based reconstruction methodology. She gives historical credence to the figure of Jesus whilst at the same time stressing the symbolic and mythic origins of the Jesus of Christianity,[82] which perhaps represents a significant development to her earlier position. She draws attention to the selective and partial interpretations of Jesus, and also to the employment of the different images of Jesus. She locates her own theological perspective in *Saving Jesus From Those Who Are Right* as being firmly within this process. Very importantly, she does not argue that her own interpretation of Jesus should be considered truthful or in any way definitive, merely that this is the Jesus of her belief. She uses small capital letters when using the term JESUS to stress the nature of her usage of it as essentially a human construct, that is, as interpreted and situated.[83] As will be explored in later chapters, this creative, if sometimes frustrating, strategy of representing words in alternative or challenging visual formations is used by feminist informed theologians quite often. It is an attempt to draw attention to the limitations of what have been interpreted as essentially gendered language and to challenge this with alternative, constructive suggestions. One of the problems of such a strategy, however, is that it is in danger of creating an internal and essentially elitist code or discourse, largely inaccessible to most people. A code or discourse that can only be known and accessed by insiders.

One of the interesting methods employed by Heyward in her work, and especially her approach to christology, is her use and reliance on terms and concepts that in their origins at least have a very firm base in the Christian tradition and in Christian theology. She purposefully takes established theological concepts and recasts them in the light of her own explicit and very focused concern to develop a theology of mutual relation. The ministry of Jesus, as understood by Heyward, is a ministry of revelation, a ministry that makes available to humanity an understanding of what it means to be fully human.[84] She struggles with expounding the meaning and understanding of Jesus, his humanity, divinity and relationship to God, but attempts to address this by proposing a relocation of significance. Heyward moves from a christology of meaning in who Jesus was, to a functional christology.

Seen in these terms, Jesus was, for Heyward, a "justice-loving brother",[85] a prophet, a teacher, a social activist and religious leader.[86] She claims that the focus of Jesus' criticism of injustice and also of his ministry was both religious and political. One of the most illuminating concepts offered by Heyward in her reflections on christology is the notion of Jesus' story as "a window into our own".[87] What she seems to mean by this term is that what we see in the Jesus story are the possibilities for our own lives. Perhaps inevitably, Heyward argues for a fluid understanding and interpretation of christology. For example, in explaining her choice of the title *Saving Jesus From Those Who Are Right* for her 1999 text she claims that it is not simply, perhaps as expected, a reference to the religious right of America, but is also a reference to all people who claim a fixed and inflexible understanding of Jesus, and Christianity in general. She claims influence from postmodernist thinking here, and especially from the insights that human perceptions and understandings are necessarily fluid and partial.[88]

Despite this clarification of the title of *Saving Jesus From Those who are Right*, a clear challenge is posed to the religious right by Heyward in her feminist informed theology. She argues that the religious right incorporate and give political and theological significance to capitalism, nationalism and patriarchy,[89] which for her constitutes a small step to fascism. Which she in turn describes as, "a theo-political commitment to and a systematic effort to secure the 'self' as the one and only image of God, and the self's possessions, desires, and worldview as sacred".[90] Such a worldview, in her opinion, influences a Christ who is authoritarian and moralistic,[91] which in itself is used to sanction an insular, authoritarian fear of others. In rejecting such an interpretation, she offers new images of Jesus which sanction not an authoritarian and moralistic stance but one of mutual relation.

At the heart of Heyward's christology is the attempt to overcome separation and alienation. Separation not only between humanity, but also between humanity, God, Jesus and the rest of creation. This is similar to Mercy Amba Oduyoye's description of the approach of African women theologians, who she claims, "...think in inclusive terms, hence the emphasis on Jesus for all and particular contexts, peoples and all situations".[92] Heyward's approach, as she understands it, is a shift away from an authoritarian christology, concerned to stress and incorporate the distance between humanity and the divine, to a christology that stresses the humanity of Jesus. Heyward recognises that this might be read as a denial of the divinity of Jesus, but rejects both this claim and the underlying assumptions based on separateness:

> Am I denying the divinity of JESUS? No. I am denying the singularity of his status as the Son of God. I am affirming the presence of divinity in him and moving through him. I am affirming his participation in the divine life and God's participation in him. I am affirming JESUS' "god-ness". I believe that those who knew and loved him knew and loved God. I also imagine that whenever he knew and loved others, individually and collectively, he too was knowing and loving God. I have no doubt that you and I are as much God's daughters and sons as JESUS was and, moreover, that this has been true not only of human beings but of other creatures too, from the beginning.[93]

So, what does this mean? What Heyward seems to be rejecting here is the implication of a stress on the particularity of Jesus. Daphne Hampson, as outlined earlier, has identified this as fundamentally problematic for feminist analysis, and in particular the claim that God was uniquely revealed at one particular point in history. Heyward's problem with the authoritarian emphasis on the uniqueness of Jesus is that it incorporates an essential and unbridgeable distinction between humanity and God, which she claims is not reconcilable with a stress on mutual relation and connection. For Heyward, Jesus' participation in divinity is shared by all of humanity. It is not distinct and is not unique. An interpretation which might be said to constitute a radical rereading, and even rewriting of christology. Accordingly, in Carter Heyward's scheme, sacred power is not so much invested in Jesus, or discovered in him, as in relationship:

> ...*we find our sacred power neither "in" JESUS nor "in" ourselves but between and among us.* God is *in* the dynamic, sparking moment among and between us, within and beyond us, beneath and above us. God is *with* all of us at once and *with* everyone else as well. This all true, but there is more. And this "more" I believe, is the key to liberating Christology and saving JESUS.[94]

For Heyward, then, the significance of Jesus is in terms of the connections made and in the relation of mutuality, which she argues, was evident in his life. This mutuality is the source of liberation and the basis of human life. God, then, is power in mutual relation, and so, given Heyward's overall theological scheme, should be understood as the source of liberation.[95] Mutual relation is power as the source of liberation, relational theology focuses on this power and on the dynamic of justice through relation. Heyward talks of relation as "radical connectedness",[96] which refers not just to the connectedness of humanity but to all of reality. Theologies of mutual relation, then, are concerned to work towards mutuality and out of this the possibilities of reordering life as justice-centred. And the significance of Jesus is to be located here, "...Jesus historical significance, his Christic, or redemptive, meanings, originated in the power that he experienced in relation to sisters and brothers".[97] The focus and intention of faith, then, becomes the transformation of power. All of which depends almost entirely on this reinterpretation of the Jesus symbol as being of primarily Christian theological significance in terms of the possibilities for mutual relationship rather than perhaps more traditional or classical theological understandings of atonement or redemption.

Connection, mutuality and participation in justice seeking ways

Heyward is insistent that the inclusion of a focus on the Jesus story does not necessarily amount to "an adoration of JESUS of Nazareth whom we have named 'CHRIST'".[98] Rather, the reason for engaging in a retelling of the Jesus story is empowerment, it is about connection, about how making connection is possible, and to encourage us to engage likewise with the aim of community-building. The power she refers to here, the power at the centre of the Jesus story and at the centre of our possibilities, is relational power. Rather than a stress on the uniqueness of Jesus, Heyward actually argues that the reason the Jesus story is so significant for us today is that it is constantly echoed in our lives:

> We remember the death of JESUS not because the circumstances that brought him to it were exceptional but because they were so utterly commonplace. Then and now, our crucifixions of one another remain a deep, troubling dimension of our common spiritual predicament.[99]

What the Jesus story, rather than Jesus himself, offers us is the opportunity to reimage ourselves in relation. With this, she makes use of the body imagery of the Pauline writings, and stresses that we must take seriously our own bodies as well as the body of Jesus, so stressing humanity. So, what does Heyward understand about the nature of Jesus? For her, what is of particular significance, and the reason why we should focus on him, is not his uniqueness of nature, but rather his passion:

> I believe that JESUS was following the *dictates* of neither simply a god above him nor only his own inner voice. I believe that the "something special" about JESUS was his *passion*: the fullness of his embodied life, the depth and power of his embodied spirit, the openness of his body to risk and struggle in the spirit of God. I believe that JESUS lived in this passionate spirit of One who was both with and in him – and *other* than him; the God who was with and in him – and with and in *others*, the Holy Spirit of love in history, the sacred energy moving through JESUS, stirring among the people, acting through them all, and even today as much with and for one of us – JESUS – as for us all.[100]

Heyward constantly stresses the connection, and not the difference, between divinely and humanity, captured clearly in her claim that, "Like JESUS, and in his Spirit, we are created to god",[101] and this is precisely "...why we are here to god",[102] where "to god" seems to be strongly related to justice. Questions of distinctions and boundaries between humanity and divine are clearly blurred if not close to obliterated in such a reading. Set against such an apparently radical departure in theological interpretations of Christianity and in particular christology, Heyward uses trinitarian imagery to explore the theological meaning and implications of mutuality. The strategy employed by Heyward here and elsewhere of using traditional language and imagery and recasting it is especially effective and illuminating with her use of trinitarian imagery, and is an excellent example of Heyward's methodology of investing traditional theological concepts and imageries with feminist meaning resulting in a feminist based strategy of radical reinterpretation. Isherwood comments on the implications of Heyward's approach for Christian theology and for christology in particular:

> Re-imaging may mean letting go of tradition. One such letting go is realizing that Jesus only really matters if he was human and if we view his incarnation as a "relational experience". Heyward believes it is a crippling mistake to see Jesus as a divine person "rather than a human being who knew and loved God"...By re-imaging Jesus she also re-images human beings through realizing the amazing power and relation that lies dormant in human nature.[103]

Heyward argues that early theological reflections on the trinity were used to emphasise the understanding of God in relation, in relation to Jesus and humanity. Alongside this, she does recognise that trinitarian imagery has also been used in an oppressive way, to support patriarchal and androcentric power relations. Of particular interest to Heyward, however, are the possibilities offered by trinitarian imagery with its essentially fluid implications, allowing for a changing and transformative understanding of mutual relation and the implications this brings for understandings of humanity, God and Jesus:

> The Trinity is an image of dynamic movement, rather than static unchanging being, as the very essence of God; an image of passion and yearning, rather than dispassion or apathy, at the heart of the Sacred; an image of wholeness and holiness woven through diversity and multiplicity, rather than through sameness.[104]

For Heyward to live in trinitarian faith is to break away from restraints of authoritarian religion that constantly distort what it means to be human. She places blame with the Church authorities for distorting the connectedness of humanity, Jesus and God, with their stress on a removed, divine Christ rather than a relational, connected Christ. This is quite similar to the approach of Janet Martin Soskice who whilst recognising the problematic associations made by feminist critics between trinitarian imagery and theology and the inherent maleness of God and associated implications for women, she argues that even this doctrine can be recovered and renewed:

> Despite these criticisms it can still be argued that it is the doctrine of the Trinity which saves the Christian doctrine of God from stifling androcentrism. Custodians of the tradition would be quite wrong to dismiss the feminist criticisms as simply failing to understand the doctrine. It would be more accurate to see these as a clarion call for its renewal.[105]

Heyward characterises the human condition as being one of loneliness, and an intense need to overcome this loneliness in right relation,[106] and it is here that the significance and possibilities for christology become most clear, as humanity seeks right relation. The Jesus story is about right relation, about the struggle and passionate desire for mutual relation. This is fundamental to Heyward's theology and her understanding of Christianity and a justice-seeking or justice based faith. In that she incorporates it into her understanding of God, "we honestly can describe God *as* the desire for justice and compassion, solidarity and friendship. Indeed, not only is God "in" the depths of our longing for mutuality and justice-loving, God *is* the depths."[107] Heyward characterises two aspects of the suffering of humans. The first relates to what she terms "the *unfinishedness of creation*"[108] and by this she means fear, disease and loss. She contrasts this with the suffering related to moral, spiritual and political issues,[109] that she terms the "*brokenness of creation*".[110] It is out of a concern with both of these, the unfinishedness of creation, and the brokenness of creation, Heyward argues, that theologies of atonement and incarnation arose, with Jesus completing the unfinished creation through both living and dying. Importantly, Heyward argues that a stress on christology does not mean that the values of suffering, death and struggle are overplayed. By choice, Heyward prefers to speak of Jesus rather than Christ, associating the use of the latter with imperialism and exclusivism.[111] For her, this is not the Jesus that she is concerned with, and if used, "Christ" must be understood differently:

> If we are to speak of CHRIST at all as a healing and liberating Spirit, "CHRIST" must be a synonym for the risen, ongoing, spiritual presence of JESUS with us as fully creaturely brother, or sister, seeking to be in right – mutually empowering – relation with other creatures. If we are committed to "CHRIST" in this sense, then we realize that we, like JESUS, are lured by the Spirit of justice-love into a shared commitment to be Christic – liberating, God-bearing – characters together in history.[112]

Christianity, then, or the Jesus movement, as she sometimes refers to it, in the context of human lives, and of suffering, is "...a revolutionary political call and a spiritual home.[113] Salvation, as understood by Heyward within the scheme of the theology she outlines, refers to liberation and healing, in material, political, spiritual, social and personal terms:[114]

> We cannot enjoy the spirituality that truly is of God unless we are enjoying the struggle for justice-love, compassion, non-violence, and forgiveness in the world. And we cannot stay in the struggle unless we are drawing personal strength from God whom JESUS loved, however we may experience and image this sacred power.

Participation in justice seeking ways is clearly a part of moving towards mutuality and especially within a Christian theological framework that focuses on the mutual relation of the Jesus story. This, for Heyward, is passion. Passion fuels the desire for mutual relation and the accompanying justice seeking.

> *Passion* is a theological term that denotes this "going with" and "going for" God, this godding, this real presence in life and in God. Passion is also an ethical term of agency or power. As such, passion is our sacred energy for going with and, if need be, going for one another into the joy and sorrow of making justice-love with compassion.[115]

She also holds on to the symbol of the cross, seeing it as a symbol "*of what it cost him and what it costs all who suffer because they love*".[116] Similarly, she takes on board the notion of atonement and broadens its meaning, "Whenever God is incarnate (made flesh) in any context of violence or injustice ...atonement is underway":[117]

> ...incarnation and atonement are not inseparable redemptive events or images but rather are the same passionate moment, again and again, throughout history.[118]

Not only does Heyward broaden their frame of reference but also places their meaning as firmly within the social and political sphere:

> Participation in incarnation and in atonement as the act of solidarity is not only a spiritual event. It is also a political, social, ecological, and pastoral movement of liberation from larger and smaller forces that are cruel, violent, apathetic, or ignorant of what humans and other creatures need in order to live and thrive. Such participation in incarnation and atonement is steeped in a passion that is God's own and that we catch, through glimpses and intimations, in the JESUS story.[119]

Throughout, Heyward's understanding of the significance of Jesus is tied closely to the social and political. Similarly, she describes her use and reading of the Bible in socio-political terms, as a critique of structures of power.[120] This is not to place issues of justice and relatedness solely in the political and social spheres, but to avoid introducing hierarchical differentiation between the spiritual and the political. Heyward claims that through reading the biblical texts, she comes to a knowledge of Jesus as one who sides with the poor,[121] and similarly to an understanding of God as "…a spiritual force, an energy, a drive, and in that sense a relentless yearning for justice.[122] To this end, Heyward finds the image of Jesus as engaging in boundary-breaking activities.[123] In this sense, she argues that atonement begins in Jesus at the point at which he engaged in justice-seeking activities, not with death. This is the true passion of Jesus, which drives the individual towards such activity, with, potentially, revolutionary implications. Such action as it stands in defiance of boundaries should not lead to accusations of disrespect for convention or society, but should be seen in theologically creative terms:

> In each of these revolutionary, boundary-breaking moments, our lives give birth to God, and Sophia (God's wisdom) is incarnate again among us here and now. Because she is here, the foundations of our life together will always be shaken whenever injustice lingers or cruelty and indifference still abound.[124]

Heyward claims that the distinguishing feature of a theology or perspective, and the mark of "the embodied, boundary-breaking passion of JESUS and his disciples"[125] is compassion. It is compassion that is the distinguishing mark of the sacred. In Heyward's understanding, faith is the realization that God is good and is the root of human passion. Similarly, Christians are called to remember Jesus, because in so doing they remember their own power and potential to heal and liberate.[126] From the brokenness of the world as described by Heyward in its disconnectedness, she argues that hope lies in forgiveness, which is both spiritual and political. Heyward claims that the most complete experience of mutual relation is friendship, with other people and with the rest of creation. Friendship is fuelled and sustained by compassion,[127] it is about right relation. To forgive means to let go of resentment, to forgive both others and ourselves.[128]

Conclusion

Heyward's writings are marked by the conviction that committed action is needed in the face of injustice, and that such action should not be delayed or promised as something for the future. There is a very strong stress here on responsibility. For example, writing in relation to responding to the ways in which people with AIDS and HIV are treated by society, she equates non-action or silence as complicity,[129] and it is interesting that a number of her key texts are actually collections which include many sermons. Heyward has a very strongly social based understanding of justice, as a justice for here and now.[130] Love, justice and theological understandings of these must be particular and historical. She claims that, "it is only in history and in time that human beings can realize who we are as lovers of humanity and of God as well".[131]

Authority is both important and problematic for Heyward, and in her writings she has attempted to address the meaning of authority in relation to the lives of those disempowered both within Christianity and by Christianity. Heyward stresses the importance of not professing an interpretation of Jesus and claiming authority for it. But despite this, the question does have to be raised as to whether this is not in fact what Heyward herself effectively does. She does seem to give normative status to a particular approach to christological interpretation with the words that, "The wisest among us will move with the currents of the chaos, not resisting them, but rather letting ourselves be washed in time onto new shores".[132] Tradition is understood by Heyward as open and diverse. The antagonistic relationship that she perceives herself to be in with the traditions and institutions of Christianity is not a problem for her:

> It is ironic, though understandable in terms of sin, that just as Jesus, a Jew found himself in confrontation with Judaism, we Christians today find ourselves confronting Christianity. God is love and this love is inclusive of justice and human rights and has a call over the rules and laws of societies.[133]

She continues to employ the term "feminist" in description of a work, but is increasingly incorporating the critical insights of contemporary reflection on the problems associated with feminisms and feminist informed theologies.[134] Nevertheless, like many other feminist thinkers Heyward comes very close to claiming special significance for the experiences and insights of women, as opposed to men, which when set within the Christian context has particular theological implications:

> *I see women as the single most creative force within the Christian Church.* We, as a group, are those challenged most immediately with the task of *renewal* – of making new what is old – within and beyond ourselves in the Church and elsewhere.[135]

She counteracts the implications of this with the claim that women's insights into justice possibilities are a result of their own lived experiences, based in society's marginalised and denigration of women. Heyward's theology of mutual relation, and in particular her stress on the reinterpretation of Jesus, constitutes a departure in thinking through the employment of traditional concepts with radical feminist based reinterpretations. Heyward has also made some use of the controversial concept and term "Christa" in exploring what it means to develop a feminist informed christology. Edwina Sandys' sculpture of a female crucified figure titled "Christa" has inspired theologians like Heyward and Rita Nakashima Brock to develop the theological image and to reclaim christology for feminist informed Christian theology in such a way that Christa becomes "an iconoclastic image that shatters the maleness of Christ".[136]

Heyward has not so much identified a strand or aspect of the Christian tradition and engaged in a feminist reclamation of this, as employed the language and imagery of Christian theology and offered radical re-readings of them in the light of her concern for mutuality. For Heyward Jesus is prophet and pastor,[137] and stands at the centre of Christianity and so necessarily at the centre of Christian theology, which is expressed succinctly in her words that, "...we who are Christian speak of Christ...."[138]

Notes

[1] Heyward, C., (1984), *Our Passion for Justice: Images of Power, Sexuality and Liberation*, New York: Pilgrim Press.
[2] Heyward, C., 1994:xiv.
[3] Heyward, C., (1999b), *A Priest Forever*, Cleveland, Ohio: The Pilgrim Press, p.17.
[4] Heyward, 1999b:32.
[5] Heyward, 1999b:v.
[6] Heyward, 1999b:viii.
[7] Heyward, 1999b:x.
[8] Heyward, 1999b:xi.
[9] Heyward, C., (1989), *Speaking of Christ: A Lesbian Feminist Voice*, New York: Pilgrim Press, p.42.
[10] Heyward, C., (1999b), *A Priest Forever*, Cleveland, Ohio: The Pilgrim Press.
[11] Thorne, H., (2000), *Journey to Priesthood: An in-depth study of the first women priests in the Church of England*, Bristol: Centre for Comparative Studies in Religion and Gender.
[12] Thorne, 2000:148.
[13] Cornell, J.C., (2000), *Women Priests, Assimilation and Transformation:* Oxford: Oxford Brookes University.
[14] Thorne, 2000:134-135.
[15] Heyward in Thatcher, A., and Stuart, E., (eds.), (1996), *Christian Perspectives on Sexuality and Gender*, Gracewing, p.75.
[16] Heyward, 1989:41.
[17] Heyward, C., (1979), "Speaking and sparking, building and burning: Ruether and Daly, theologians", *Christianity and Crisis*, 39(2), pp.66-72.
[18] Heyward, C., 1984:11.
[19] Heyward, 1999b:5.

[20] Heyward, 1999b:5.
[21] Heyward, 1999b:74.
[22] Heyward, 1984:8.
[23] Heyward, 1999b:5.
[24] Heyward, 1999b:6.
[25] Heyward, 1989:10.
[26] Heyward, 1989:11.
[27] Heyward, 1995:50.
[28] Heyward, 1999b:21.
[29] Isherwood, I., (2001), *Introducing Feminist Christologies*, Sheffield: Sheffield Academic Press, p.62.
[30] Heyward, 1995:114.
[31] Nelson, J.B., (1992), *Body Theology*, Louisville, Kentucky: Westminster/John Knox Press, p.9.
[32] Heyward, C., (1982), *The Redemption of God: A Theology of Mutual Relation*, University Press of America.
[33] Heyward, 1982:xvii.
[34] Heyward, 1982:xvii.
[35] Grey, M., (2001), *Introducing Feminist Images of God*, Cleveland, Ohio: The Pilgrim Press, p.51.
[36] Heyward, 1982:1.
[37] Maitland, S., (1983), *A Map of the New Country: Women and Christianity*, London: Routledge & Kegan Paul, p.19.
[38] Heyward, 1982:2.
[39] Heyward, 1982:1.
[40] Heyward, 1982:2.
[41] Heyward, 1982:3.
[42] Heyward, 1982:5.
[43] Heyward, 1982:6.
[44] Heyward, 1982:9.
[45] Heyward, 1982:10.
[46] Goldenberg, 1979:4.
[47] Heyward, 1999a:85.
[48] Heyward, 1999a:85.
[49] Heyward, 1999a:86.
[50] Heyward, 1999a:91
[51] Heyward, 1982:15.
[52] Heyward, 1989:25.
[53] Goldenberg, 1979:22.
[54] Hampson, D., (1990), *Theology and Feminism*, Oxford: Basil Blackwell., p.59.
[55] Hampson, 1990:65.
[56] Johnson, E.A., (1993), "Redeeming the Name of Christ", 115–137 in Lacugna, C.M., (ed.), (1993), *Freeing Theology: The Essentials of Theology in Feminist Perspective*, p.119.
[57] Grant, J., (1993), in Stevens, M., (ed.), *Reconstructing the Christ Symbol: Essays in Feminist Christology*, New York: Paulist Press, p.61.
[58] Swidler, L., (1971), "Jesus Was a Feminist", *Catholic World*, January 1971, 177-83.
[59] Ruether, R., (1981), *To Change the World: Christology and Cultural Criticism*, London: SCM Press.
[60] Hopkins, J., (1995), *Towards a Feminist Christology: Jesus of Nazareth, European Women and the Christological Crisis*, London: SPCK.

[61] Grant, J., (1989), *White Women's Christ and Black Women's Jesus: Feminist Christology a Womanist Response*, Atlanta, Georgia: Scholars Press.
[62] Douglas, K.B., (1994), *The Black Christ*, Maryknoll, NY: Orbis Books.
[63] Schussler Fiorenza, E., (1995), *Jesus: Miriam's Child, Sophia's Prophet: Critical Issues in Feminist Christology*, London: SCM Press Ltd.
[64] Isherwood, L., (2001), *Introducing Feminist Christologies*, Sheffield: Sheffield Academic Press.
[65] Ross, S.A., (2001), *Extravagant Affections: A Feminist Sacramental Theology*, New York: Continuum, p.39.
[66] Isherwood, 2001:9.
[67] Chung, Hyun Kyung (2000), *Struggle to be Sun Again*, London: SCM Press, p.73.
[68] Hopkins, 1995:9.
[69] Heyward, 1982:31.
[70] Heyward, 1984:229.
[71] Heyward, 1982:31.
[72] Heyward, 1982:34.
[73] Heyward, 1989:13.
[74] Heyward, 1989:14.
[75] Heyward, 1989:14.
[76] Heyward, 1989:15.
[77] Heyward, 1989:21.
[78] Heyward, C., (1999a), *Saving Jesus From Those Who Are Right: Rethinking What it Means to be Christian*, Minneapolis: Fortress Press.
[79] Heyward, 1999axii.
[80] Heyward, 1999a:1.
[81] Heyward, 1999a:1.
[82] Heyward, 1999a:2.
[83] Heyward, 1999a:4 – 5.
[84] Heyward, 1999a:8.
[85] Heyward, 1999a:9.
[86] Heyward, 1999a:9.
[87] Heyward, 1999a:10.
[88] Heyward, 1999a:52.
[89] Heyward, 1999a:14.
[90] Heyward, 1999a:15.
[91] Heyward, 1999a:17.
[92] Oduyoye, M.E., (2002), "Jesus Christ" in Parsons, S.F., (ed), *The Cambridge Companion to Feminist Theology*, Cambridge: Cambridge University Press, p.167.
[93] Heyward, 1999a:57.
[94] Heyward, 1999a:61.
[95] Heyward, 1999a:61-62.
[96] Heyward, 1999a:62.
[97] Heyward, 1999a:66.
[98] Heyward, 1999a:111.
[99] Heyward, 1999a:114.
[100] Heyward, 1999a:126.
[101] Heyward, 1999a:71.
[102] Heyward, 1999a:71.
[103] Isherwood, 2001:59.
[104] Heyward, 1999a:72.

[105] Soskice, J.M in Parsons, S.F., (ed), *The Cambridge Companion to Feminist Theology*, Cambridge: Cambridge University Press, p.139.
[106] Heyward, 1999a:20.
[107] Heyward, 1999a:22.
[108] Heyward, 1999a:23.
[109] Heyward, 1999a:24.
[110] Heyward, 1999a:24.
[111] Heyward, 1999a:32.
[112] Heyward, 1999a:33.
[113] Heyward, 1999a:36.
[114] Heyward, 1999a:37.
[115] Heyward, 1999a:130.
[116] Heyward, 1999a:122.
[117] Heyward, 1999a:121.
[118] Heyward, 1999a:149.
[119] Heyward, 1999a:122.
[120] Heyward, 1999a:134.
[121] Heyward, 1999a:135.
[122] Heyward, 1999a:136.
[123] Heyward, 1999a:137.
[124] Heyward, 1999a:140.
[125] Heyward, 1999a:140.
[126] Heyward, 1999a:149.
[127] Heyward, 1999a:165.
[128] Heyward, 1999a:178.
[129] Heyward, 1989:35.
[130] Heyward, 1982:17.
[131] Heyward, 1982:19.
[132] Heyward, 1999b:33.
[133] Heyward, 1989:9.
[134] Heyward, 1999a:42.
[135] Heyward, 1999b:3.
[136] Heyward, C., in Russell, L., and Shannon, J., (ed.), (1996), *Dictionary of Feminist Theologies*, London: Mowbray, p.40.
[137] Heyward, C., 1989:9.
[138] Heyward, 1989:11.

Chapter Four

Remembering and Valuing: Elisabeth Schüssler Fiorenza

Introduction

From identification and analysis of the strategy of feminist informed reinterpretation developed by Carter Heyward, this chapter moves on to examine the strategy of feminist Christian encounter based in the historical location, recovery and reconstruction of "authentic Christianity" of Elisabeth Schüssler Fiorenza. Schüssler Fiorenza's is an approach that is guided by feminist criticism and insights, and informed by feminist values and understandings of justice. And against the backdrop of over thirty years of contemporary feminist theological discourse the contribution of Schüssler Fiorenza to the development and sustaining presence of feminist informed theologies is outstanding. The approach that she has developed to facilitate feminist Christian encounter in her theology is one that attempts to establish a clear historical based relationship to the Christian tradition through feminist critique and reconstruction. This strategy is employed, though in a number of different guises, by many theologians concerned with addressing issues of gender and Christian theology. The reasons for examining this strategy of the recovery of authentic Christianity in relation to the work of Schüssler Fiorenza, rather than any other theologian, is that first, its use is very clear and explicit in her work, and second, through her work it has exercised a major influence on the methods of feminist Christian encounter.

Background

As Krister Stendahl Professor of Scripture and Interpretation at Harvard Divinity School Elisabeth Schüssler Fiorenza has an international standing in contemporary Christian theological scholarship and education that few women engaged with theology and gender can make claim to. In addition to her current post, she has also held teaching posts at the University of Notre Dame, Episcopal Divinity School, Union Theological Seminary and the University of Tubingen. Schüssler Fiorenza is without doubt one of the most visible of contemporary feminist informed Christian theologians. Reflecting in 2002 on the two main locations of her theological activity, Germany and North America, she describes how she has "...chosen to remain a 'resident alien' in the United States in order to be able to do my work from such a social location of partial identification"[1], and claims that such a positioning has brought criticisms from both Europeans and Americans in a similar way that her cross-disciplinary scholarship brings criticisms in contradiction[2] from different parties.

Schüssler Fiorenza has maintained a significant presence in the field of feminisms, gender studies and Christian theology since the 1970s and is a prolific writer with a large number of books and articles to her name. The combination of wide-reaching academic standing and her clear feminist commitment leads her to a space that in itself has given rise to a sometimes ambiguous reading of her work, both from those engaged with the spectrum of liberative theological activity and those working from within the specifically disciplined base of academia. And this is an ambiguity of which Schüssler Fiorenza is well aware. For example, writing in 1990 in *Christian Century*,[3] and reflecting on the development of her thinking, she drew attention to the specific criticisms raised by feminist critics about the style she employed in one of her most significant texts to date, *In Memory of Her*, she noted that:

> Even today, feminist students will occasionally accuse me of "male scholarship" because my book *In Memory of Her* is full of footnotes and written in a "logical-linear" style. Although I can understand such a sentiment, given the bad experiences women have had in academic institutions, I could never share this view. It tends to replicate the cultural stereotype that restricts logical thinking and disciplined intellectual work to men and thereby prohibits women from producing knowledge and from defining the world.[4]

Schüssler Fiorenza claims that she is not prepared to concede to limiting or stereotypical understandings of the possibilities of Christian theology, whatever the source of such understandings.

Giving description to the depth and importance of Schüssler Fiorenza's contribution to the development and shaping presence of feminist theological discourses is difficult, and one of the reasons for this is that her work has had an impact on a number of different aspects of feminist informed theologies and Christian theology as a whole. In fact, versatility and a willingness to engage with the contemporary and often contentious issues of feminist theological discourse are two characteristics of her approach and are in themselves reasons for her continuing influence within a field that is characterised by an increasing visibility and significance of a diversity of voices. She has made a significant contribution to the theoretical frameworks of feminist theological discourse and particularly to the critical discussion surrounding the ambiguous and often problematic place and understanding of women's experiences within feminist informed theologies. In addition to this, she has engaged very openly with the claim that the visible and dominant faces of feminist informed theologies incorporate exclusions and underlying presumptions that replicate some of those of traditional theologies, which have been so heavily criticised by feminist informed theologies. Undoubtedly, however, it is in the field of biblical studies, and in particular the development of critical feminist biblical hermeneutics, that her work has received most critical recognition and has, arguably, had most transformative impact on

Christian theology and practice, and, also, is specifically the focus here for exploring her strategy for feminist Christian encounter. Given the authoritative place of the Bible in Christian testimony, and particularly, as argued by feminist based criticism, in the justifying and sanctifying of gender based injustice and inequalities, it is not surprising that it has received a large amount of critical attention in the development of feminist informed theologies. Yet even within the great variety and depth of critical feminist analysis that has emerged here, Schüssler Fiorenza's work claims particular prominence. She is acclaimed not only for her critical analysis of traditional Christian theological scholarship and her identification of the androcentric perspective of Christian scripture, but also for the development of her reconstructionist methodology for the recovery of women's Christian past, which is of particular interest to this study of the strategies of feminist Christian encounter. Over the last thirty years Schüssler Fiorenza has developed a feminist informed Christian theology of liberation that incorporates a radical approach to biblical interpretation and one that explicitly places issues of gender based injustice, and the need to overcome such injustices, at the forefront of analysis and critical concern. At the same time her theology is one that is clearly concerned to move beyond the critique of traditional Christian theology and Christianity as gendered and exclusive to a more constructive feminist informed Christian theology that seeks to engage the Christian tradition in justice seeking ways.

One of the most interesting things about Schüssler Fiorenza's feminist informed theological approach, from a methodological perspective, and one of the reasons that her theology attracts so much attention, is her concern to maintain a careful tension between the traditions of Christianity and feminist informed radicalism. In many ways she can be seen to employ a quite radical feminist based approach whilst at the same time drawing on the findings of more traditional theological methods and retaining a very clear sense of commitment to her Christian heritage. This is one of the key reasons for the influence of her theology because it pays heed to the insights of feminist criticism, taking on board, developing and applying the often radical insight to theological perspectives, yet claims a direct and for many, unambiguous, relationship to the Christian tradition. In Schüssler Fiorenza's own words:

> Although I fully shared the trenchant feminist critique of the Christian tradition, I never felt such an irreconcilable contradiction between my Christian and my feminist identity. In my experience some Christian teachings had offered a religious resource for resisting the demands of cultural feminine roles.[5]

Here, then, she shares with Carter Heyward an understanding of Christianity as certainly affected and distorted by gender based injustice, but also as being in some way open to the possibility of recovery or transformation from such injustice. Schüssler Fiorenza places her theology very firmly within the Christian tradition with the kinds of claims and presuppositions she makes. On one level then, a straightforward reading of Schüssler Fiorenza's method sees it as traditional, if compared for example with the approaches of such as Daly or Hampson, in its claim to be based firmly in the Christian tradition but radical in both its understanding of this tradition, and the approach taken to it. And it is the explicit attempt by Schüssler Fiorenza to maintain this tension as creative and not problematic, or rather as not insurmountable that is the key point of interest here in terms of the strategies employed to maintain this tension.

Feminist biblical studies and the reconstruction of early Christian history

In exploring the implications and possibilities of feminist analysis and criticism for Christian theology Schüssler Fiorenza offers the image of the feminist informed theologian as a "troublemaker, as a resident alien".[6] This, then, moves away from a stress on the critical dependency of feminist informed Christian theologies on a conflictual or marginal relationship with "mainline" Christian theology. It understands feminist informed Christian theologies as theologies in their own right, and in some ways moves away from the concept of boundary living, which is used quite extensively by some feminists and feminist informed theologians to stress the often ambiguous and often marginal space so often occupied by feminisms:

> Feminist theologians should not situate their theological work on the boundaries and in the margins but should move it into the center of academy and religion. Women, who for so long have been excluded from the production of scientific and theological knowledge, must claim the center of theory and theology in order to transform it. We must do so in order to undermine the tendencies of androcentric world views and theological languages that have relegated us to the margins, the periphery, and the boundaries for much too long.[7]

Schüssler Fiorenza articulates this double play in terms of being bilingual,[8] which is a useful concept when considering the multiple discourses in which scholars like Schüssler Fiorenza inevitably participate. And it encapsulates something of the ambiguity of feminist informed Christian theologies in relation to both academic and ecclesial institutions. Throughout her feminist biblical work the negotiating and envisaging of this ambiguous existence is a driving and shaping force of her theology. This is seen clearly, for example, in the two early texts that established Schüssler Fiorenza's influential place within the development of feminist informed theologies, *In Memory of Her: A Feminist Theological Reconstruction of Christian Origins* which was first published in 1983 and *Bread Not Stone* published in 1984. In both of these theological texts the approach that she employs does much more than simply analyse from a feminist perspective those biblical passages concerned with women, although this fundamental feminist theological task is incorporated into her approach. Rather, she offers what for many have proved to be groundbreaking perspectives on the possibilities of reclaiming women's biblical and early Christian experiences as important contemporary critical liberative resources.

In *Bread Not Stone* Schüssler Fiorenza argues that a key task of feminist informed theology in terms of biblical analysis and interpretation is to directly and explicitly question the authority of oppressive, androcentric or "patriarchal" texts and to ask how the Bible can be employed as a liberative resource for women. That is, as a resource that is justice seeking rather than justice denying. This then, constitutes in part the nature of the radical reformist feminist approach to Christianity to which she has committed herself over the last thirty years. It is concerned with the understanding and function of the Bible in the struggles of women's self-identification and liberation in the face of gender based injustice. As such the task of feminist informed theologies, as articulated by Schüssler Fiorenza, is intrinsically political. Schüssler Fiorenza argues that in approaching biblical texts women are faced with a very difficult task because androcentric biblical language and perspectives, which she claims characterise these biblical texts, do not highlight or record women's experiences and history, which according to feminist analysis are fundamentally different from the experiences of men. She argues that in fact, when women *are* mentioned in the biblical texts it is generally only when they are distinguished or are being represented as being in some way difficult or problematic. She also claims that the experiences of exclusion are compounded by the workings and presuppositions of most biblical exegesis, which she argues assumes that the early Christian communities were organised and led by men. She recognises that many feminist approaches reject the possibilities for biblical texts being employed in a liberative way because of the part they have played so far in the oppression of women and the legitimisation of this oppression. And whilst Schüssler Fiorenza recognises and acknowledges the negative ways in which these texts have been used, she nevertheless argues that biblical texts can and must be recovered as a positive resource. What she is concerned with, then, is not simply accepting the Bible as authoritative but with submitting it to a critical evaluative process to discern what is and what is not liberative, and more specifically, what does and what does not support gender based justice. This critical task, according to Schüssler Fiorenza, is essential before authority can be placed with such texts.

In these earlier works Schüssler Fiorenza makes extensive use of the term "patriarchy" in her critique of church and society. Even at this stage in her thought she is careful to stress that she uses the term not simply to refer to gender based inequalities in which men exercise power in an oppressive way towards women. Rather, for her, it refers to a whole organisational system, social, political, economic and religious, which are characterised by "graded subjugations and oppressions".[9] Patriarchal images and symbols then are seen not only to define people according to gender but also according to race, religion and class. By this, women are separated not only from men but also from other women and placed in hierarchical relationships with each other, for example, on the basis of colour, sexuality, ethnic origin, religion and economic or social class. Although "patriarchy" has proved to be a very contentious term in feminist analysis, which, as will be seen in this chapter, is something which Schüssler Fiorenza responds to in her later work, she is quite thorough in her analysis and use of the term even in her earlier theological works. With clarification and precision she is very radical in her understanding of the "patriarchal" influences and conditioning of the Christian biblical and early traditions. She depicts early Christianity as being fundamentally and systematically transformed, and indeed, distorted by the patriarchal cultural influences on the developing Christian Church.

Schüssler Fiorenza draws on contemporary tools and methods of biblical scholarship in the development of her feminist informed approach to biblical interpretation and she places particular emphasis on the need to incorporate a recognition both of the context in which texts arose and the context in which they are now used in order to understand their liberative possibilities. This explicit employment of the tools of contemporary biblical scholarship is in part why her theology gains recognition from the wider theological community, and, as noted earlier, the reason why her approach has been criticised by some feminist informed theologians. Schüssler Fiorenza argues that the Bible must be subjected to a process of critical evaluation which takes note of its value and possibilities for contemporary society and, very importantly, for specific contexts. Biblical texts cannot be understood, or their value assessed, in isolation from either the historical context out of which they arose or from the contemporary concerns of situations, which they are called upon to address. The very difficult task at the heart of feminist hermeneutics is the need to go beyond, or to interpret what have been identified as the silences of texts, a task which seems almost by definition, the interpretation of silences, to be a non-starter. The feminist paradigm here then, is not only about recovery but also about creative and critical reappriopriation of the past. Schüssler Fiorenza's approach is one, which determines the authority of the text according to its interpreted liberative content, and so the whole process rests on the criteria used to make such an evaluation. The determination of the criteria of evaluation is the focus or location of authority.

Feminist biblical hermeneutics

In detailing her understanding and contribution to the development of the methodologies of feminist informed theologies, Schüssler Fiorenza has argued that feminist biblical interpretation involves a series of hermeneutical tasks. These include a hermeneutics of suspicion, a hermeneutics of proclamation, a hermeneutics of remembrance and historical reconstruction, as well as a hermeneutics of creative actualisation.[10] This is a very useful elaboration or breakdown of her vision of what actually constitutes the feminist informed critical approach to the Christian Bible, and in particular, the various aspects or elements to her own approach and as such is worth a more detailed examination here.

In adopting or employing a *hermeneutics of suspicion*, feminist informed theologies do not simply accept Christian biblical texts as divine revelation, but instead, they are seen to have functioned according to and have been shaped by patriarchal interests, which have either made women invisible or have depicted them according to patriarchally determined stereotypes.[11] Given this, feminist informed theologies, with their hermeneutics of suspicion, challenge the authority that has traditionally been accorded to the Bible. For Schüssler Fiorenza the very fact of the patriarchal influences on the Bible, as claimed and determined by feminist analysis, and the reading of the history of the Bible as participating in or being used as a tool of the oppression of women means that such authority cannot simply be accorded to the Bible in the ways it has in the past and largely continues to be today. Kwok Pui-lan recognises the significance of Schüssler Fiorenza's approach here, and shares her commitment to a hermeneutics of suspicion and to being constantly aware of both context and function:

> Conversely, I support Elisabeth Schüssler Fiorenza's suggestion that a feminist interpretation of the Bible must "sort through particular biblical texts and test out in a process of critical analysis and evaluation how much their content and function perpetuates and legitimates patriarchal structures, not only in their original historical contexts but also in our contemporary situation." The critical principle lies not in the Bible itself, but in the community of women and men, who read the Bible and who, through their dialogical imagination, appropriate it for their own liberation.[12]

Schüssler Fiorenza understands feminist informed theologies here as having the task of examining the validity and liberating function of texts and identifying those that do not support gender based justice. The starting point of such a hermeneutics of suspicion is the conviction that both biblical texts themselves, and interpretations of these texts, are androcentric and so reflect an exclusively, or predominantly, androcentric perspective.[13] She explains or justifies such an interpretation with the claim that it is men who are largely understood to have authored the biblical texts and men who have largely interpreted these texts in influential ecclesial and academic settings. The place of women in relation to both of these tasks is largely hidden and unknown and so the appropriate response to such exclusion is rightly one of suspicion. She draws a revealing analogy here between the work of the feminist critic and the woman in the parable of the lost coin:

> Just as the woman in the parable sweeps the whole house in search of her lost coin, so feminist critical interpretation searches for the lost traditions and visions of liberation among its inheritance of androcentric biblical texts and their interpretations.[14]

The suspicion named in this phrase of Schüssler Fiorenza extends to the methods and approaches that have been developed to interpret the biblical texts. She argues that just as the writing of these texts was influenced by the context and perspectives of the biblical authors, so the context and perspectives of both critics and interpreters also needs to be taken into consideration and explicitly acknowledged by both the critics and interpreters themselves and their readers or listeners.[15] She offers an interesting, and for some very challenging perspective on what kind of relationship to the biblical tradition a hermeneutics of suspicion actually leads to. Within this she places great importance with the necessity of recognising how language works and claims that the feminist task here is not to cover up what she calls "sexist language".[16] A hermeneutic of suspicion is by no means an approach exclusive to feminist informed biblical interpretation and is to be found in many different liberation theologies and liberation movements. However, it is often associated with the feminist informed theological response to gender based injustice. And as Julie Hopkins has pointed out, a hermeneutics of suspicion does have particular significance in the work of Schüssler Fiorenza:

> In her book "In Memory of Her", Elizabeth Schüssler Fiorenza uses the tools of biblical criticism, sociology, linguistics and women's history to break through the silence of the New Testament text concerning the praxis and authority of the first Christian women. She argues that the theological meaning of the Jesus movement and the Early Christian Missionary Movement cannot be grasped until a hermeneutic of feminist suspicion is applied to the New Testament canon. Hidden beneath the text and in clues in the text is the silenced suffering and power of our spiritual foremothers. To recover and retell their story for Womenchurch is to reclaim women's memory, a memory which challenges the epistemological and religious framework of Western power and knowledge.[17]

The *hermeneutics of proclamation* that Schüssler Fiorenza also identifies as being part of feminist biblical interpretation seems to involve the Bible being subjected to careful examination to assess its possible significance and function for contemporary Christian communities.[18] In this way, then, it focuses on the significance of the biblical texts for contemporary faith communities. Within such a process, those biblical texts which are assessed as being oppressive, and more specifically, in terms of Schüssler Fiorenza's specific contextual focus, those texts which are assessed as reinforcing gender based injustice, are rejected, and Schüssler Fiorenza proposes that they should have no place in the life of the worshipping community. This, then means that the contemporary significance of biblical texts plays a key role in the critical assessment of the liberative value, and so continuing relevance, of texts and it involves "...a political-critical feminist evaluation to assess the interaction of patriarchal texts with contemporary culture".[19] The knock on effects of identifying texts that do not function in a positive (justice seeking) way are real and quite dramatic. Those texts that are seen to go beyond androcentric concerns and perspectives should be given a "proper place"[20] in the life of the Church and worshipping communities and those that do not should not play any role in Christian worship. Again, this places particular significance and determining authority with the feminist process of assessment.

Countering the potentially very radical implications of such a hermeneutics of proclamation Schüssler Fiorenza argues that the *hermeneutics of remembrance* of feminist biblical interpretation considers all traditions of the Bible from a feminist reconstructive perspective approach. It does not relinquish androcentric traditions, as such, but seeks to go beyond the oppressive elements "to the history of women in biblical religion".[21] The hermeneutics of remembrance does not forget women's Christian past with its suffering and oppression. The past experiences of women are identified and critically recovered. It does not seek to move beyond the historical experiences of women but seeks to reclaim the historical experiences of women through the subversive power of memory. She claims that this not only gives voice to and celebrates the struggle of women but "allows for a universal solidarity among women of the past, present, and future",[22] which seems to be an argument for seeing the experiences of gender based oppression as a unifying experience of women. Heritage is paramount for the feminist informed theological task here as envisaged by Schüssler Fiorenza:

> In short, a feminist hermeneutics of remembrance has as its primary task to keep alive the *memoria passionis* of biblical women as well as to reclaim our biblical heritage.
>
> The history and theology must not be allowed to cancel out the memory of the struggle, life, and leadership of biblical women who spoke and acted in the power of the Spirit.[23]

Such is the influence of the traditions of oppression and injustice not only on the recording, transmission and interpretation of biblical texts, but also on the historical processes of canonical inclusion or exclusion, that Schüssler Fiorenza also identifies the need to cast the feminist net beyond the accepted canon of the Bible,

> ...I seek to work out a process and method for a feminist political reading that can empower women who, for whatever reason, are still affected by the Bible to read "against the grain" of its patriarchal rhetoric. Moreover, such a critical feminist interpretation is not limited to canonical texts but can be equally applied to extracanonical sources and traditions.[24]

Finally, a *hermeneutics of creative actualisation* as detailed by Schüssler Fiorenza places and celebrates women as part of the ongoing biblical story. A story that, for Schüssler Fiorenza, is a story of justice or liberation.[25] A hermeneutics of creative actualisation is the participation of women in the biblical story, the ongoing biblical story. In this way, then, women today become part of the biblical story. This involves the creative retelling of biblical stories from a feminist perspective and brings with it a stress on the importance of criticism needing to be matched by creative and constructive theologizing. Here we encounter Schüssler Fiorenza's understanding of the process of "creative revision"[26] which draws on many tools and insights to "amplify"[27] liberation feminist remnants. The creative participation of women in the biblical story retells the biblical story in such a way as to "reformulate"[28] patriarchal elements and include feminist interpretation. This may involve the renewal of stories, rituals, new symbols, images and language and may be radically creative, if not actually transformative of the transmitted Christian tradition. But again, this is justified if not in fact fundamentally necessitated by the nature of the inherited tradition. Injustice demands a radical response guided by feminist values and visions.

The hermeneutical process that Schüssler Fiorenza seems to be envisaging here that will take place according to the feminist paradigm of biblical interpretation is one in which questions determine answers and in which texts are formative in answering questions. The Christian community assesses texts today, according to its experiences and situations, and only those texts that are deemed as not perpetuating gender based injustice can continue to be used by the Christian community. This, then, places huge responsibility and authority with feminisms, and very significantly with those employing feminist insights and values. Schüssler Fiorenza notes that the task of contemporary feminist informed theological assessment and interpretation of the Bible is difficult and problematic and she is also quick to point out that she is not trying to "...save the Bible from its feminist critics".[29] It is a proposed paradigm of biblical interpretation concerned to free the gospel from patriachalism, and it is about the experience and power of women as community, past and present. Its aim, then, is not to forget the patriarchal past, but to reclaim the "subversive power of the 'remembered past'",[30] women's past of oppression and struggle.

Schüssler Fiorenza's stress on the importance of experience in critical and constructive theologising leads her to a number of very important methodological insights into the nature and representation of theological scholarship. Along with many feminist informed thinkers in theology, she rejects the view of theology as objective, value-free scholarship. She argues that theology is very much the product of each writer's experience, and so is determined in form and content by the historical and social context of the theologian. All theology and theological texts are culturally conditioned and contextually shaped and employed. As such, theology can be said to reflect or serve the interests of a particular group or individual.[31] Theology not only has the responsibility of acknowledging its partisan nature, but as Schüssler Fiorenza understands it, it has the task specifically of reflecting and serving the interests of the marginalised and oppressed. This, then, reflects Schüssler Fiorenza's own understanding of theology and of the specific nature of Christian theology as an advocacy theology, "Only when theology is on the side of the outcast and oppressed, as Jesus was, can it become incarnational and Christian. Christian theology, therefore, has to be rooted in emancipatory praxis and solidarity".[32] Schüssler Fiorenza's understanding of Christian theology as an advocacy theology leaves it with clear and specific responsibilities. She also here very clearly places her liberative reading of Christianity at the very centre of the faith tradition by aligning it so closely with the figure of Christ. Schüssler Fiorenza, then, has a very specific understanding of Christianity as justice based and of Christian theology as concerned with detailing and working through this justice concern. This is a very particular reading of Christianity, as concerned with justice, and more specifically, gender based justice. Questions then rightly need to be asked of whether at the same time this particular reading does not in fact claim more than particular contextual relevance. Or whether, as some suspect, it in fact claims universal relevance and significance. These questions will be explored in more depth in Chapter Six.

Feminist reconstruction and women's Christian heritage

One of the key areas of feminist theological concern in which Schüssler Fiorenza's work has had most impact is in the area of the early Christian Church studies. She has proposed and developed, particularly in her earlier studies, a radical reconstructionist approach to the recovery and elaboration of women's Christian history and heritage. This reconstructionist approach underlies and sustains the strategy of feminist Christian encounter that she has developed. As part of the argument that she has forwarded for both the legitimacy and possibility of feminist informed Christian theologies Schüssler Fiorenza has stressed that women's history and experience must not only be remembered (as opposed to being forgotten) but also that they must be reclaimed as women's own. Within the context of her own approach and detailing of continued Christian commitment in the face of the radical critique of feminisms, this stress on heritage seems to be particularly important, and for some critics of Schüssler Fiorenza, particularly problematic. She is concerned, she emphasises, not to give up women's Christian past too easily, and argues that post traditional feminist informed theologies often reinforce the idea that women did not have a significant role to play in the development of early Christianity. An interpretation that she very firmly rejects. The continuing influence of biblical religion on many women's lives is reason enough, according to Schüssler Fiorenza, for giving serious critical address to the contribution of women to the early Christian movement, and to make it a legitimate focus of feminist informed theological activity:

> Insofar as biblical religion is still influential today, a cultural and social feminist transformation of Western society must take into account the biblical story and the historical impact of the biblical tradition. Western women are not able to discard completely and forget our personal, cultural, or religious Christian history. We will either transform it into a new liberating future or continue to be subject to its tyranny whether we recognize its power or not.
>
> Feminists cannot afford such an ahistorical or antihistorical stance because it is precisely the power of oppression that deprives people of their history.[33]

What Schüssler Fiorenza seems to be arguing here is that the very fact of history and the cultural influence of heritage on human lives, however the underlying history and heritage have traditionally been interpreted and represented, is reason enough to stay and work with these traditions. The rationale of such an argument is clearly problematic when the feminist understanding of the gender based nature of such tradition and heritage sees them as denying the full humanity of women. However, Schüssler Fiorenza argues that the alternative response, to relinquish this heritage, simply reasserts the dominance of the androcentric nature of traditional Western society:

> ...relinquishing our biblical heritage merely reinforces the androcentric reality construction of Western culture according to which male existence and history is the paradigm of human existence and human history.[34]

Fundamental to her understanding of the need to recover and reconstruct early Christian history is the conviction that the picture of early Christianity that we have is not the full story, an interpretation she claims is supported by historical-critical scholarship.[35] The feminist informed Christian methodological response to the realisation of gendered history and the impact of this on understandings and representation of Christian history, and Christianity itself, is one that involves a degree of creative rewriting based in feminist consciousness. Schüssler Fiorenza argues that the task of feminist critical approach "...can be likened to the work of a detective insofar as it does not rely solely on historical 'facts' nor invents its evidence, but is engaged in an imaginative reconstruction of historical reality":[36] The task is necessarily based in creative imagination and reconstruction, "In the attempt to make the past intelligible the historian must go beyond the events in an act of 'intellectual re-creation'".[37]

Feminist methodology and authority

Within the feminist informed model of biblical interpretation and reconstruction or early Christian history that Schüssler Fiorenza proposes the Bible as the textual base of Christian authority is inevitably radically reassessed. In Schüssler Fiorenza's understanding the Bible cannot be attributed complete and unconditional authority because of its past and continuing role in the gender based oppression of women. This leads Schüssler Fiorenza to an approach that attempts to accept the revelatory significance of the biblical texts, whilst at the same time acknowledging the androcentric nature, as understood by feminist criticism, of these texts. This, then, again enables Schüssler Fiorenza to maintain the crucial tension between feminist informed radicalism necessitated by centuries of injustice and the need to retain a clear relationship to the Christian tradition.

> The historical-theological insight that the New Testament is not only a source of revelatory truth but also a resource for patriarchal subordination and domination demands a new paradigm for biblical hermeneutics and theology. This paradigm must not only shed its objectivist pretense of disinterestedness but also its doctrinal neo-orthodox essence-accidents model of interpretation.[38]

The experience of those oppressed by biblical texts affirms, according to feminist informed Christian theological analysis that the Bible, in part at least, is not liberating, and so it must be subject to careful and extensive critical assessment. Consequently, only those texts, which function positively for women, can be attributed with authority and can be accorded with contemporary religious significance. The paradigm that Schüssler Fiorenza is proposing for feminist biblical interpretation in response to such an assessment is one which neither simply sees the Bible as the Word of God[39] nor only as an historical document of the past. Rather, the Bible is understood, in Schüssler Fiorenza's words, as a "historical prototype", a collection of texts which were written and gathered at a certain point in history, and which reflect, and were to some extent motivated, by historical, social, political and religious circumstances.

For Schüssler Fiorenza, in describing the Bible as prototype she seems to mean that it is not a closed or static authority, but is something, which can, and indeed must, remain open to change and critical development. Given her interpretation of the gendered nature of biblical texts and traditional biblical interpretation, she is concerned with developing a heuristic model, which enables her to go beyond what she has described as the androcentricism of Christian scriptures and reinterpret the silences of biblical texts. This then involves a very different assessment of the authority of the Bible from that found in much of traditional Christian theology. Her specifically feminist based methodology places authority for the evaluation and interpretation of biblical historical traditions firmly with women. The Bible is engaged as a source among sources and, very importantly, Schüssler Fiorenza argues that the androcentric biblical texts and patriarchal traditions are not identical with Christian revelation. So, what happens to those texts that are deemed to be androcentric according to Schüssler Fiorenza's scheme of critical assessment? She argues that because of their androcentricity, these texts should be denounced and the authority that has traditionally been accorded them, stripped away. Such texts should then be replaced by texts that function in a justice affirming and seeking rather than denying way. Biblical authority, as such here, is very clearly bound up with experience, and in particular, the specific experiences of women seeking to overcome gender based injustice:

> ...the revelatory canon for theological evaluation of biblical androcentric traditions and their subsequent interpretations cannot be derived from the Bible itself but can only be formulated in and through women's struggle for liberation from all patriarchal oppression.
> ...The personally and politically reflected experience of oppression and liberation must become the criterion of appropriateness for biblical interpretation and evaluation of biblical authority claims.[40]

Schüssler Fiorenza does see beyond the experiences of women as the critical base of discernment here, but at the same time she does seem to prioritise the experiences of those who are oppressed and seeking to overcome this oppression. She seems to regard such experiences as in someway offering special insight in seeing through the tainted aspects of the Christian tradition to discern authenticity through its alignment with justice. And even within this broader sweep of justice seeking experiences the experiences of women, in Schüssler Fiorenza's theology, have particular significance. Also, in arguing against ascribing authority to the Bible without first subjecting it to a critical examination from a feminist perspective, she gives special significance to feminisms and the processes of feminist informed theological analysis and critique. In particular, and perhaps most importantly in terms of this analysis of the strategies of feminist Christian encounter, Schüssler Fiorenza places authority with her own specific understanding of the nature of the true Christian message via the interplay between women's experiences and the Bible as they work together in a critical yet essential unity. Authority comes to the Bible through a critical process that involves both evaluation and transformation, in which feminist insight and women's experiences clearly have a determining place. As suggested earlier, then, the claims that Schüssler Fiorenza seems to be making for feminisms and women's experiences in her theology have important consequences for questions of authority in feminist informed Christian theologies and for authority and even orthodoxy as a whole.

In the context of feminist informed theologies, then, in effect, Schüssler Fiorenza identifies women's experiences as the determining factor in assessing what is and what is not liberating in the Christian tradition and so, (according to her understanding of Christianity) what is and what is not authentically Christian:

> A feminist theological hermeneutics having as its canon the liberation of women from oppressive patriarchal texts, structures, institutions, and values maintains that – if the Bible is not to continue as a tool for patriarchal oppression of women – only those traditions and texts that critically break through patriarchal culture and "plausibility structures" have the theological authority of revelation.[41]

This places with women's experiences, and so with the feminist approach, the discerning power of locating authenticity and the proper functioning of the 'true' Christian message. The feminist approach, then, becomes the tool or even the location of truthfulness in terms of religious truth. It also places authority with Schüssler Fiorenza's understanding of the nature of the true Christian message.

From the depth of the critical claims made by Schüssler Fiorenza about the effects of patriachalism on the Christian tradition, the question arises as to how then she proposes to move beyond such insights or claims to the position of affirmation of the Christian tradition. Or, put another way, within the midst of such androcentrism and patriachalism of biblical texts and the Christian tradition overall, as claimed and detailed by Schüssler Fiorenza, what is it that enables her still to talk of the possibilities of a Christianity that is justice seeking and affirming rather than justice denying? What does Schüssler Fiorenza identify as a possible aspect or tradition of Christianity that can be recovered from its patriarchal influences? Whereas Carter Hayward focuses on the symbol of Jesus Christ, with all of its possibilities through radical reinterpretation, Schüssler Fiorenza locates the revelatory basis of the Christian tradition as Christ's ministry and life and also 'the movement of women and men called forth by him'.[42] So, despite recognizing the depth of androcentric influences that were at play in the development and writing of the biblical traditions Schüssler Fiorenza argues that there are still glimpses of the egalitarian Christian tradition. And these glimpses are in themselves good reason for hope:

> Although the canon preserves only remnants of the nonpatriachal early ethos, these remnants still allow us to recognize that the patriachalization process is not inherent in Christian revelation and community but progressed slowly and with difficultly.[43]

Her approach then is not primarily about radical reinterpretation but the reconstruction of claimed historical tradition. For Schüssler Fiorenza, this "Christian revelation and community" refers to the vision of equality upon which the response to Christ was initially based, which she names as the "discipleship of equals". Here, then, there is an important correlation between justice and authentic Christianity or even truth. According to Schüssler Fiorenza's understanding, Christianity or the original Christian message was one of liberation and justice, which contemporary critical feminist informed Christian theologies have the task of rediscovering and recovering. She is very careful here not to set up the ministry and response to Jesus in conflictual opposition to Judaism, as justice seeking as opposed to justice denying, recognising the potential anti-Semitic tendencies or implications of such an approach:

> The praxis and vision of Jesus and his movement is best understood as an inner-Jewish renewal movement that presented an *alternative* option to the dominant patriarchal structures rather than an oppositional formation rejecting the values and praxis of Judaism.[44]

Schüssler Fiorenza's reconstruction of women's early Christian history, then, is based on this egalitarian model or reading of early Christianity. She criticises both the theological and anthropological models on which the reconstruction of early Christian history has traditionally been based, and proposes an egalitarian model in its place. Her feminist based reconstructionist model aims to liberate the "egalitarian impulses" of the early Christian movement and engage them in a constructive and justice seeking way. She claims that her approach, "...does not seek to distill the 'historical Jesus' from the remembering interpretation of his first followers, nor does it accept their interpretation uncritically and without question".[45] Her understanding of Christianity is dependent upon this interpretation of the biblical message as involving an egalitarian vision. It is this understanding of Christianity as fundamentally egalitarian in nature which legitimises her commitment to the Christian tradition despite what she has assessed as its patriarchal nature. As Susan Ross in *Extravagant Affections: A Feminist Sacramental Theology* has argued:

> Yet Schüssler Fiorenza, while agreeing that Catholicism is in serious need of transformation, observed that within it there exist practices and traditions that are nevertheless supportive of and inspirational to women. The message of Jesus as one of liberation, rejection of hierarchy, and inclusivity remains alive despite the tradition's institutionalization and patriachalization.[46]

Schüssler Fiorenza argues that the vision of Jesus focuses on the *basileia* of God,[47] and this, as she understands it is a radically inclusive vision, as seen within the God-Sophia wisdom tradition.[48] The evidence that she offers to support her interpretation of the radically inclusive discipleship of equals in the vision and ministry of Jesus and in the responses to those around him has been variously received by scholars working in this and related areas. At the heart of her claims here is the belief that "Rather than reproducing the patriarchal relationships of the 'household' in antiquity, the Jesus movement demands a radical break from it...".[49] She argues, for example, that the Markan saying (10:15) "Truly, I say to you, whoever does not receive the kingdom of God like a child shall not enter it" evidences the kind of social reversal that she understands to underlie the radical discipleship of equals and she offers Mark 9:35-37, Matt. 18:1-4 and Luke 9:48 as further evidence of this. The early Christian missionary movement has also been a particular focus of Schüssler Fiorenza's critical attention, as she has attempted to interpret and move beyond what she claims are the often silent biblical texts to an understanding of women as key participants in the missionary activity of the early church. She claims that the Pauline literature allows such a reading of women as "...prominent leaders and missionaries who – in their own right – toiled for the gospel".[50] In *In Memory of Her* Schüssler Fiorenza attempts to reconstruct the early missionary movement placing the activity and contribution of women at the very centre.

Within the reconstructed early Christian movement that Schüssler Fiorenza offers, Gal 3:28, "There is neither Jew nor Greek, there is neither slave nor free, there is neither male nor female; for you are all one in Christ Jesus" takes on a key role. She notes the significance of discussions surrounding the interpretation of this verse but moves to an understanding of it as having vital significance as a baptismal announcement to an early Jewish-Hellenistic community.[51] She argues that the sentiment and key message of this declaration is found repeatedly in Pauline texts, including, 1 Cor 6:20, 7:23, Gal 5:1, Gal 5:13 and 2 Cor 3:17:[52]

> Paul's interpretation and adaptation of the baptismal declaration Gal 3:28 in his letters to the community of Corinth unequivocally affirm the equality and charismatic giftedness of women and men in the Christian community. Women as well as men are prophets and leaders of worship in the community. Women as well as men have the call to a marriage-free life. Women as well as men have mutual rights and obligations within the sexual relationship of marriage.[53]

Whilst recognising the ambiguity of the Pauline texts towards women Schüssler Fiorenza traces the increasing patriachalisation of the early Christian Church through the post-Pauline literature,[54] which she argues was increasingly influenced by "...the Greco-Roman patriarchal order of the house with its injunctions to subordination and submissions of the socially weaker party".[55] This she contrasts with the message of equality that she associates with Jesus' ministry and the earliest Christian movement. She argues that the key shift influenced by social factors took place in the second century:

> The shift...was not a shift from charismatic leadership to institutional consolidation, but from charismatic and communal authority vested in local officers, who – in time – absorb not only the teaching authority of the prophet and apostle but also the decision-making power of the community. This shift is, at the same time, a shift from alternating leadership accessible to all the baptized to patriarchal leadership restricted to male households; it is a shift from house church to church as the "household of God".[56]

The justice denying framework in which Christian tradition presents itself was a cultural, historical phenomenon wrapped around and distorting the authentic justice seeking heart of the Christian message.

The ekklesia of women

In her early work Schüssler Fiorenza's conclusions for the possibility and direction of a feminist informed biblical spirituality in the light of her analysis of the absence of women's experience from Christian texts and history bring her to the conviction that such a spirituality must be both critical and communal:[57]

> A feminist Christian spirituality, therefore, calls us to gather together the *ekklesia of women* who, in the angry power of the Spirit, are sent forth to feed, heal, and liberate our own people who are women. It unmasks and sets us free from the structural sin and alienation of sexism and propels us to become children and spokeswomen of God.... It enables us to live "for one another" and to experience the presence of God in the *ekklesia* as the gathering of women. Those of us who have heard this calling respond by committing ourselves to the liberation struggle of women and all peoples, by being accountable to women and their future, and by nurturing solidarity within the *ekklesia* of women. Commitment, accountability, and solidarity in community are the hallmarks of our calling and struggle.[58]

This places the understanding of women in terms of their response to Christ and to the call to the discipleship of equals[59] at the centre of contemporary Christian living. It articulates a vision in which all alienating separations between people will be overcome. It also stresses that women do have a history and place within the Christian tradition. For Schüssler Fiorenza, the ekklesia of women describes "....the movement of self-identified women and women-identified men in biblical religion"[60] the collective experience of women as Church. It places women, despite their apparent lack of visibility and presence in Christian history and practice, firmly within the Christian tradition. Anne Carr has argued that:

> ...Schüssler Fiorenza offers an egalitarian model of early Christianity as a conflict movement, based on the discovery that Christianity was neither originally patriarchal in itself nor integrated into patriarchal society.[61]

> These discoveries lead Schüssler Fiorenza to argue that the norm of feminist theology cannot be found in particular biblical texts, since all the texts are part of an androcentric tradition. Neither can it be found in an abstract, timeless theological principle or an ahistorical prophetic principle.... Instead, the only adequate criterion for feminist theology is the women themselves who struggle for liberation, transcendence, and selfhood in remembrance of their heritage.[62]

Schüssler Fiorenza's concept of ekklesia of women or women-church remembers and aspires to the early Christian experience of equality of community. Her elaboration and use of women-church indicates well the combination of radicalism and tradition that is intrinsic to feminist informed Christian theology, and also the difficulties and tensions found there in its treatment and understanding of the past and present. For her, the ekklesia of women, as a vision of freedom based on the Christian discipleship of equals, calls women to challenge oppressive patriarchalism in religion and society. It is a vision and experience of freedom based on equality, and as such stands as a new model for Christianity. "To link ekklesia of church with women makes explicit that women are church and always have been church".[63] Mary Grey recognises the significance of this and shares something of Schüssler Fiorenza's vision here:

> Fiorenza herself has described her vision of Women-Church as that of "discipleship of equals". This is close to the image which I am proposing. The discipleship of equals evokes a deeper level of community than the claiming of equal rights of liberal individualism – the level at which the ordination debate is frequently conducted. Fiorenza evokes mutuality-in-relating as the vision of the Jesus movement, which, through the centuries (she claims) has never been totally lost sight of.[64]

Women-church calls upon an alternative vision or experience that is necessarily community-based.[65] It must remain both critical and communal,[66] remembering the past experiences of oppression and liberation, and operate at the creative heart of Christianity today.

The authority that Schüssler Fiorenza claims for Christian women as women-church is based in the life and ministry of Christ, and the experiences and praxis of the early Christian Church. This authority, then, depends on Schüssler Fiorenza's understanding of God's action and presence in the world, and also, very importantly in the experience of oppression. God is understood to be a liberating God, and women-church the remembered experience of oppression and move towards justice, "The spiritual authority of women-church rests on the experience of God's sustaining grace and liberating presence in the midst of our struggles for justice, freedom and wholeness of all.[67] On one level, the force behind women-church as a contemporary experience comes from Christian women's decisive theologising and praxis today, and their attempt to determine their own existence as Church.[68] Their experiences, however, as Schüssler Fiorenza understands them, are rooted firmly within the Christian tradition, within the tradition of the ministry of Jesus, and with the experiences of the early Christian Church. Schüssler Fiorenza claims legitimacy for her feminist informed methodology not only by her emphasis on the necessary historicity of religious feminism (or the need for women to base their religiosity in history) but also by the extensive claims she makes for the early Christian community. She places a great deal of authority with her reconstruction of the experiences of the early Church. Ultimately, however, her argument for the possibility of the feminist task in Christian theology is dependent on an understanding of the experiences of the early Christian community as egalitarian, an understanding or reading that would be challenged by some feminist critics. Schüssler Fiorenza is aware of the possible descriptions of her approach her, and places her own work as distinct from the neo-orthodox feminist approach[69] that she claims characterises the work of feminist informed scholars such as Letty Russell and Rosemary Ruether, in their search for "...a canon within the canon",[70] or the "useable past"[71] of Christianity. She seems concerned here that such approaches offer idealised interpretations of some traditions of

Christianity and in so doing removing such traditions from critical feminist scrutiny.[72] It is possible to argue, however, as will be discussed in Chapter Six, that Schüssler Fiorenza is quite similar in her own approach, in some ways, to such scholars as Russell and Ruether.

The kinds of claims that Schüssler Fiorenza makes for women's contributions and roles in the development of the early Christian Church and the significance that she has placed with these experiences for women today has brought important, and often understandable, criticisms of her work. For example, Luce Irigaray in an article "Equal to Whom?"[73] which reviewed *In Memory of Her* critiques the underlying values and assumptions of Schüssler Fiorenza's feminist informed reconstruction of early Christian history. Whilst welcoming the feminist work of Schüssler Fiorenza in relation to Christianity she is sceptical of her findings and the resultant Christian feminist informed theology. She questions [74] her readings of Jewish and Greco-Roman cultures and her claims for the significance of women to the ministry and life of Jesus.[75] A lot of this comes down to the interpretation given to the evidence offered by Schüssler Fiorenza. Irigaray argues, "...woman's role in the Gospels isn't really as "central" as Schüssler Fiorenza would have us believe".[76] The issue here is one of the reading and acceptance of feminist based theological creativity when set against its own reading of recorded history as so steeped in and shaped by androcentricism that such creativity is needed.

Daphne Hampson also criticises Schüssler Fiorenza's engagement with feminist informed reconstruction of early Christian women's experiences.[77] In "On not remembering her" published in 1998 in the journal *Feminist Theology* Hampson questions some of the underlying claims and insights of her approach found in *In Memory of Her*. Hampson recognises the difficulty for feminist informed scholars, critics and thinkers who take different positions of actually engaging in debate with each other, but stresses the need for such critical engagement.[78] She focuses particularly on Schüssler Fiorenza's valuing and central reclamation of women's heritage as an important source of power for contemporary feminist movement.[79] She challenges the possibility and validity of the links that Schüssler Fiorenza seems to be making with the experiences of first century Christian women, and asks why women today should engage in such a project. At the heart of this is her questioning of the appropriateness of valuing "historical memories".[80] Hampson calls for a need to explore critically the central feminist claim for heritage as power, because of the nature of this heritage:[81]

> But why is one ever in the position of wanting to find something in the past, in this period, to which one should look? Here we arrive at the heart of the matter. The only reason for identifying with these women can be that one is Christian...
>
> Why look to these particular women? Because they made a reference to Christ. As a Christian one has to make some reference to Christ. The best way to do this, as a woman, is to look to the community of women who acknowledged him.[82]

Hampson, then, acknowledges the logic of Schüssler Fiorenza's approach given her Christian heritage but challenges the validity of it from a feminist perspective. Grace Jantzen also questions the continuing priority that Schüssler Fiorenza accords to the biblical traditions in her approach, asking that if she recognises the need to adopt a hermeneutics of suspicion to the Bible and given the traditions of injustice that such an approach seems to uncover, then why does she persist in staying with these traditions?

> ...if on the other hand Fiorenza really means it when she says that the biblical texts, especially those of the life and teaching of Jesus, are not normative, then why (especially in view of the bleakly patriarchal nature of so much scripture) focus so much attention on it? Why not just let it go, and let women's experience serve as a fresh revelatory source?
>
> If Fiorenza's reason for continuing to privilege the Bible is a reason of *strategy*, then it is not obvious that such a strategy will actually work for liberation rather than unintentionally presenting the oppression with a tool of recuperation. A great deal depends on an assessment of what religion is, and its relationship with culture, language and society.[83]

Jantzen goes on to argue that the reason for this is indeed not strategy but principle,[84] and claims that as a result "she is on much more dubious ground".[85] Such readings of the underlying motives or functioning of Schüssler Fiorenza's strategies see the attraction and focus on biblical traditions not in terms of their liberative potential or inherent justice seeking vision, but simply because of Schüssler Fiorenza's continuing commitment to that tradition. Hampson claims that in effect Schüssler Fiorenza fails to face up to the central issues and addresses "neither the question of the truth of Christianity, nor that of its acceptability to women".[86] She argues that Schüssler Fiorenza's position leads to the conviction that as it is impossible to get away from biblical influence that women need to accept the situation and try to improve it. Hampson rejects that this is the case. However, she is not so much challenging the continuing influence of biblical traditions on contemporary western lives as much as accepting that the only response to this is to accept its influence and sees the need to distinguish between the influence of the traditions and remaining controlled by these traditions. She also argues that Schüssler Fiorenza's approach veers towards essentialism in its pleas to the past experiences of a particular group of women, concluding that her enterprise in feminist terms is meaningless, "We shall never progress in our theology by piecing together the history of biblical women".[87] Schüssler Fiorenza has rejected such readings of her work and in *But She Said* she argues that she has been misinterpreted in her early work. She challenges readings of her work that see:

> ...a reading in terms of simplistic continuity between women-church and the discipleship of equals not only overlooks the tension between the "already" and "not yet", between the reality and vision of the *ekklesia* of women. It also neglects the contradiction and conflict between egalitarian democratic understandings of community and the dominant reality of patriarchy as an interlocking system of

discriminations and subordinations. Furthermore, this tension and conflict did not begin with the emerging Christian movements but can be traced back to classical Greece, as well as to early Israel. It is this tension and contradiction that provides for a fragile continuity of struggle. Indeed, emancipatory movements such as the early Christian "discipleship of equals" have always positioned themselves within this history of conflict and struggle.[88]

Without reservation, then, Schüssler Fiorenza rejects the claim that her understanding of the discipleship of equals and the *ekklesia* of women leads to the privileging of a particular group,[89] and also clarifies her reasons for participating in such debates, claiming that:

> Although I am writing as a Christian theologian, I am neither attempting to persuade women to remain members of biblical religions nor am I arguing that they should read the Bible, or why. Rather, I seek to work out a process and method for a feminist political reading that can empower women who, for whatever reason, are still affected by the Bible to read "against the grain" of its patriarchal rhetoric. Moreover, such a critical feminist interpretation is not limited to canonical texts but can be equally applied to extracanonical sources and traditions.[90]

More recent major texts of Schüssler Fiorenza in the field of feminist informed biblical interpretation, *But She Said: Feminist Practices of Biblical Interpretation* (1992) and *Sharing Her Word* (1998), clarify and illustrate her approach. These two texts mark the further development of Schüssler Fiorenza's feminist informed biblical hermeneutics and the development of her critical recovery and development of the wisdom literature for feminist informed theology. However, her commitment to feminisms and understanding of the implications that such commitment brings remains firm:

> Feminism is thus best understood as a theoretical perspective and a historical movement for changing sociocultural and religious institutions and structures of domination and exploitation. Christian feminism attempts to do so both by seeking full citizenship for wo/men in church and society, and by reformulating the study of scripture, tradition, theology and community in feminist terms.[91]

In a number of respects Schüssler Fiorenza has developed the theological concepts and ideas that she employed in her earlier work in such a way as to address critical insights that have been raised more recently as feminist based critical perspectives have developed. For example, from early feminist gender based analysis and theologising she has moved to what she has described as a "kyriarchal" vision and theology, in an attempt to express and draw out the complex nature of oppressions. In *But She Said* she explains her use of the term "kyriarchy":

> Kyriarchal power operates not only along the axis of gender but also along those of race, class, culture, and religion. These axes of power structure the more

general system of domination in a matrix – (or better, patrix-) like fashion, or in what bell hooks calls the interlocking systems of oppression.[92]

Kwok Pui-lan notes the significance of this clarification or development in Schüssler Fiorenza's work:

> Responding to the challenges of women of colour, biblical scholar Elisabeth Schüssler Fiorenza proposes to shift from patriarchy, based on gender dualism, to kyriarchy (the rule of emperor/master/lord/father/husband over his subordinates), to signal more comprehensive, interlocking and multiplicative forms of oppression.[93]

In a similar way, then, Schüssler Fiorenza has also made some revision to the way in which she understands and employs the notion of women-church. Instead of "*ekklesia* of women" she now uses the term "ekklesia of wo/men":

> When I speak of the ekklesia of wo/men as the hermeneutical center of feminist biblical interpretation and christological construction, I do not speak of a women's church that excludes men. Nor do I speak of one group of women as a unitary entity or mean to argue for women's integration into the kyriarchal institutions of the church. Nor do I want to restrict the notion of the ekklesia of wo/men to the interpretive theological community that articulates christological discourse. Rather, the "reality" and vision of the ekklesia of wo/men is a hermeneutical, discursively constructed articulation that seeks to make conscious that cultural "common-sense" patriarchal religion and malestream democracy have been exclusive of women, be they human or divine.[94]

Her concern, evident through her articulation and explanation of ekklesia of wo/men, is to develop a theoretical framework and to delineate[95] a space marked not by kyriocentric concerns and values but a space characterised by justice, a liberative radical democratic space. Both developments respond to concerns about the kinds of claims, both implicit and explicit, that feminist visions and understandings make for women, and the resulting kinds of privileged oppositions that are set up. She has shown herself to be aware of the problems of subjectivity and naming for feminist informed thinkers and the instability of postmodern analysis of fragmented and multiple identities.[96] Increasingly, Schüssler Fiorenza is drawing on postmodernist and poststructuralist insights. But in some ways this does not sit all that easily with the claims she seems to make for her liberationist reading of Christianity. In *Jesus: Miriam's Child, Sophia's Prophet* (1995) she claims that the kind of approach that she advocates is one that can not be described simply as either positivist or postmodern but rather stresses the continued relevance and centrality of a hermeneutics of suspicion to her approach.[97] She is attempting to focus on the critical action of her approach rather than the underlying presumptions or implications. This then keeps her visions and workings fluid yet grounded, they are based in the historical struggles of women. They retain links to and values of a particular tradition, whilst at the same time approaching this tradition in a very critical way and stress the need for dialogue and conversation.[98]

She also retains stress on the significance of being critically aware of perspective and context. In *But She Said* she develops her approach to biblical interpretation with an emphasis on a critical feminist rhetorical approach to biblical interpretation.

Elizabeth Castelli claims[99] that this employment of rhetorical analysis by Schüssler Fiorenza, "...is an explicitly value-laden one, rejecting Enlightenment's privileging of value-free objectivity; it is an ethical stance, and one grounded in theology..".[100] There are clearly different possible readings of Schüssler Fiorenza's methodology, which need themselves to be recognised as being influenced and indeed determined by the contextual concerns and perspectives, including faith perspectives, of the critic.

Reclaiming traditions of wisdom

One area that is becoming increasingly significant in feminist Christian encounter generally, and in particular, the work of Schüssler Fiorenza is the tradition and concept of divine wisdom, where a particular focus is being placed on the biblical wisdom traditions. Texts of significance here include, Proverbs, Ecclesiastes, Job, the Song of Songs, the Apocryphal books of Sirach and the Wisdom of Solomon, and the four Gospels. The feminist theological focus on divine wisdom has so far been concerned with the development of feminist spirituality which employs the biblical resources of the figure and traces of wisdom variously expressed as Sophia, Shekhina or Chokma. Over the last few years a number of important publications illustrate the way in which divine wisdom is emerging as an important and versatile aspect of feminist informed Christian theological engagement. For example, Schüssler Fiorenza *Jesus: Miriam's Child, Sophia's Prophet* (1995), Athalya Brenner and Carole Fontaine (eds.) *Wisdom and Psalms: A Feminist Companion to the Bible* (1998), and Marcia Pilar Aquino and Elisabeth Schüssler Fiorenza (eds.) *In the Power of Wisdom: Feminist Spiritualities of Struggle* (2000). *In the Power of Wisdom* is an important collection as it engages the traditions and possibilities of divine wisdom in a variety of social, political and religious contexts with a concern for developing feminist informed spiritualities of struggle. The collection includes articles by Nami Kim who explores spiritualities of struggle in Korean society, Susan Starr Sered who focuses on Jewish informed feminisms and the Shekhina, and Mary Condren who focuses on Catholicism in Ireland and Celtic religion. Schüssler Fiorenza captures something of the radical possibilities envisaged in the traditions of divine wisdom by feminists in her editorial comment:

> ...the individual articles probe the possibilities for articulating a political Wisdom spirituality that sustains rather than mutes struggles for survival and liberation. The contributions focus on religious resources for such a spirituality and centre on issues of sacred power and justice. They articulate a spiritual vision that not only expresses wo/men's struggles to survive and transform relations of domination but also critically identifies religious traditions and resources for such a

discernment of the Spirit-Shekhina-Sophia's working in different global contexts.[101]

The focus on wisdom literature and tradition is one important way in which Christian feminist encounter has employed radical feminist informed mechanisms to explore the impact of gender based imagery and language used for God in the biblical texts. It demonstrates the way in which radical critical tools of analysis and reconstruction have been developed by theologians drawing on feminist critiques and analyses and employed in such a way as to claim a clear base in the traditions of Christian theology and practice. As with all of the texts and traditions that have been subject to such constant critical attention, questions need to be asked as to why these this particular tradition is proving such an important resource for theologians who are attempting to identify and recover potentially liberative aspects of the Christian tradition that might be used to support and inform a feminist based spirituality or religiosity. One reason for this is, as Silvia Schroer points out, the identification of divine wisdom as, "...a female figure who is immediately associated with Israel's God and who advances a divine claim".[102] From this are perceived radical possibilities for the functioning of divine wisdom in relation to the biblical images for God:

> Sophia, as an authentic biblical image of God, offers remarkable possibilities for breaking up the petrifactions and ontologizations of androcentric God language, and for doing so on the basis of a Jewish tradition. Her attributes are the attributes of God; when she speaks, God speaks; what she proclaims and does is God's will. She is the "wholly other", yet she makes herself known.[103]

This quest for female representations and traces of female links to the divine, and for female language used in relation to the divine, is found throughout feminist informed theological engagement. For example, one of the characterising features of goddess thealogy is the reconstructive search to locate and engage symbols and traditions of the past and often such activity has been open to accusations of historical inaccuracy. However, the task is often understood by those involved as an explicit attempt to address perceived processes of marginalisation and silencing in a creative and constructive way. In many feminist informed Christian theologies the combination of radical reconstructive methodology and an appeal to "tradition" or "orthodoxy" is a constant feature of feminist Christian encounter. An appeal which is sometimes made explicit within the approach and at other times is not quite so visible.

William Abraham in *Canon and Criterion in Christian Theology: From the Fathers to Feminism* (1998), for example, highlights the role that canon and an interest in canon have played in contemporary feminist informed Christian theology. He argues that despite expectations and some initial reading, the notion of canon lies at the heart of feminist theological activity. And that within such activity comes the potential for reconsidering approaches to Scripture and canon:

> Buried in the debate evoked by feminist criticism lies the possibility of developing a much more adequate interpretation of canon........Feminist theologians have stumbled on to a vision of canon which has been long lost in the theories of the West.[104]

> The crucial concern that governs feminist interest in Scripture initially is that any relevant canon must be a means of liberation. We might say that this is a fundamental conception of canon that governs the initial approach of feminist theology to Scripture.[105]

Abraham recognises just how important the feminist informed work in this area is:

> The challenge to the Christian tradition posed by this stream of feminist criticism can be expressed in this fashion. Does the complex canonical heritage of the Church, when it is rightly used, provide healing for the sins of patriarchy and androcentricism? This is not an epistemological issue. Translating it into an epistemological problem merely ensures that its resolution will be dependent on the addressing of philosophical questions that yet await an adequate answer. It is a soteriological and moral problem, one of the many problems that the Christian tradition has had to resolve in its long pilgrimage throughout history.[106]

Traditions and sacred texts are engaged, then, but not without a radical hermeneutic of suspicion and a creative approach towards the recovery and contextualisation of such traditions and texts.

> Schüssler Fiorenza's contribution to the development and self-understanding of feminist theologies is outstanding. Her theological work has been at the forefront of biblical feminist hermeneutics and reconstruction. Schüssler Fiorenza argues that wisdom has become a resource for "articulating a political wisdom spirituality that sustains rather than mutes struggles for survival and liberation".[107]

What is of interest here is the way in which the wisdom tradition has been identified and then taken and emphasised as a resource for struggle today. In her earlier work, a similar pattern of critical feminist informed engagement is evident in Schüssler Fiorenza's approach the "discipleship of equals", where she proposed a radical reconstructionist approach to the recovery and elaboration of women's Christian history and heritage. Schüssler Fiorenza employs this understanding and criteria of recovery to the traditions of divine wisdom and reflects the depth of the problem posed by the processes of recording and transmission that such traditions have been subject to. Her concern is to develop an approach that will enable the traditions of divine wisdom to be imaginatively reconstructed so that they might become a resource in the feminist informed theological task of overcoming injustice in its many forms and articulating alternative Christian discourses:

> How can we reconstitute this tradition in such a way that the rich table of Sophia can provide food and drink, nourishment and strength in the struggles for transforming Kyriarchy?[108]

Schüssler Fiorenza traces the development of the wisdom traditions from Jewish literature to early Christian literature and attempts to address the apparent absence of the figure of divine wisdom in early Christian literature. She argues that despite this lack of visibility of the tradition an attentive, discerning approach to biblical texts will discover:

> ...that a submerged theology of Wisdom, or sophialogy, permeates all of Christian Scriptures. Early Jewish discourses on Divine Wisdom provided a theological linguistic matrix that was activated by early Christian communities.[109]

In articulating the task facing feminist informed Christian theologians here she draws on Adrienne Rich's analysis of feminists as miners, digging and searching for traces and evidence of this tradition. One criticism of such an approach, and a criticism that has been levelled particularly at such selective reconstructive methodologies, is that it in effect essentialist or neo-orthodox. Schüssler Fiorenza is concerned to stress that her own approach is not designed to simply locate, recover and then revere the core tradition of Christianity acceptable to feminists. Rather:

> I want to explore how feminist critical interpretations challenge the whole Christian community to engage in theological struggles to find appropriate language about the divine.[110]

For Schüssler Fiorenza, then, the tradition of divine wisdom is appropriated and justifiably engaged in a critical constructive search. In *Jesus: Miriam's Child, Sophia's Prophet* Schüssler Fiorenza writes that:

> By naming Jesus as the child of Miriam and the prophet of Divine Sophia, I seek to create a "women" – defined feminist theoretical space that makes it possible to dislodge christological discourses from their malestream frame of reference.[111]

In identifying the early Christian discourse of divine wisdom Schüssler Fiorenza is concerned to make explicit and traceable links between her understanding of divine wisdom and the possibilities that a feminist informed understanding of the tradition might offer.[112] She is concerned to make clear the relationship between the traditions of Christianity and the feminist articulated resource of divine wisdom. She draws attention in particular to the grammatical focus for wisdom as gendered form in both Hebrew (*Chokmah*) and Greek (*Sophia*) and she explores texts such as Proverbs 31 and Proverbs 9 to establish and build up a picture of the place and reference given to divine wisdom. Schüssler Fiorenza explains and justifies the authoritative and critical significance given to divine wisdom by a textual based characterisation of the tradition. This establishes divine wisdom as participating in divine activity, as understood by the Christian tradition, in such a way as is consistent with and supportive of feminist values and concerns:

> She is the glory of God (Wisd. 7:25-26), and mediator of creation (Wisd. 8:5-6) and shares the throne of G*d (Wisd. 7:25-26). She rules over kings and is herself

all powerful. She makes everything, renews everything, and permeates the cosmos (Wisd. 7:23, 27; 8:1, 5). "She is but one, yet can do everything, she makes all things new" (Wisd. 7:27). She is "intelligent and holy, free moving, clear, loving what is good, eager, beneficent, unique in her Way" (Wisd. 7:22). She is a people-loving spirit (Wisd. 1:6) who shares in the throne of G*d and in the ruling power of G*d (Wisd. 9:10). She is an initiate into the knowledge of G*d, collaborator in G*d's work, the brightness that streams from everlasting light, a pure effervescence of divine glory, and the image of G*d's goodness. In short, Divine Wisdom lives symbiotically with G*d (Wisd. 8:3f; 7:26). Kinship with Wisdom brings immortality and friendship with her, resulting in pure delight (Wisd. 10:17).[113]

From identified biblical evidence for a feminist critical recovery and engagement of divine wisdom, Schüssler Fiorenza and other feminist informed theologians offer the reconstructed tradition as a tool of justice. In this way the tradition is articulated as a key Christian resource for addressing situations of injustice. For example, Mary E. Hunt in "Sophia's Sisters in Struggle: Kyriarchal Backlash, Feminist Vision":[114]

> In the beginning, Sophia struggled.
> The struggle continues, as feminists inspired by her Wisdom seek to bring about religiously informed justices in society at large and in Christian churches in particular.[115]

It is specifically the qualities of divine wisdom as perceived by Christian feminist theologians that makes the tradition such an important resource. These qualities include divine wisdom as powerful, creative, loving and justice seeking. Maria Pilar Aquino's comments express this understanding clearly:

> The presence of Divine Wisdom, because it excludes oppressive and dehumanizing relationships, fosters and supports a world in which life is worth living. Divine Wisdom sees the spiritualities, actions and attitudes of the kyriarchal elites as deserving of condemnation for dominating and exploiting humankind and the environment. So, for critical Wisdom, justice is the foundation of understanding, discernment, and the practice of an ethical way of life that can be considered right, honest, reasonable, and just. In these traditions, Divine Wisdom not only deliberately appears within social groups suffering under and resisting injustices but also empowers them to struggle against these injustices for liberation and its objectives.[116]

Divine wisdom is an increasingly prominent discourse of feminist informed Christian theology. The wisdom traditions, as seen in the work of Schüssler Fiorenza, are being recovered from the Jewish and Christian sources in a feminist creative process of reconstruction and used as a tool to address and transform contemporary situations of injustice. The viability of divine wisdom as such a tool of justice is linked to its roots in the traditions of Christianity, and particularly in terms of its links with biblical texts. These traceable roots, combined with a correlation between the characteristics of divine wisdom and the concerns, values and approaches of feminism, has lead Christian feminist theologians to articulate a vision of divine wisdom as a powerful and relevant justice based, transformative element of Christianity.

Conclusion

The voice of Schüssler Fiorenza has been a persistent and brave one. In 1994 in introducing *Jesus: Miriam's Child, Sophia's Prophet* Schüssler Fiorenza acknowledged the cost of this persistence at this particular time, "…it costs much psychological and spiritual energy to write a feminist theological book at a time when the backlash against feminists is in full swing".[117] In 1990 she wrote, "It is gratifying not to have been tamed."[118] And she speaks of feminist informed women scholars. She speaks of women feminist scholars as "resident aliens":[119]

> The notion of resident alien positions one as both insider and outsider: inside by virtue of residence or family affiliation to a citizen or institution; outsider in terms of language, experience, culture, and history. The metaphor of "resident alien" seems an apt figure for a feminist movement and politics that seek to open up a theoretical space and socio-political; position from which critical feminist scholars in religious studies can speak.[120]

She talks of the ambiguity of feminist informed theological positions but accepts the challenges that such positions bring:

> Since the institutional location of feminist studies in religion is that of malestream scholarship, feminists, I argue must not only deconstruct hegemonic academic discourses but also must construct a different feminist discursive space. They must conceptualize feminist studies as critical; rhetorical-political practices for liberation. When one is conscious of wo/men's socio-political location in the academy, it becomes apparent what is at stake in the theoretical construction of such a discursive position. Feminists who as "outsiders" or "aliens" engage in religious studies in order to transform the patri-kyriarchal discourses of church and academy, can do so only if they can manage to both become qualified *residents* within religious institutions and remain *foreign speakers* at one and the same time.[121]

In her earlier work Schüssler Fiorenza's reading and engagement of the Christian tradition have been interpreted by some critics in essentialist terms. The claim here is that her approach seeks to locate a liberative aspect or tradition of Christianity that she understands as having effectively been unaffected or as being substantially different to prevailing and subsequent cultural and religious ethos that she understood as patriarchal. This, then, becomes the critical focus of Schüssler Fiorenza's feminist biblical hermeneutics and her Christian feminist informed reconstructionist approach. Her articulation of this position and her responses to criticisms of this approach are important here for understanding the development of Christian feminist theologies. And so the first part of this chapter focused on her earlier works such as *In Memory of Her* and *Bread Not Stone* to explore the strategies that Schüssler Fiorenza can be seen to employ in her attempt to bring the insights and critical perspectives of feminism to bear on Christianity. In her more recent work she has developed and carefully articulated some of the central and yet contentious aspects of her feminist informed liberation theology. However, despite the careful refutation of the validity of such criticism and the subsequent development of her work, there remains at the heart of Schüssler Fiorenza's approach a vision of justice rooted in an understanding or priority of Christianity as a political, social and religious force. However, both the development and consistency of her methodology can be described by a shift in her theology concerned with a feminist informed vision of women-church to a vision of ekklesia of wo/men. But at the heart of both of these is a recognition and critique of oppression and a vision of justice that gives significant and unrivalled space to Christianity or the early Jesus movement as she describes it. What is clear is that Schüssler Fiorenza is not ready to give up on women's Christian heritage:

> ...to reject religion as totally oppressive and to neglect it as a positive source of empowerment and hope in creating a better future for wo/men would mean to relinquish religion to the ownership claims of reactionary right-wing fundamentalism.[122]

Also, the radicalism of Schüssler Fiorenza's approach to Christianity in her proposals for a feminist informed theology based in the Christian religion is clear if seen from the perspective of inside the Christian tradition. She is both thorough and consistent in her application of a feminist informed critique to the New Testament and is insistent that women do not have to reject biblical religion but, rather, that they have the opportunity to reclaim and engage positively their own Christian heritage. Her heuristic approach not only incorporates women's history (or herstory) as oppressed people but also their own experiences or history of community in the early Christian movement. She demonstrates a dynamic creativity in her assessment of what is liberating in Christian scripture, and so what might be relevant to a new feminist informed Christian canon. This combination of critique and positive recovery is precisely why her theology represents such an important development in feminist informed methodology. The contribution of both Schüssler Fiorenza's assessment of the presence of feminist consciousness in Christianity and the development of her own reconstructionist methodology is outstanding. As a Christian theologian, strongly influenced by feminisms, Schüssler Fiorenza shows great awareness of and commitment to maintaining a careful balance between the radical and the traditional. Feminist informed Christian theology by definition is faced with the very problematic task of combining the often radical and always challenging feminist critique with commitment to tradition. And Schüssler Fiorenza's strategy of feminist informed recovery and reconstruction of the egalitarian Christian tradition is one possible feminist informed method that attempts to combine commitment to tradition and radical creativity. Schüssler Fiorenza places a great deal of significance with her reconstruction and understanding of the experiences of the early Church. Her approach locates authority firmly in the interplay of experience and mainstream and fringe traditions and writings of the Christian faith. This takes Schüssler Fiorenza's feminist informed theology firmly beyond simply being a comment on, or critique of historical Christianity to the realm of critical and constructive feminist informed theology, where women's experience is of the highest significance and authority is experientially based. For Schüssler Fiorenza the choice to stay within the Christian tradition is a claim to Church, a claim to historical and continued participation in the Christian religion:

> To choose organized religion as a site of struggle for liberation presupposes a sense of ecclesial ownership as well as repentance of complicity with patriarchal religion. Such a feminist strategy needs to abandon both the dualistic conceptualization of women as mere victims of patriarchal religion *and* the submissive collaboration of women in patriarchal religion and church. Only when women understand ourselves *as* church and not as passive bystanders in the church can we reclaim the church as the *ekklesia of women*.[123]

Notes

[1] Schüssler Fiorenza, E., (2002), "Thinking and working across borders: the feminist liberation theologians, activists, and scholars in religion network", *Journal of Feminist Studies in Religion*, 2002, 18(1), pp.72.
[2] Schüssler Fiorenza, 2002:73.
[3] Schüssler Fiorenza, E., (1990), "Changing the paradigms", *The Christian Century*, Sept. 5-12, p.798.
[4] Schüssler Fiorenza, 1990:798.
[5] Schüssler Fiorenza, 1990:798.
[6] Schüssler Fiorenza, 1994:10.
[7] Schüssler Fiorenza, 1994:11.
[8] Schüssler Fiorenza, 1994:11.
[9] Schussler Fiorenza, E., (1984), *Bread Not Stone: The Challenge of Feminist Biblical Interpretation*, Boston: Beacon Press. Schüssler Fiorenza, E., p.5.
[10] Schüssler Fiorenza, 1984:15.
[11] Schussler Fiorenza, 1984:16-17.
[12] Kwok Pui-lan in Sugirtharajah, R.S., (ed.), (1991), *Voices From the Margin: Interpreting the Bible in the Non-Biblical World*, London: SPCK, p.312.
[13] Schüssler Fiorenza, 1984:15.
[14] Schüssler Fiorenza, 1984:16.
[15] Schüssler Fiorenza, 1984:16.
[16] Schüssler Fiorenza, 1984:17.
[17] Hopkins, J., (1995), *Towards a Feminist Christology: Jesus of Nazareth, European Women and the Christological Crisis*, London: SPCK, pp.72-73.
[18] Schüssler Fiorenza, 1984:18.
[19] Schüssler Fiorenza, 1984:18.
[20] Schüssler Fiorenza, 1984:19.
[21] Schüssler Fiorenza, 1984:19.

[22] Schüssler Fiorenza, 1984:19.
[23] Schüssler Fiorenza, 1984:20.
[24] Schussler Fiorenza, 1992:7.
[25] Schüssler Fiorenza, 1984:20.
[26] Schüssler Fiorenza, 1984:21.
[27] Schüssler Fiorenza, 1984:21.
[28] Schüssler Fiorenza, 1984:21.
[29] Schüssler Fiorenza, 1983:XVIII.
[30] Schüssler Fiorenza, 1983:31.
[31] Schüssler Fiorenza, 1975:616.
[32] Schüssler Fiorenza, 1975:616.
[33] Schüssler Fiorenza, 1983: XIX.
[34] Schüssler Fiorenza, 1983:28.
[35] Schüssler Fiorenza, 1983:69.
[36] Schüssler Fiorenza, 1983:41.
[37] Schüssler Fiorenza, 1983:69-70.
[38] Schüssler Fiorenza, 1983:30.
[39] Schüssler Fiorenza, 1975:616.
[40] Schüssler Fiorenza, 1983:32.
[41] Schüssler Fiorenza, 1983:33.
[42] Schüssler Fiorenza, 1983:41.
[43] Schüssler Fiorenza, 1983:35.
[44] Schüssler Fiorenza, 1983:105.
[45] Schüssler Fiorenza, 1983:103.
[46] Ross, S.A., (2001), *Extravagant Affections: A Feminist Sacramental Theology*, New York: Continuum International Publishing Group, p.85.
[47] Schüssler Fiorenza, 1983:119.
[48] Schüssler Fiorenza, 1983:134.
[49] Schüssler Fiorenza, 1983:147-148.
[50] Schüssler Fiorenza, 1983:161.
[51] Schüssler Fiorenza, 1983:209.
[52] Schüssler Fiorenza, 1983:209.
[53] Schüssler Fiorenza, 1983:235.
[54] Schüssler Fiorenza, 1983:245.
[55] Schüssler Fiorenza, 1983:245.
[56] Schüssler Fiorenza, 1983:286-287.
[57] Schüssler Fiorenza, 1983:351.
[58] Schüssler Fiorenza, 1983:346.
[59] Schüssler Fiorenza, 1983:349.
[60] Schüssler Fiorenza, 1984:xiv.
[61] Carr, A., in LaCugna, C.M., (ed.), (1993), *Freeing Theology: The Essentials of Theology in Feminist Perspective*, San Francisco: Harper, p.20.
[62] Carr, in Lacugna, C.M., (ed.), 1993:21.
[63] Schüssler Fiorenza, 1990:799.
[64] Grey, M., (1993), *The Wisdom of Fools: Seeking Revelation for Today*, London: SPCK, pp.123-124.
[65] Schüssler Fiorenza, 1983:345.
[66] Schüssler Fiorenza, 1983:351.
[67] Schüssler Fiorenza, 1984:xvi.
[68] Schüssler Fiorenza, 1984:6.

[69] Schüssler Fiorenza, 1983:14-18.
[70] Schüssler Fiorenza, 1983:14.
[71] Schüssler Fiorenza, 1983:16.
[72] Schüssler Fiorenza, 1983:17.
[73] Reprinted in Gill, R., (ed.), (1995), *Readings in Modern Theology: Britain and America*, London: SPCK, pp.198-214.
[74] Irigaray, in Gill, R., (ed), 1995:200.
[75] Irigaray, in Gill, R., (ed), 1995:201.
[76] Irigaray, in Gill, R., (ed), 1995:201.
[77] Hampson, D., (1998), On not remembering her, *Feminist Theology*, 19, pp.63-83.
[78] Hampson, 1998:64.
[79] Hampson, 1998:66.
[80] Hampson, 1998:68.
[81] Hampson, 1998:69.
[82] Hampson, 1998:70.
[83] Jantzen, 1998:107.
[84] Jantzen, 1998:108.
[85] Jantzen, 1998:108.
[86] Hampson, 1998:73.
[87] Hampson, 1998:80.
[88] Schüssler Fiorenza, 1992:6.
[89] Schüssler Fiorenza, 1992:7.
[90] Schüssler Fiorenza, 1992:7.
[91] Schüssler Fiorenza, 1998:4.
[92] Schüssler Fiorenza, 1992:123.
[93] Pui-lan, K., in Parsons, S.F., (ed.), (2002), *The Cambridge Companion to Feminist Theology*, Cambridge: Cambridge University Press, p.29.
[94] Schüssler Fiorenza, 1994:27.
[95] Schüssler Fiorenza, 1994:24.
[96] Schüssler Fiorenza, 1994:24.
[97] Schüssler Fiorenza, 1994:30.
[98] Schussler Fiorenza, 1994:31.
[99] Castelli, E.A., (1994), "Heteroglossia, Hermeneutics, and History: A Review Essay of Recent Feminist Studies of Early Christianity", *Journal of Feminist Studies in Religion*, 10(2), pp.73-98.
[100] Castelli, E.A., 1994:84.
[101] Schüssler Fiorenza, E., (2000), in Aquino, M.P., and Schüssler Fiorenza, E., (eds), *In the Power of Wisdom: Feminist Spiritualities of Struggle*, London: SCM Press, p.7.
[102] Schroer, S., "The Justice of Sophia: Biblical wisdom Traditions and Feminist Discourses", in Schüssler Fiorenza, E., (ed.), *Searching the Scriptures: Volume Two: A Feminist Commentary*, London: SCM Press, 1994.
[103] Schroer, S., in Schüssler Fiorenza, E., (ed.), *Searching the Scriptures: Volume Two: A Feminist Commentary*, (London: SCM Press, 1994.
[104] Abraham, W.J., (1998), *Canon and Criterion in Christian Theology: From the Fathers to Feminism*, Oxford: Clarendon Press, p.433.
[105] Abraham, 1998:434.
[106] Abraham, 1998:464-465.
[107] Schüssler Fiorenza, E., in Aquino, M.P., and Schussler Fiorenza, E., (eds.), 2000:7.
[108] Schüssler Fiorenza, 1994:133.
[109] Schüssler Fiorenza, 1994:139.

[110] Schüssler Fiorenza, 1994:132.
[111] Schüssler Fiorenza, 1994:3.
[112] Schüssler Fiorenza, 1994:133.
[113] Schüssler Fiorenza, E., *Jesus: Miriam's Child, Sophia's* Prophet, (1994), 135-136.
[114] Hunt, M.E., 'Sophia's Sisters in Struggle: Kyriarchal Backlash', Feminist Vision in Aquino, Mariá Pilar and Schüssler Fiorenza, E., (eds), *In the Power of Wisdom: Feminist Spiritualities of Struggle*, (London: SCM Press, 2000), 23-32.
[115] Hunt, "Sophia's Sisters in Struggle", 2000:23.
[116] Aquino, M.P., in Aquino, M.P., and Schussler Fiorenza, E., (eds.), (2000), *In the Power of Wisdom: Feminist Spiritualities of Struggle*, London: SCM Press., p.132.
[117] Schüssler Fiorenza, 1994:ix.
[118] Schüssler Fiorenza, 1990:800.
[119] Schüssler Fiorenza, 1998:44.
[120] Schüssler Fiorenza, 1998:45.
[121] Schüssler Fiorenza, 1998:42.
[122] Schüssler Fiorenza, 1998:27.
[123] Schüssler Fiorenza, 1990:799.

Chapter Five

In Context and in Dialogue: Being Indecent with Marcella Althaus-Reid

Introduction

In this third and final of the chapters that focus in depth on a key strategy of feminist Christian encounter through detailed exploration of the work of particular theologians, the strategy of feminist theological engagement of the radically contextual queering of Christianity will be identified and critically explored. This strategy of contextual queering differs significantly from the other two strategies already examined, in terms both of method and the place and authority that it gives to feminist insights and values. It uses feminist informed insights and criteria, alongside other deconstructive tools, to queer Christianity with specific liberation concerns.

To queer, in this context, is not only to challenge the boundaries and structures of Christianity, but to deliberately turn Christianity inside out, to imagine the unimaginable in a liberation theological approach to situations of injustice. It proposes and attempts the subversion of the orders of Christianity out of recognition of the problems that these orders have so far brought. And it doesn't so much prescribe the intended outcome of this subversion, as attempt to leave spaces open for new and potentially exciting possibilities. Such spaces are imagined as free from constraints, whatever their origin or form, that serve to oppress or limit. The strategy as it will be explored here, is grounded and remains grounded, in specific cultural, historical and social situations of injustice. That which informs the encounter is a basic concern to overcome injustice, and feminisms are one tool of queering in this process rather than the specific vision of justice advocated to replace the current unjust one. In this chapter the strategy of the contextual queering of Christianity will be examined in relation to the relatively recent and very challenging work of Marcella Althaus-Reid, a Latin American theologian who now lives in Scotland and teaches at the University of Edinburgh. The reasons for examining this third strategy in relation to her theological work, as opposed to any other theologian, is that hers is a radical example of the employment of this strategy, and it is one that actually represents a very important contemporary departure in the strategies of feminist Christian encounter.

Marcella Althaus-Reid sees Christian theology in fundamentally radical terms. For her it is a, "...passionate and dangerous business, a *laberinto de pasiones* (a labyrinth of passions) of historical struggles between blind, consuming desires.[1] Her approach is multidisciplinary and at times quite radically interdisciplinary, and the guiding light or determining factor in her theological approach is the concern to overcome injustice, which is largely addressed, and perhaps even understood, in situational terms. Her concern is unrelentlessly with the practical and contextual and she captures something of the praxis-orientated emphasis of her theology in her statement on her personal profile page of Edinburgh University's website, where she describes the grounded approach that she takes not only to theological engagement but also to theological education:

> I want to encourage students to do theology, more than to repeat theology, and to learn to do theology in dialogue and in community. Every class in New College is for me a theological community and our starting point for action and reflections.[2]

As will be explored in the course of this chapter, within Althaus-Reid's liberation theological approach, no core tradition or key symbol is identified or reconstructed as such, unlike the other two strategies of feminist Christian encounter examined in chapters three and four. Also, feminisms are not apparently accorded unique or even outstanding significance. Rather, they are seen very much as tools of engagement rather than a set of defined values that need to be adhered to. This, however, does not detract from the feminist informed nature of her work, in terms of its concern with gender based injustice. Rather, given the problems that have arisen from the hypostasising of feminisms as a universally applicable system of justice, potentially it offers a more eclectic and selective approach to feminisms in which their use is determined on a functional basis which has the potential to free feminisms from some of the constraints that have so far limited their effectiveness and appeal. Authority, within Althaus-Reid's theology is very firmly with experience, with the situation of oppression, and with the concern to overcome injustice, rather than with the tool or form of analysis.

Indecent theology

Althaus-Reid is currently Senior Lecturer in Christian Ethics and Practical Theology in the School of Divinity, New College at the University of Edinburgh. She completed her first degree in Buenos Aires at ISEDET (Union Theological Seminary) during the 1970s[3] in an environment in which political, social and theological commitment was very clearly to the causes and methodologies of liberation theology as was developing in Latin America at the time. And even though her current geographical base is now Scotland, to some extent her theological focus remains in Latin America. Her work so far has considered a number of issues and topics but overall there is a concern with injustice, within which liberation theology has a determining place:

> I have taken Liberation Theology as my basic theological reference because this is my theological stand, in which I have been professionally educated and from

which base I worked with deprived communities both in Latin America and Britain. I still emphatically affirm the validity of Liberation Theologies as crucial in processes of social; transformation and superior to idealistic North Atlantic theologies. However, Liberation Theology needs to be understood as a continuing process of recontextualisation, a permanent exercise of serious doubting in theology.[4]

Marcella Althaus-Reid's most significant publication to date, and the place where this key strategy of the feminist informed radical queering of Christian theology is most clearly to be seen is her 2000 text *Indecent Theology: Theological Perversions in Sex, Gender and Politics*. The impact of this book is only just beginning to be felt but it undoubtedly introduces the work of Althaus-Reid in uncompromising, and even confrontational terms. The reviews of the text and responses to it suggest that whatever the reader's theological or political position it is generally being experienced as both provocative and engaging. In brief, *Indecent Theology* challenges Christian theology to answer the charges levelled at it from a number of critical bases, but with the underlying claim that Christianity in Latin America has functioned as an agent of constraint by compelling people, and in particular, poor women, to behave and conform according to perceived orders of decency. This amounts to a theologically justified and supported system of control that regulates behaviour and compels conformity. *Indecent Theology* is thorough and persistent in its critical base and visionary in its push towards a radical feminist informed reconceptualising of the possibilities of Christian theology. Something of the challenging nature of *Indecent Theology* is captured by Jeremy Carrette in his description of it which highlights both Althaus-Reid's unrelenting questioning of Christianity and the provocative edge to her work:

> You read *Indecent Theology* with either disgust or delight (perhaps always both), but either way, as Foucault recognised in 1963, you are always drawn into a space where theological limit and theological transgression are seen as mutually dependent.[5]

The methodological base of *Indecent Theology* is radically diverse and at times even eclectic. Althaus-Reid employs the methodologies and insights of a range of relevant and revealing approaches as necessary to her understanding of the challenges facing contextual liberation theology. Among the approaches drawn on are those of postcolonial criticism, liberation theologies, sexual theologies, queer theologies and feminist informed theologies. All of which come together in a radically grounded piece of contextual theology. As Althaus-Reid herself describes, "*Indecent Theology* is a book on Sexual Political Theology intended as a critical continuation of Feminist Liberation Theology using a multidisciplinary approach".[6] She is influenced in particular by the body theology of James Nelson, the gender and queer thinking of Judith Butler, the queer theological work of Robert Goss and the thinking of Adrienne Rich on compulsory heterosexuality.

The concern of *Indecent Theology* both in terms of subject and methodological shape begins and remains with the streets of Argentina and tries out new and at times obscure ideas, in an intentionally shocking and explosive dialogue between Christian theology and indecency. As a deconstructive theological project it engages in a challengingly indecent analysis of the bases of power and their theological constituents and manifestations in Latin America. The methodological mix of *Indecent Theology* is a response to the complexity of the situation that Althaus-Reid is engaging with. The situation is one in which multiple forms of oppression are at work, and so the theological critique and response necessitate a methodology that uses a variety of tools to effectively analyse and challenge this injustice. Any one specific tool of analysis and subversion employed by Althaus-Reid, be it Marxist, feminist or liberation theological, is not sufficient to address the complex reality of the context that she is concerned with:

> *Indecent Theology* is a book on Sexual Political Theology intended as a critical continuation of Feminist Liberation Theology using a multidisciplinary approach and drawing on Sexual Theory (Butler; Sedgwick; Garber), Postcolonial criticism (Fanon, Cabral, Said), Queer studies and theologies (Stuart; Goss; Weeks; Daly), Marxist studies (Laclau and Mouffe; Dussel), Continental Philosophy (Derrida; Deleuze and Guattari; Baudrillard) and Systematic Theology.[7]

Her aim in writing the book is one of exploration of the hermeneutical circle, that questions and deconstructs liberation theologies in a process of "...recontextualisation, a permanent exercise of serious doubting in theology",[8] this, then, according to Althaus-Reid is a task of re-contextualising of liberation theology. The theological basis of *Indecent Theology* is liberation theology but the context is the day to day lives of the people of Latin America:

> The everyday lives of people always provide us with a starting point for a process of doing a contextual theology without exclusions, in this case without the exclusion of sexuality struggling in the midst of misery.[9]

Her focused theological address in *Indecent Theology* is to the restraints and limitations that women face in Latin America. She identifies and critiques restraints that she claims are experienced by women theologians in Argentina and women lemon vendors selling lemons on the streets of Argentina. And in doing this she is engaging the theological in confrontational analysis with the aim of explicitly uncovering and indecently undressing the traditional restraints that have functioned in a hypocritical, repressive way. She wants to unpack the hidden, underlying structures that support the repressive orders of decency which she sees as the root cause or factor underlying the multiple layers of oppression facing women in Latin America. So, what she does is to bring out into the open the hidden relationship between the sexual and the theological. The mutually supportive and enhancing, yet essentially masked, relationship that she claims has been at work, and which she understands as effecting the traditions of repression, particularly of women, in Latin America. She approaches this daunting task with the explicitness that she is demanding of all theologies and all theologians and this is seen most clearly in the opening of *Indecent Theology*:

> Should a women keep her pants on in the streets of not? Shall she remove them, say, at the moment of going to church, for a more intimate reminder of her sexuality in relation to God? What difference does it make if that woman is a lemon vendor and sells you lemons in the streets without using underwear? Moreover, what difference would it make if she sits down to write theology without underwear?[10]

As such, *Indecent Theology* can be described as a theological act of radical contextual reflection on Latin America, and the deconstruction of the orders of decency that determine, limit and repress the lives of women, of, for example, the lives of the women lemon vendors, on the streets of Buenos Aires. The history of Christian based decency that operates repressively in the lives both of the women lemon vendors and the women theologians in Argentina is one that involved the fragmentation of Latin American civilisation through the *Conquista*. Which, Althaus-Reid argues, in effect signalled the end of the Grand Meta Narrative of Latin America and the imposition of European Christian rule:[11]

> The daughters of the Inca Empire lost their narratives. They now worship the medieval dressed figurine of the Virgin Mary with its oversize crown and God-prince in its arms. Few of them may be able to decode the intricacy of the Virgin Mary's ancient European dress and mantle. Besides, the Virgin Mary is a fashion figurine, a dress and a cloak, decorated with a face and two hands (the hands are useful to sustain a rose, or some beads or a child). The Virgin Mary is overdressed, and contrary to the lemon vendors the smell of her sex (even if statues were alive) would be difficult to perceive.
> ...The outcome of the destruction of the Grand Meta-narratives of Latin American high civilisations can be seen in the everyday lives of women such as the lemon vendors and the women theologians in the streets of Buenos Aires. The everyday lives of people always provide us with a starting point for a process of doing a contextual theology without exclusions, in this case without the exclusion of sexuality struggling in the midst of misery.[12]

According to Althaus-Reid Christianity played a key part in the process of displacement which took place with the imposition of the European Grand Narrative, in that it supported the economic, social and sexual systems of exploitation.[13] The ensuing system is one in which "Christianity in Latin America imposed a sexual economic order or usury, of usage of people in relationships",[14] where heterosexuality is the rule of decency and the currency of the order and the law of the regulation of sexuality and indeed human lives. What is needed, in Althaus-Reid's understanding is a break with all of this, a theology that challenges this sexual, economic and theological order of decency. And whilst Latin American liberation theology has attempted to address some of the problems of Christian imperialism, in Althaus-Reid's understanding, it has so far failed to offer any significant challenge to this oppressive order of decency.

The problem with Latin American liberation theology, as Althaus-Reid understands it, is that whilst it has attempted to address some of the layers of oppression it has failed to address the underlying and supporting order of decency that underpins the decent, oppressive order.[15] She talks of liberation theology, such as that which is usually associated with theologians such as Gutierrez, as "traditional and conventional",[16] and criticises it for being a "commercial enterprise"[17] with the claim that as it gained recognition and publicity in Europe it ended in, "church tourism and theological voyeurism".[18] It failed to recognise that within the category of 'poor' lay women and people of diverse sexualities, its concern with decency, influenced by Western theological patterns, damaged its potential for creativity and radicalism. In effect it failed to break with the orders of decency. It also drew on the energies and resources of women without giving support and recognition in return.[19] In fact, Althaus-Reid argues that women actually came not just to be excluded but also exploited by liberation theology[20] through a process of idealisation in which she argues women were anonymous or in her words, "fetishisations, reified phenomena extrapolated from the reality of people's lives".[21] Instead of the white middle-class woman idealised elsewhere the model of women that came to be idealised was of "the poor, ignorant but faithful Christian mother".[22] A model that failed to take account of the desires and needs of many women. This critique, as will be seen later, is also extended to feminist theologies of liberation.

This critique of liberation theologies, such as Latin American Liberation Theology, as having in some way failed to include the experiences, needs and concerns of women, as was seen earlier, is shared by many explicitly addressing issues of gender and theology and who have employed feminist based insights and critiques to do this. However, whilst Althaus-Reid is not alone in articulating this concern, what is perhaps distinct about her critique is her understanding of the extent to which liberation theology has excluded women and the way in which it has done this, through compliancy with the orders of sexual decency:

> Their model of poor women excluded our rebellions, our vocations and struggle to be whatever we wanted – poor but intellectual women, active in theological praxis, informed by serious study and reflection. The model of womanhood constructed by the liberationists was as deceptive in their benignity as the Jesuitical reduction models of Paraguay and the north of Argentina....In reality, we poor Christian women were supporting that theological enterprise that was Liberation Theology, but were not supported by it in equal terms.[23]

Latin American liberation theology has failed the women of Latin America, and Althaus-Reid bases this assessment, in part, on her own experiences. She does not, however, propose a complete move beyond the methodological and ideological base of liberation theology, but, in the light of such experientially based analysis, proposes to take it somewhere else, beyond the restrictions and decencies of its established orders.

Sexuality and Christian theology

Indecent Theology aims to challenge heterosexist hegemonies and, using Althaus-Reid's terminology, puts Christian theology very firmly into bed with God in a sexually active[24] way. For Althaus-Reid theology does not simply aim to address or have a concern at some level with the sexual, instead, she describes theology in very radical, and quite surprising terms, as "a sexual act".[25] The concern of *Indecent Theology* with theology and the sexual is persistent, and its methodological approach to this is very challenging and even deliberately provocative in its use of terminology and displaced juxtapositioning of concepts. As Althaus-Reid understands it, theology is not only concerned with the sexual but it also has an inherent address, it seems, to some kind of assumed appropriate or decent behaviour, "Theology is a sexual ideology performed in a socialising pattern: it is a sexual divinised orthodoxy (right sexual dogma) and orthopraxy (right sexual behaviour); theology is a sexual action".[26] The theologian, then, given this description of theology as a sexual act, is the performer of sexual acts. Althaus-Reid claims that when the sexual is spoken of in theological discourse it is often represented as if it is without lust, yet she claims that lust needs to be acknowledged and to be given its appropriate place in theological engagement, as the sexual without lust is an attempt to cleanse or purify it on a public level. In order to give lust its proper place in the sexual order Althaus-Reid argues that there is a need to challenge the limited and repressed approach that theology depicts itself as having. And as part of this she talks of the need to queer God. Such an act, of queering God, can only happen when theologians move away from the schizophrenic approach that has traditionally been taken by theologians, in which a split is apparently enforced between the public and the private. According to Althaus-Reid, all theologians, whatever their own sexual practices and preferences, need to come out of the closet and publicly incorporate the sexual into their theology. They need to make explicit and to acknowledge that which is already there, that which has a direct influence on the theologian's work:

> ...God cannot be Queered unless theologians have the courage to come out from their homosexual, lesbian, bisexual, transgendered, transvestite or (ideal) heterosexual closets. Out-of-the-closet theologians do not leave the personal aside, and that always implies a risk, but neither do the closeted kind. It would be delusory to believe that closeted theologians can compartmentalise their lives so easily. The difference is that the closeted theologians indulge permanently in duplicity between the realms of a public and a private theology. They build schizophrenic spiritualities, those which require to be put aside at meal times, as the late Juan Luis Segundo said. Can we keep carrying the burden of a theology which leaves us alone when having sex?[27]

Althaus-Reid is not alone in recognising and stressing the importance of the sexual for theology and in particular, in challenging the unrealistic split between the private and the public. Discourses of the human body and especially human sexuality have increasingly become part of Christian theologies in the last twenty years. They are now to be found in a number of different theologies, including feminist informed, body, sexual and queer, and are a part of the recognition of the contextual and situated nature of all theologies. These theologies, and their associated methodologies of the inclusion of the sexual, incorporate and reflect the ways in which discourses of sexuality and the body are increasingly and explicitly public as opposed to private. Human sexualities and reflection on these sexualities have become visible and celebrated aspects of Christian theologies. Many aspects of human sexuality that have traditionally been seen as taboo or problematic are now being openly discussed and are becoming the appropriate focus of critical theological attention. And one of the most interesting and often most contentious aspects of this shift is the claim that human erotic experiences far from being a problematic area of human living that Christian theology needs to deal with, or rather not deal with, are now being identified and claimed as possible sites for experiencing the divine. In many ways such significant shifts in the way in which theology is viewing and valuing the sexual can be seen to foreshadow, and in part, be incorporated into, Althaus-Reid's approach to human sexuality in *Indecent Theology*.

The question of why the sexual has traditionally so often been denied a public and positive place in theology is an interesting but complex one. As has been well documented, the Christian Church in many historical forms, geographical contexts and denominational types, seems to have struggled profoundly with the realities of human sexualities. In recent times this focus has so often been centred on the issue of same-sex sexual relationships and the many related issues, either imagined or actual, that accompany these. However, human sexualities in all their types and realities (and not just those concerned with same-sex sexual relationship) remain deeply problematic for Christianity, and indeed many religious traditions. And yet given the centrality of sexuality to human experience, the absence of or negative pitch on human sexuality found in many theologies is troubling when attempting to make sense of human experience. This perhaps explains in part why, in recent years, so many theologies, across the theological spectrum, have expressed a clear concern with the sexual, to try and make sense of this apparently conflictual relationship between religion and the sexual, and to try and address the seemingly relentless negativity of religion towards human sexuality.

At the heart of many Christian theologies which are attempting to offer a positive reading of the sexual and to incorporate the possibility that human sexualities as a site for experiencing the divine, is a necessary juxtaposition between the very negative valuing and understanding of human sexualities in traditional Christian theologies and the valuing and understanding of the sexual in these contemporary theologies. The traditions of negativity and denial of human sexualities seem all too familiar in Christianity and theologians who are attempting a more positive assessment of human sexuality often incorporate into their work an analysis of the processes of development and crystallisation of such traditions of negativity towards the sexual, with particular reference to key figures. This serves to illustrate how the heritage of negativity towards the sexual in Christian theology developed, and also, how essentially contextual and personal in terms of being grounded in individual's experiences and concerns, this tradition is. Such individuals and traditions that are seen to have contributed most clearly to this are often the same as those cited by feminist informed theologians as having shaped the Christian traditions of gender-based inequalities. Most notable here are the Hellenistic, Jewish and Pauline traditions, Marcion, Origen, Augustine, Tertullian and Luther.[28] These are often depicted as traditions or individuals who in part incorporate a stress on the need to transcend the human body, its desires, functions and form, effected through a dualistic, hierarchical valuing of the human body (with all of its associated desires and activities) and the spiritual. Such dualistic hierarchicalism is seen to celebrate and elevate the spiritual as the pure, godly realm and the bodily and the sexual as the base, limiting realm that humanity needs to escape. In contrast, those attempting to move away from such a framing of the world and human experience interpret such dualistic orders in negative and even destructive terms. This perceived split, between the spiritual and the sexual, for sexual, body, feminist informed and queer theologians is problematic, but the blame for underlying dualistic tendencies can not always be as readily as is sometimes thought, placed so clearly at the door of either Christianity or the cultures and traditions which are understood to have influenced it especially in its earlier days. And neither is the picture of Christianity's negativity towards the body and the sexual always so straightforward, as Ruether has pointed out in relation to the Catholic tradition's understanding of the sexual:

> Roman Catholic Christianity is sometimes presented as suffering from a solely negative view of sexuality, rooted in hostility to women. This view is sometimes contrasted with robust and positive views of sexuality in the "pagan" and the Jewish worlds, although the negative Catholic views are sometimes also blamed on Platonism, supposedly in contrast to the positive Jewish views. These negative views are seen to have been overcome either by Protestantism which embraced sexuality as good and/or modern "enlightened" views, allowing modern Europeans to embrace sex as innocent and happy pleasure.
> The reality of this historical trajectory is, predictably, much more complex. Neither Judaism nor the Greek and Roman cultures viewed sex as unambiguously good.
> ...Western European and North American cultures operate out of a deep split personality toward sexuality.[29]

Contemporary theologies that are stressing a more positive valuing of the sexual often incorporate a criticism that the emphasis of dualistic theologies is so often not on the here and now, but rather is on the future. The human body, and the sexual, are not a part of this and are also actually distractions from the more appropriately spiritual concerns and focus of human living. The Christian traditions are often seen to be fundamentally hostile to the body and sexualities, and this is seen to be embedded theologically in the Christian tradition. Such an interpretation is seen, for example, in James Nelson's detailing of the "Seven Deadly Sins" of Christianity found in his influential and groundbreaking text *Body Theology*.[30] Nelson identifies the seven ways in which he claims Christianity has in effect sinned towards humanity, the human body and human sexuality – (1) spiritualistic dualism, (2) patriarchal dualism, (3) heterosexism, (4) guilt over self-love, (5) legalistic sexual ethic, (6) a sexless image of spirituality and (7) privatized sexuality.[31] It is possible to use Nelson's "Seven Deadly Sins" or "distortions of tradition" to build up a picture of the place and understanding of sexuality that Nelson is trying to advocate in his theology. All seven of these sins have as their underlying concern the negative valuing of human sexuality, especially in the theological or spiritual realm, which Nelson interprets as fundamentally wrong, hence the use of the term "sins". For Nelson Christianity is characterised by incarnation, it is a religion of incarnation. And as such he is concerned to develop a theology in which incarnation, understood in its widest sense, stands at the very centre of Christian practice and thought. His understanding of incarnation is one of individual lived reality, where incarnation is both apparent and experienced in the bodiliness of each individual human being. He claims that when humanity becomes concerned with what have traditionally been perceived as the spiritual things then this in practice often amounts to a move away from an ability to connect and communicate with others. This move to disconnection is problematic as connection, as opposed to fragmentation, stands at the centre of human experience. Human life, according to Nelson's understanding, is about relationship.

Nelson's body theology incorporates a very positive approach to sexuality in that he gives quite a high profile to sexuality within his theology because for him, sexuality is a fundamental part of human experience and existence. It is not a problematic in the scheme of Christian theology, not something to be hidden away or denied an explicit place in the theological picture of humanity. Sexuality is something to be celebrated, it is fundamental to who we are as persons, and its significance in theological terms is that it reveals our essential nature as relational. Sexuality, then, far from being an obstacle or barrier to spirituality is an appropriate way to know God. He claims that God can be known in authentic sexual relationship or experience. The body, then, in Nelson's scheme of things, is the location of great possibilities:

> Body theology is not primarily a theological description of the body. Nor is it principally an ethical prescription for how we ought to express ourselves physically. Rather, and most simply put, it is doing theology in such a way that we take our body experiences seriously as occasions of revelation.
>
> An incarnational faith boldly proclaims that Christ is alive. In other words, God continues to become embodied in our common flesh in saving, healing, liberating, justice-making ways.[32]

A very important methodological characteristic of many contemporary Christian theologies which now incorporate a positive approach to the human body is the claim that Christianity, its ethical prescriptions and theological visions, and sexuality are not radically different and necessarily distinct. Instead, attention is often drawn to the fact that many religious traditions do in fact celebrate human sexualities as positive, in some quite significant ways. As such, the theologically imaginative and creative relationship between religious experience and sexuality is not without precedent. And the feminist informed, body, sexual and queer positive theological valuing of human sexuality is not so much a break with tradition, as a particular emphasis. So, the case for Christian theologies incorporating human sexualities is further substantiated by the claim that the theological interpretation being articulated is not seen to be radically breaking from tradition or moving away from the perceived theological roots of Christianity. Rather, it is often understood to be consistent with the Christian story, with particular emphasis placed on a celebration of the incarnational nature of Christian theology. For example, Isherwood and Stuart draw attention to the centrality of bodiliness and embodiment in Christian scriptures. Whilst they acknowledge the ambiguity of the Pauline traditions, at the same time they also argue that:

> Christian Scriptures naturally have embodiment at their heart. From the moment when Mary agrees to give birth to a special child, bodies become sites of revelation and redemptive action.[33]

The kind of theological shift that is taking place here is one from a private sexuality to a more public one, with the contextual recognition that the self, the contextual, particular self, is how we experience God. This then leads to a stress on celebrating the self, including the bodily and sexual self in theological terms. Philip Sheldrake in *Befriending Our Desires* argues that human spirituality and experiencing of the divine are about addressing and dealing with the range of our needs and desires. Sexuality, then, given such a description, can not be left out of the equation, as this would lead to an incompleteness. He argues for the need to see desire as part of the spiritual journey, and claims that, "Only by attending to our desires are we able to encounter our deepest self – the image of God within us".[34]

Queer theory has had a significant impact on approaches to understanding and reenvisaging human sexuality. Since the late nineteen eighties it moves on from the identity politics of sexuality that have characterised such understandings for so long to a much more fluid approach. Despite what is often assumed, queer theologies and queer thinking do not limit themselves to a concern with lesbian, gay, bi or transgendered sexualities. Queer is an inclusive approach to sexualities that have been posited as outside of normative heterosexuality which has been constructed or defined in a constraining way. Reflecting on the theological employment of the term, Mary Hunt describes queer theology as the third stage in the "evolving effort to bring the experiences of lesbian, gay, bisexual, transgendered mainstream on their own terms".[35] The first stage that she places as from 1972 to 1982 is "the homosexual stage"[36] and this was characterised by the challenging emphasis found in the work of theologians such as Sally Gearhart and John McNeill on same-sex sexuality and theology, which often meant male experiences. From this developed what Hunt describes as the "lesbian/gay/bisexual stage"[37] in the years 1982 to 1992 which was concerned with the different sexualities of men and women and so opened up the category of homosexual, challenging that had become to be seen as primarily male experiential bading to a wider spectrum, emphasising female as well as male experiences. Within this stage HIV and AIDS developed as key concerns. Hunt describes the third stage as "queer theology"[38] which she places as from 1992 onwards. She too recognises the place of feminisms in queer thinking and theology and stresses the attention to difference of queer. In recent times theologians such as Robert Goss and Elizabeth

Stuart are developing queer informed Christian theologies with some very challenging results.[39]

Indecent theology and sexuality

The indecent theology of Althaus-Reid refuses the exclusions of sexuality from theology and alongside such writers as Nelson, Sheldrake and Stuart states the centrality of sexuality to human experience and so to theology. As has already been seen, it interprets Christian theology as a sexual act and as having traditionally reinforced sexual orthopraxy. Althaus-Reid argues that out of the closet theologians place the personal and sexual at the centre of theology. Indecent theology celebrates and reclaims the everyday of sexuality that has traditionally been deemed as unacceptable. With echoes of Carter Heyward it sees theology as passionate and dangerous and as radically marginal. At the heart of Althaus-Reid's proposal of indecent theology is a challenge to the perceived constructed sexual order and to the multiple bases of power as political, economic, sexual and gender based. It is a challenge to closed sexualities, and a critique of the violence of religious colonialism and the ensuing control on sexualities in their diversity. It criticises liberation theologies for the exclusion of human sexualities and argues that such theologies because of this do not break with the orders of decency. She draws on queer theory and queer theology to inform the indecent approach that she takes, not just to sexuality but also to theology, politics and economics. The refreshing contribution of Althaus-Reid to this field of investigation is her concern not just to focus on the inclusion of same-sex sexualities in all of their diversities but with the wider spectrum of human sexuality. She is concerned with bringing the heterosexual theologian out of their closet along with the lesbian, gay and bisexual theologian.

So, what does Althaus-Reid mean when she talks of the indecenting of Christianity? What is it exactly that she is trying to do? First of all, it is clear that she wants to challenge the traditional apparent exclusion of the sexual from the Christian story and from the theological. For Althaus-Reid sexuality stands at the centre of every theology. Her theology, however, does not stand still on the matter of sexuality at that point. She has a fundamental concern to challenge the orders of theological decency, as she perceives them:

> If God or Jesus Christ cannot be called faggots it is simply because we cannot see the divine outside the reductive structures of a Systematic Sexual Theology which knows little about love outside decent regulatory systems of controllable sexual categories.[40]

The sexual is not a compartment of human experience, according to Althaus-Reid. It can not be contained and spoken of in clearly structured and delineated ways. She sees the sexual in much more fundamental and extensive terms:

> The point is that the political and economic constructions of this world are based on sexual experience, or the interpretation of sexual experience. Theology is from that perspective a sexual act participating in the ideological construction of God from the idealist discourse of what it is supposed to be going to bed with God, the regulations and control discourses based on some heterosexual falsifications or alienations of what is due to reality, and to the people who live under the threats of the naturalisation of sexuality or decency codes in theology.[41]

Indecent theology with its recourse to the wider range of human experiences celebrates transient sexualities. It welcomes and embraces sexual dissidency, fetishism and sadomasochism and argues that decent heterosexuality is central to exploitative hierarchical systems of power and that Christianity supports exploitative sexual configurations:

> Theology is a sexual ideology performed in a sacralising pattern: it is a sexual divinised orthodoxy (right sexual dogma) and orthopraxy (right sexual behaviour); theology is a sexual action. Theologians, therefore, are nothing else but sexual performers who need to take many ethical and sometimes partisan sexual decisions when reflecting on God and humanity, because theology is never innocuous or sexually innocent or neutral.[42]

When Althaus-Reid talks of theology as a sexual act she seems to mean that sexuality lies at the very heart of Christian theology, and more than that, an exploitative heterosexual Christian theology:

> Women, and sexual dissidents in general, are merely depicted for the consumption of a constructed male heterosexual reader. Their images may be fixed in situations of pain and sexual torture, but these are acceptable in the history of Christianity.[43]

The response of indecent theology to this is uncompromising, it has to undress, to deconstruct the theological enhancement and justification of repressive controlling orders of heterosexuality which she sees as underlying political and economic structures:

> Indecent Theology forces a Soft-Core Porno Theology (namely, Systematic Theology) to assume its real hard-core nature and to come out with the crudeness of its sexual constructions...indecenting, that is, denouncing the real hard-core sexual nature of Systematic Theology while announcing gender and sexual deconstructions which could carry precious meaning to our lives in relation to the sacred, and the political implications of theology as ideology, is considered scandalous and immoral.[44]

She argues that far from being absent from theology, as we might be lead to believe, sexual lust is at the heart of theology in terms of the control, denial and stipulation of lust. Indeed, she goes so far as to argue that even notions such as sin and grace are bound up with sexual desire.[45] Exploring Paul Tillich's apparent sexual inclinations, as revealed through Hannah Tillich's reflections, Althaus-Reid speaks of the need for integrity in making explicit the desires, lusts and preferences of the theologian, as being in someway essential for Christian theology. We might ask of Althaus-Reid, why is this? Why do we need to know about Tillich's sexual practices and desires in order to understand or engage with his theology? In Althaus-Reid's understanding, it is because "...theology is never innocuous or sexually innocent or neutral".[46] In some ways this goes back to the fundamental feminist insights that the personal is the political. Theology is not removed from the personal, it does not take place in isolation from the grounded experiences of the theologian, but it has a clear and dramatic relationship to the individual theologian. It is radically contextual, where contextual takes on its fullest meaning. It is, however, more than this, it is also the underlying claim of Althaus-Reid of exploitation, that controlling systems of sexual decency underpin the histories of Christian theology and so controlling systems of decency, underpinned by theology, act as a regulating force upon humanity, taking on social, religious, economic forms. In this way, then, Althaus-Reid talks of Christian theology as "an imperial sexual act".[47]

Indecent theology forces an acknowledgement of the inherently sexual nature of Christian theology. It challenges and at times forces theology to spell out the full implications of its controlling heterosexist agenda, and to face up to its imperialistic mechanisms of operation. The imperialism and orders of decency that she is talking about have essentially imposed strict limitations, the effects of which are seen especially in the lives of women. Althaus-Reid criticises the way in which feminist informed theologies have focused on gender rather than sexual activity or sexuality in their address to the oppression of women, and she claims that it is more than just gender, it is also inherently and indistinguishably sexual. The purity claims of theology, then, in this way, extend also to liberation and feminist informed theologies. For example, in exploring constructions of christology she notes that liberation theologies have attempted to represent and identify Jesus in such a way that people can identify more easily with him, but argues that indecent theology must go further than this:

> ....but an Indecent Theology must go further in its disrespect for the interpellative, normative forces of patriarchal theology. It must go beyond the positive identification with a larger Christ. It must have the right to say not only that a lesbian can identify herself with a liberator Christ but that it must sexually deconstruct Christ too. Then indecent theologians may say: "God, the Faggot; God, the Drag Queen; God, the Lesbian; God, the heterosexual woman who does not accept the constructions of ideal heterosexuality; God, the ambivalent, not easily classified sexually".[48]

This is necessary because these theologies too have been caught up in the need for decency, hence the need for a theology of indecency and to talk for example, of God as "Faggott; God, the Drag Queen".[49] This juxtapositing of the theological and the sexual in such pairings is part of her strategy of confrontation. It uses language in such a way as to invite shock and then for the reader to begin to unpack why the use of language in this way has this impact. For example, she talks of, leather salvation,[50] Soft-Core Porn Theology,[51] Vanilla theologians,[52] a Bi/Christ[53] and French-kissing God.[54] Carrette comments of this strategy:

> Many uninitiated into the realms of Sexual theologies could be forgiven for thinking that the words of a book on pornography and Liberation theology have become mixed up in the publishing of Althaus-Reid's text, but that would be to miss the very important theoretical motivation behind the work.[55]

So, having established that Althaus-Reid identifies the need to move beyond the heterosexist theologies of decency in a radical act of indecency we need to establish what it is exactly that this indecency amounts to and how it functions within her scheme of theology and to examine it in terms of the contextual frame of reference in which Althaus-Reid operates in *Indecent Theology*. So, why does she propose an indecent theology for Latin America, and more specifically, for the women of Buenos Aires? Such a question really takes us to the very heart of Althaus-Reid's liberation theological approach and to the heart of this assessment of Althaus-Reid's strategy of feminist Christian encounter.

Feminist theology and the need for indecency

Indecent theology, as proposed by Althaus-Reid, is a theology that accepts the feminist analysis that women, both historically and still today, have experienced widespread injustice. This is seen, for example, in her analysis of the experiences of women in Latin America, and, in particular, her analysis of her own experiences of trying to gain access to theological education. Feminist informed theology, then, in this sense, has an important contribution to make in identifying and challenging gender based injustice. However, what is distinct about Althaus-Reid's approach is that her understanding of injustice, which sees the sexual, and in particular, the constructed order of sexual decency, as the determining and sustaining cause of this injustice. The gender focused approach of feminist informed theologies, claims Althaus-Reid, has failed to take into account the sexual base of women's oppression, choosing to focus instead on the relatively safe category of gender. As such, feminist informed theology also comes in for criticisms from Althaus-Reid with her claim that it "...follows liberationist decency based on tight sexual constructions".[56] In her own, uncompromising words, she challenges what she seems to read as the concern with purity of feminist informed theologies and asks some very probing questions of such theologies, in terms of their radicalism and their implications:

> Has Liberation Feminist Theology stopped eating divine phalluses?...Does Feminist Theology have a quest for purity still, for singleness of desire and hegemonic resurrections? The quest for transcendence in Feminist Theology, even in the context of political theologies, is still a quest for an out-of-body experience of purity.[57]

> If purity is a common base for Liberation Feminist Theologies, or to put it differently, if purity is to Liberation Feminist Theologies as colonial thought is to Christianity, the frame we are dealing with is indeed very limited.[58]

Feminist informed theologies, then, it seems, in Althaus-Reid's understanding, as they have so far been conceived and developed, have either not been aware of or not been prepared to address the fuller picture of injustice, as she sees it. Like Latin American and other liberation theologies, feminist informed theologies, in not recognising or failing to acknowledge the sexual base of injustice, in effect, participate in the very orders of decency that perpetuate the injustices that women in particular are so often subject to. This, she expresses in expectedly uncompromising words of, "The gap between a Feminist Liberation Theology and an Indecent Theology is one of sexual honesty".[59] Given all of this, something more, in Althaus-Reid's understanding, is required. Something that is more than, or goes beyond, liberation theology, and something that is more than, or goes beyond, feminist informed theologies. In Althaus-Reid's words, "...something that will require us to take our pants off at the moment of doing theology".[60] This something that Althaus-Reid speaks of is a theology which:

> ...problematises and undresses the mythical layers of multiple oppression in Latin America, a theology which, finding its point of departure at the crossroads of Liberation Theology and Queer Thinking, will reflect on economic and theological oppression with passion and imprudence. An Indecent Theology will question the traditional Latin American field of decency and order as it permeates and supports the multiple (ecclesiological, theological, political and amatory) structures of life in my country, Argentina, and in my continent.[61]

The repressive orders of decency, that she claims underpin the injustices of Latin American life, need to be subverted theologically because they are infused with theological authority and meaning. One of the key differences between Althaus-Reid's approach here and the other two strategies examined in earlier chapters in relation to the theologies of Carter Heyward and Elisabeth Schüssler Fiorenza, is in terms of the kinds of claims that seem to be made for both Christianity, and indeed feminisms, in relation to justice. Both Schüssler Fiorenza and Heyward seem to see Christianity as some kind of exceptional, if not unique, site for hope. Or, as some kind of inherent justice based or justice orientated tool, that once the layers of patriarchalism, kyriarchalism or gender based oppression, have been stripped away, will serve to overcome injustice and seek justice. In Althaus-Reid's approach, this sense of commitment to authentic or original Christianity, as inherently justice seeking is not so apparent. Indeed, the substance of her analysis is the damage that theologically infused orders of decency have done. This is seen, for example, in her description of the way in which she uses the term indecent:

> ...in a positive, subversive sense, referring to a counter-discourse for the unmasking and unclothing of the sexual assumptions built into Liberation

Theology during the past decades but also today when confronting issues of globalisation and the neo-liberal world order.[62]

Also, in Althaus-Reid's approach there seems to be no distinction between the historical forms of Christianity and some understanding of an original or authentic Christianity. Which is so important as it allows the vital, although sometimes suspiciously convenient, distinction to be drawn between justice denying and justice seeking Christianity. What she is concerned with is the cultural/religious context of women's experiences of injustice in Latin America. It is the functioning of theology which is of concern, as the location of injustice, and the focus of her indecenting, rather than Christianity as such. So, she is not so much concerned with reconstruction or reinterpretation of an identifiable tradition or symbol that stands at the heart of Christianity, as the process of opening up spaces through deconstructive indecenting. She seems to make no moves to reject Christianity from a value standpoint, but neither does she seem to make any claims for it as having inherent justice seeking qualities or possibilities. She is not advocating a feminist informed vision of Christianity or even an indecent Christianity as the solution to gender based injustice. It is more a theological act of subversion, than a systematic theology of liberation. It seems to offer no structure for a revised Christian based justice story as highlight and subvert the constraints that have functioned to support injustice. Her concern is with the functioning of theology rather than with the possibilities of the Christian religion. She is not so much interested in content as function, it is a critically reflective discourse of indecent theology.

This, in part, explains her criticisms of feminist informed theological attempts to reconstruct out of silence, which, for example, results, in her words, in the "…obsession…in the studies of women in the primitive church…".[63] For her, theology is radically hostile to women, and the kinds of methodologies that have been proposed to address this, so far, have simply not been effective enough:

> It is sad to say that theology as a text is a deathbed where the woman author has never existed, and has been aborted. Indecent theologians are usually found glancing at these deathbeds, pondering what to do with the remains. Shall the corpse be buried or preserved in alcohol? It is from there that methodological problems arise such as the question of women's silence as a hermeneutical challenge. However, feminist methodology has a tendency to obscure the point that women in Christian theology are "dead girls"….Death is part of the aboutness of Feminist Theology, and its understandable obsession. This obsession is manifested, for instance, in the studies of women in the primitive church, assessing their supposed equality with men.[64]

A further criticism that she levels at feminist informed theologies relates to the kinds of claims that it has made as being in some way universally relevant. She stresses the need to remain grounded at all times. To be contextual is absolutely fundamental to her theological understanding and approach and she argues that feminist informed theologies cannot be dislocated, theoretical theologies; they must be grounded if they are to avoid the imperialism of hegemonous feminisms:

The problem is that in the discourse of liberation, women are already disembodied in the category of the poor woman, which is a romantic conceptualisation, a universal which fits the invention of women and the invention of the poor at the same time. In a theological materialist feminist analysis, women need to be studied in certain contexts, and not from a mere struggle of ideas about womanhood constructed in opposition to hegemonic definitions, say by reading life in opposition to the Bible, but by a process of de-abstractionism or materialist reversal.[65]

Interesting questions have been asked of Althaus-Reid, of her indecent theology and of the underlying concerns of this theology. Kwok Pui-lan has raised an interesting point about Althaus-Reid's interpretation of theology as sexual, she welcomes the insight but goes on to ask what this actually means. Should we stick with this reading of theology or should other visions and approaches be developed to challenge and displace this?[66] Pui-lan is not so much challenging Althaus-Reid's interpretation as asking what comes after the moment of deconstruction in what she suggests is a concern for, "...stretching our theological imagination".[67] She also shares Althaus-Reid's use of post-colonial criticism but is concerned about her use of theologies of the North such as Daly[68] and points out that Daly has an exclusivist "colonial tendency in her representation of Third World women as victims",[69] and she invites Althaus-Reid to engage in fuller dialogue with other Third World thinkers, and makes some quite challenging criticisms of Althaus-Reid:

While she criticizes her male colleagues in Latin America for writing for the consumption of the white academy, her heavy reliance on white queer theory and theology and continental philosophy may also be open to similar criticism. I do not subscribe to the nativistic position that one should not use Western theories, but I think one should be constantly vigilant of their racial and even colonial biases. As someone who has grown up in an Asian culture which constructs sexuality and gender in different ways, I cannot help but think that some of the queer theorists, such as Judith Butler, are Eurocentric.[70]

Yet, even given this, she still acknowledges the significance of Althaus-Reid's book, and says that she has "written a wild and courageous book".[71] Jeremy Carrette asks of the place of fetishism and sadomasochism in *Indecent Theology*, he describes her work in this area as "theological voyeurism"[72] by which he means "looking (at safe distance) at fetish images",[73] what he asks is what kind of practice emerges from this and suggests that she "remains at times in the (orthodox) theological closet".[74]

Feminist and Indecent?

Given the kinds of criticisms that Althaus-Reid makes of feminist informed theologies, in terms of its limitations and fundamental failure to address the full (sexual) nature of the theologically infused constraints that determine the orders of society, the question needs to be asked of how can Althaus-Reid's theology said to be feminist informed? Or, to place the emphasis slightly differently, the question needs to be asked of whether the inclusion of her approach in this analysis of the strategies of feminist Christian encounter be justified and be said to be appropriate to Althaus-Reid's understanding of her own theological approach and position? Raising such questions brings this study to the beginnings of the important, but difficult task, of raising the question of what actually constitutes a feminist approach and in particular a feminist informed approach in theology? This is undoubtedly both a difficult and problematic question to ask, as the whole matter of describing particular approaches, whether theological or not, and using particular terminology, can be said in part to be of ambiguous and even dubious benefit. A key reason for this is that potentially all such labels and designations might be seen as limiting or unreflective of the reality of the scope of the approach. It has been seen from the brief history of feminist theologies and from the analysis of the development of feminisms and feminist informed theologies so far, that the category of "feminism" is fundamentally unstable. In that not only are feminist informed theologies ever changing but also that in the process of establishing themselves as an identifiable approach, as an approach that facilitates the application of feminist ideas and analysis to theological issues and questions, the definition of feminist informed theology has proved not only limited as a frame of reference but also as limiting and even alienating for those addressing issues of gender based inequalities.

The reason that this question of characterising the feminist informed approach can be raised, and really needs be raised here, is that Althaus-Reid's approach is so multidisciplinary (and even on first analysis so explosive of methodological boundaries) that the issue of definitions and appropriateness of descriptions demands consideration. As does the wider question of the developing, changing identity of feminist informed theological engagement, especially in the light of the weight of the accumulative evidence of the failure or shortcomings of feminist informed theologies. As the future of any coherent notion of feminist informed theology seems on a number of levels questionable. So, drawing on the analysis carried out so far, but in particular, the analysis in the mapping out exercise in Chapter One it is possible to identify a number of characteristics that tend to be found in the approach and ideas of those who by both self-definition and critical identification have been described as feminist:

1. The first identifiable feature of "feminisms" is the claim or recognition that women have experienced exclusion or marginalisation. This claim is variously made in relation to a wide diversity of cultures, historical periods, organisations and groups, and a number of different explanations are given for this.
2. The next characterising feature of feminisms follows on from this first characteristic and is the claim that this initial recognition of gendered exclusion or marginalisation is in some way unjust or problematic. Because the shaping, governing and determining of the power bases, whatever the sources, whether economic or theological, have largely been

in the hands of men, and women, by means of their perceived gender based difference, have been excluded from these areas. So, difference here has been interpreted hierarchically and has been employed as the basis of a mechanism, of exclusion. In theological terms, this exclusion or marginalisation is seen to have specific implications and manifestations. Such implications and manifestations include, for example, the language, images, mediating roles and the representation of the divine, which it is argued, are gendered in such a way as to marginalise or make invisible the experiences of women. One of the most obvious examples here is the role of the priest in Christianity. The ordained priestly role in many Christian denominations and groups has been out of bounds for women and this means that what has been traditionally interpreted as the essentially important mediatory, representation, and organisational roles of the priest have been denied to women.

3. Given these implications and manifestations of gender based exclusion, particular challenges and responses are needed to challenge these limiting implications, in order to effect change. As change is usually a specific outcome of the feminist research it does not usually stay with analysis and so can be identified as the third characteristic of a feminist informed approach. Feminist informed analysis does not usually stay with analysis. It usually has an aim or understanding of justice, perhaps not specific, built into the concept of injustice. So, the idea that women have been excluded from major roles needs identification and uncovering, perhaps the necessary outcome of feminisms is that this is exclusivist and problematic. What the specifics of the answer are takes many diverse forms, from the inclusion of other roles, to the changing of all roles.

So, how does Althaus-Reid's theology fit in with this? Throughout her work she is clearly concerned with identifying and challenging injustice, and in her own grounded conceptual concerns with the women of Latin America, and her analysis of the historical forms of injustice, gender is a prominent feature. In that she clearly understands gender to be a factor in the way in which injustice functions and so in the way in which injustice might be challenged:

> Women are the traditional consumers, not producers of theology. Other sexual identities such as bisexuality or lesbianism fall into the same economic relation of dependency, in the sense that people's lives are regulated in the market or in theology in dependence on hegemonic definitions of which goods people need, how to distribute them and for whom this model is effective in terms of satisfaction and happiness.[75]
>
> ...all the corpus of Systematic Theology including Liberation Theologies are...Sexual Theologies since they are based on a simple set of ontological and material assumptions about sexuality and women's humanity.[76]

Exclusion through gender is problematic for Althaus-Reid and she attempts to uncover and deconstruct orders which support and perpetuate such exclusions.

What is distinct about Althaus-Reid's approach is her persistent questioning of the limits and operating factors of exclusion. Gender is a factor of exclusion and injustice, but the fuller picture recognises the sexual in the everyday and feminisms are accepted and incorporated into her approach in a self-reflexive way, but certainly not the full critical category and value system.

A concern with gender, however, does not necessarily mean that her approach can be said to be informed or shaped by feminist values and insights. She focuses in on the experiences of women in order to crack open the sexual orders of decency of Christian theology. Her address in this is not just to women, but women are primarily the subjects of her contextual focus and of her historical analysis in *Indecent Theology*. A concern with women, however, as noted above, does not necessarily constitute a feminist approach. She clearly sees gender as one category of exclusion, but does not limit her understanding of injustice, in the context of Latin America, to gender. It is this recognition of factors, in addition to gender, as functional in injustice, that both raises questions about the feminist element of her approach and opens up the possibilities of the types of feminist Christian encounter.

She does seem to value feminist consciousness but has very clear problems with the systems of feminism, with the ideology, both theological and beyond. She recognises that feminist liberation theologies have made important contributions[77] but they have accepted or at least not challenged the decent sexual orders that restrain and control women and other marginalised groups. The economic and theological orders of control of women have an underlying sexual decency but feminists and feminist theologians have focused on patriarchal constructions of gender. From this they have relied and referred to liberal ideology that has imposed hegemonic readings of essential woman, which Althaus-Reid understands in a restraining way. They have not problematised the given realities[78] and so have included idealist understandings of sexuality, feminist theology, their focus has been on "sex as gender, and very rarely on sex as 'having sex'"[79] which is hugely problematic in her understanding because "sex as lust is an important conceptual category which is not new, but has dominated theology for centuries"[80] she argues, "...follows liberationist decency based on tight sexual constructions".[81] She illustrates this by talking of the decency of the place of feminist theological discourse as the female gaze and asks why should it not be instead, "...a theology 'with women's sex?'":[82]

> ...the gaze method is a yo-yo, jumping from materialist promises to historical criticism and back to idealism. The woman's gazing into male theology ends in idealism, because there has not been a sustained effort to develop a truly materialist approach which would redefine women's issues in Latin America, starting from a sexual enquiry into patterns of doing sexual theologies and confronting the abstraction process of women's life into patriarchal categories.[83]

The focus on Mary is an example of this idealising method, for Althaus-Reid Mary is an idea, "a myth of a woman without a vagina"[84], a simulacra, she talks of the Latin American Virgin Mary as "a rich, white woman who does not walk".[85]

Rather than being a source of liberation, Mary, she claims, is "part of the problem"[86] because in her words:

> ...the Virginal liberationist does theology without lust. Lust suffers a theological clitoridectomy and therefore no real sense of empowering can come from the worship of the Virgin.

She refers to the decent patterns of feminist theological engagement as vanilla theology.[87] However, very importantly, despite her criticisms of feminist theologies, she does describe *Indecent Theology* as "...a book on Sexual Political Theology intended as a critical continuation of Feminist Liberation Theology"[88] and the methodological base in doing this is queer thinking theologies, Continental thinking, Marxist studies, Sexual Theory and Systematic Theology.[89] As such, something of feminist informed theologies as they have so far developed is of value to the indecent theological approach but this cannot stand without extensive criticism. Decency is problematic for Althaus-Reid in many ways including transformation:

> Decent Christian women, unfortunately, make decent citizens too. However, it is from indecent Christian and subversive citizens that action for transformation occurs in history. Indecency may be the last chance for a surplus of Christianity to transform political structures.[90]

Change occurs through indecency, through deconstruction, which she insists is not destructive,[91] "...we need to leave decency and advocate a deviant, per/verted Sexual Theology for social change".[92] Indecency then can be a tool for women for a "...deviant Sexual Theology, which would challenge the normalcy of women's oppression in its ultimate consequences".[93]

Althaus-Reid is clearly uncomfortable with the description of feminist in relation to her work and she notes that she would consider herself to be "more a 'queer' theologian than a 'feminist'".[94] Gender based oppression in her work is not the prime focus in her theology as it is not a broad enough explanation for the situation she is concerned to deconstruct. Her explanation of decency as the basis of constraint or injustice goes beyond gender but does incorporate gender. The characteristics of the feminist based approach, then, as outlined above, are incorporated into her indecent theology but are not the defining or guiding base. She acknowledges that women have been constrained in particular by the orders of decency. She sees women as excluded from Christian theology, but does not see injustice in this way as limited to women. She is concerned to open up the understanding of the categories of exclusion and as such feminism can only really have one part in her work, because of its specific concern with the category of gender, and in particular, with the experiences of women:

> Women are the traditional consumers, not producers of theology. Other sexual identities such as bisexuality or lesbianism fall into the same economic relation of dependency, in the sense that people's lives are regulated in the market or in theology in dependence on hegemonic definitions of which goods people need,

how to distribute them and for whom this model is effective in terms of satisfaction and happiness.[95]

...all the corpus of Systematic Theology including Liberation Theologies are...Sexual Theologies since they are based on a simple set of ontological and material assumptions about sexuality and women's humanity.[96]

The workings of indecenting

Althaus-Reid demonstrates how indecenting functions in *Indecent Theology* through the indecent contextual analysis of a number of key Christian concepts from a Latin American woman's perspective, those of Jesus, Mary and what she calls, "the Gospel Family", which are all tied up with each other. The Gospel, Family, in her understanding is responsible for the "theological erasure" of women:[97]

> A whole sexual theological performance of dressing and undressing (uncovering), the dis-organisation of bodies and their recasting into naturalised pattern of relationships has been historically materialised into institutions such as the family. God has become the medieval or the capitalist family according to political mores. However, it is not only through the history of theology and ideology that this can be traced. The Gospels present us with an inner structure organised as a family economy which has contributed more to the idea of family in Latin America after the *Conquista* than anything else.[98]

She notes that some significant work has been carried out in terms of challenging some of the theological symbols that participate in the systems of decency in Latin America. For example, the radical representations of Christ, such as those of Ché Christ[99] are examples of this but don't go far enough. Deconstruction and indecenting of Jesus is necessary because of the social, theological construction of Jesus, "...Jesus is not about Jesus, but a religious system organised as a sexual utopia of the origins of heterosexuality".[100] Althaus-Reid argues that the poor woman of Latin America is forced into identification with decency, in part through identification with the Virgin Mary. But this, she argues, denies the realities of women's lives, as poor women and as sexual beings, and the danger of liberation theologies that draw on the symbol of the Virgin Mary, including feminist theologies, is that the use Mary to reinforce the order of decency that oppresses the poor woman of Latin America. As she notes such theology does theology "without lust".[101] The whole theological enterprise of the Virgin Mary demands radical attention, demystification, queering and to be made indecent because of the way in which it underpins the layers of oppression for women in Latin America, and indeed in so many places:

> The identification of "woman" and everlasting virginity, is the foundation of the theological and political enterprise of Europe in the Americas.....The Virgin imaginary in Latin America is the permanent dichotomy of lust and love: this is why poor people are presented in the Theology of Liberation as decent, that is,

asexual or monogamous heterosexual spouses united in the holy sacrament of marriage, people of faith and struggle who do not masturbate, have lustful thoughts at prayer times, cross-dress, or enjoy leather practices.[102]

The place of the Virgin Mary has long been identified as problematic for feminist informed theologies, Mary is problematic for indecent theology, as Althaus-Reid describes her in the following way:

> The Virgin Mary is not a woman but a simulacra in which the process of making ideologies and what Marx calls "mystical connections" is exemplified.
> The Virgin Mary is a theologically casuistic case presented in feminicide. A life that cannot have any choice because it is a woman's life, and no other reason, is a life which suffers many forms of assassinations.[103]

She talks about the constructed layers of decency that have been projected onto or built into Mary[104] and part of the problems with this is that these layers have been progressively imposing a non-human, or in Althaus-Reid's words, an alien, identity, to the extent that she claims that Mary actually has "more non-human characteristics than Jesus"[105], which is something radically opposed by the queering or indecency theological project. The process of indecenting the Virgin Mary has direct consequences for both the God and Jesus of Christianity and so affects the whole of the Christian theological enterprise:

> To indecent the Virgin means to indecent God and Jesus, as their identity is relational. Indecent Theology works here as a coming-out process which consists of simply doubting traditions of sexual presuppositions, a process that being public can have transformative political implications.[106]

So, what does it actually mean for Althaus-Reid to talk of indecenting the Virgin Mary? She explains this by drawing on the work of Robert Goss and in particular his 1993 text of queer christology *Jesus Acted Up*.[107] She argues that the task of queering the Virgin Mary is more complex than queering Christ, queering or indecenting here means for Althaus-Reid the "...process of coming back to the authentic, everyday life experiences described as odd by the ideology – and mythology – makers alike"[108]

> An indecent hermeneutics of suspicion, well applied, will Queer the Virgin in what counts as having sex beyond hermaphroditic patterns of sexual organs, reproductive sexuality and expectations related to biology, but also in patterns of thought and relationships with people and institutions.[109]

She sees the virginity of Mary as a denial of sexual experience. She argues that this has had the effect of elevating and exalting patriarchal motherhood so that it has become the controlling economy of women as private property[110] and Althaus-Reid's current project is a detailed indecenting of Mary.

Conclusion

To give a very brief description of her methodology, in Althaus-Reid's approach the Christian tradition might be said to be the cultural framework of indecent encounter, the inherited, lived tradition of context and the envisaged continuing framework of the encounter. Feminisms are one tool of analysis and critique to be engaged among other such tools in the process of identifying, challenging and overcoming injustice.

> ...I am aware that in theology it is not stability but a sense of discontinuity which is most valuable. The continuousness of the hermeneutical circle of suspicion and the permanent questioning of theological discontinuity.[111]

Indecent theology is not a straight forward identification with lesbian, gay, bi, queer, liberal or feminist thought and practices. *Indecent Theology* is an appropriately indecent dive into radical theology. She talks of "...that space which is a yearning, an incompleteness, which is Indecent Theology: a process that is never finished".[112] On reading *Indecent Theology* initially questions arise as to what the outcome or theological vision of Althaus-Reid actually is. This, however, on further close reading of the text, seems to be a misplaced question, arising perhaps out of expectations of a more systematic theological outcome. As Carrette has said, "...the value of Althaus-Reid's work is in setting – or, perhaps, one should say, inspiring – a new agenda, rather than fully detailing the philosophical dimensions behind her Sexual theology".[113] It is an interruption, a suggestion, a confrontation, not a worked through theology.

One of the most exciting aspects of Althaus-Reid's work is the explicit address and implications for feminist informed theologies. It takes or rather challenges feminist informed theologies to go somewhere discernibly different and refreshing, and perhaps to a place that many would agree they have needed to go for the last ten years. The question now is one of whether feminist informed theologies are ready to go to such a place of space or whether such a shift, deemed by many as necessary, would constitute a challenge to the very identities of feminist informed Christian theologies as we understand them. In some senses, there are no hiding places for feminist informed and other liberation theologies.

> Even if feminist hermeneutics has made a tremendous contribution to the course of liberation, one may have reached a full circle if we cannot do theology leaving the pattern of text-authorities aside. Theologies from the margins have a passion for justice and try to do a theology based in people's real lives, but they seldom depart critically from central definitions including a Sexual philosophy which is rarely challenged. From there, all the theo-logics which are supposed to be radical alternatives seem to carry the same dualistic notions expressed in their ecclesiologies and dogmatic power struggles.[114]

She describes her approach as a concrete materialist theology[115] that recognises and responds to the sexual nature of economics and theology. She is interested and concerned with the way in which orders of decency have controlled the poor, women, gay, lesbian, bisexual people, transgendered. So, she is not concerned solely or even primarily with women in her theology, although they do feature prominently as those who have been effected by the repressive orders of decency. Her concern is to reveal, through queer undressing, the systems that have imposed and controlled this decency and the contextual focus of her work as a woman theologian from Argentina leads her to this. Also, her focus is part of her understanding of the theological and political economies of Latin America, "The identification of 'woman' and everlasting virginity, is the foundation of the theological and political enterprise of Europe in the Americas".[116] To challenge the hegemony of the Christian story radical response is needed:

> The point is that in the self-preservation of a systematic confinement of heterosexuality, corruption is the only hope for breaking free, for allowing the integrity of heteronormativity to dissolve. Corruption like alterity spoils heterosexuality and breaks it into little pieces.[117]

Notes

[1] Althaus-Reid, M., (2000), *Indecent Theology: Theological Perversions in Sex, Gender and Politics*, Routledge, p.125.
[2] Althaus-Reid, M., The University of Edinburgh Website (no date). Retrieved on 1 June 2003 from the World Wide Web: http://www.div.ed.ac.uk/contact/staff_pages/m_althaus-reid.htm
[3] Althaus-Reid, 2000:4.
[4] Althaus-Reid, 2000:5.
[5] Carrette, J., (2001), "Radical heterodoxy and the indecent proposal of erotic theology: critical groundwork for sexual theologies", *Literature and Theology*, Vol.15(3), p.289.
[6] Althaus-Reid, 2000:7.
[7] Althaus-Reid, 2000:7.
[8] Althaus-Reid, 2000:5.
[9] Althaus-Reid, 2000:4.
[10] Althaus-Reid, 2000:1.
[11] Althaus-Reid, 2000:3.
[12] Althaus-Reid, 2000:4.
[13] Althaus-Reid, 2000:17.
[14] Althaus-Reid, 2000:20.
[15] Althaus-Reid, 2000:22.
[16] Althaus-Reid, 2000:25.
[17] Althaus-Reid, 2000:25.
[18] Althaus-Reid, 2000:26.
[19] Althaus-Reid, 2000:35.
[20] Althaus-Reid, 2000:34.
[21] Althaus-Reid, 2000:34.
[22] Althaus-Reid, 2000:34.
[23] Althaus-Reid, 2000:34-35.
[24] Althaus-Reid, 2000:23.
[25] Althaus-Reid, 2000:87.
[26] Althaus-Reid, 2000:87.

[27] Althaus-Reid, 2000:88.
[28] For example, May, M., (1995), *A Body Knows: A Theopoetics of Death and Resurrection*, New York: Continuum, p.16.
[29] Ruether, R.R., in Isherwood, L., (ed), (2000), *The Good News of the Body: Sexual Theology and Feminism*, Sheffield: Sheffield Academic Press, p.34.
[30] Nelson, J., (1992), *Body Theology*, Louisville, Kentucky: Westminster/John Knox Press.
[31] Nelson, 1992: 29-40.
[32] Nelson, 1992:9-10.
[33] Isherwood, L., and Stuart, E., (1998), *Introducing Body Theology*, Sheffield: Sheffield Academic Press, p.11.
[34] Sheldrake, P., (1994), *Befriending Our Desires*, Darton, Longman and Todd, p.11.
[35] Hunt, M., in Russell, L., and Shannon, J., (eds.), (1996), *Dictionary of Feminist Theologies*, London: Mowbray, p.298.
[36] Hunt, in Russell, L., and Shannon, J., (eds.), 1996:298.
[37] Hunt, in Russell, L., and Shannon, J., (eds.), 1996:298.
[38] Hunt, in Russell, L., and Shannon, J., (eds.), 1996:299.
[39] See for example, Goss, R.E., (1993), *Jesus ACTED UP: A Gay and Lesbian Manifesto*, San Francisco: Harper SanFrancisco; Goss, R.E., (2002), *Queering Christ: Beyond Jesus Acted Up*, Cleveland: The Pilgrim Press; and Stuart, E., (et al), (1997), *Religion is a Queer Thing: A Guide to the Christian Faith for Lesbian, Gay, Bisexual and Transgendered People*, London and Washington: Cassell.
[40] Althaus-Reid, 2000:69.
[41] Althaus-Reid, 2000:23-24.
[42] Althaus-Reid, 2000:87.
[43] Althaus-Reid, 2000:93.
[44] Althaus-Reid, 2000:93.
[45] Althaus-Reid, 2000:86.
[46] Althaus-Reid, 2000:87.
[47] Althaus-Reid, 2000:92.
[48] Althaus-Reid, 2000:95.
[49] Althaus-Reid, 2000:95.
[50] Althaus-Reid, 2000:87.
[51] Althaus-Reid, 2000:93.
[52] Althaus-Reid, 2000:109.
[53] Althaus-Reid, 2000:114.
[54] Althaus-Reid, 2000:125.
[55] Carrette, 2001:289.
[56] Althaus-Reid, 2000:36.
[57] Althaus-Reid, 2000:103.
[58] Althaus-Reid, 2000:104.
[59] Althaus-Reid, 2000:7.
[60] Althaus-Reid, 2000:37.
[61] Althaus-Reid, 2000:2.
[62] Althaus-Reid, 2000:168.
[63] Althaus-Reid, 2000:101-102.
[64] Althaus-Reid, 2000:101-102.
[65] Althaus-Reid, 2000:36.
[66] Pui-lan, K., (2003), "Theology as a sexual act?", *Feminist Theology*, 11(2), 150.
[67] Pui-lan, 2003:150.

[68] Pui-lan, 2003:155.
[69] Pui-lan, 2003:155.
[70] Pui-lan, 2003:156.
[71] Pui-lan, 2003:156.
[72] Carrette, 2001:295.
[73] Carrette, 2001:295.
[74] Carrette, 2001:296.
[75] Althaus-Reid, 2000:170.
[76] Althaus-Reid, 2000:176.
[77] Althaus-Reid, 2000:6.
[78] Althaus-Reid, 2000:52.
[79] Althaus-Reid, 2000:87.
[80] Althaus-Reid, 2000:87.
[81] Althaus-Reid, 2000:36.
[82] Althaus-Reid, 2000:37.
[83] Althaus-Reid, 2000:39.
[84] Althaus-Reid, 2000:39.
[85] Althaus-Reid, 2000:53.
[86] Althaus-Reid, 2000:46.
[87] Althaus-Reid, 2000:52.
[88] Althaus-Reid, 2000:7.
[89] Althaus-Reid, 2000:7.
[90] Althaus-Reid, 2000:170.
[91] Althaus-Reid, 2000:174.
[92] Althaus-Reid, 2000:174.
[93] Althaus-Reid, 2000:179.
[94] Althaus-Reid, M., (2003), "On Non-Docility and Indecent Theologians: A Response to the Panel for *Indecent Theology*", *Feminist Theology*, Vol.11(2), p.185.
[95] Althaus-Reid, 2000:170.
[96] Althaus-Reid, 2000:176.
[97] Althaus-Reid, 2000:100.
[98] Althaus-Reid, 2000:96.
[99] Althaus-Reid, 2000:95.
[100] Althaus-Reid, 2000:108.
[101] Althaus-Reid, 2000:49.
[102] Althaus-Reid, 2000:65-66.
[103] Althaus-Reid, 2000:39.
[104] Althaus-Reid, 2000:71.
[105] Althaus-Reid, 2000:71.
[106] Althaus-Reid, 2000:69.
[107] Goss, R., (1993), *Jesus Acted Up: A Gay and Lesbian Manifesto*, New York: Harper and Collins.
[108] Althaus-Reid, 2000:71.
[109] Althaus-Reid, 2000:74.
[110] Althaus-Reid, 2000:74.
[111] Althaus-Reid, 2000:4.
[112] Althaus-Reid, 2000:70.
[113] Carrette, 2001:291.
[114] Althaus-Reid, M., (2001a), "Outing Theology: Thinking Christianity out of the Church Closet, *Feminist Theology*, 27, pp.62-63.

[115] Althaus-Reid, 2000:6.
[116] Althaus-Reid, 2000:65.
[117] Althaus-Reid, 2000:106.

Chapter Six

Christian Tradition, Authority and Feminisms

Introduction

From the historical overview of the emergence of feminist informed theologies to the detailed unpacking of three strategies of feminist Christian encounter in relation the work of Carter Heyward, Elisabeth Schüssler Fiorenza and Marcella Althaus-Reid, this chapter moves on to ask focussed questions of the implications and effects of these strategies for the two partners in this shifting encounter - Christianity and feminisms. It asks questions of the ways in which the encounters of feminisms and Christianity are facilitated in the work of the three theologians studied, especially in terms of the roles, values and authority given respectively to feminisms and Christianity. As such, this is not a qualitative assessment of the effectiveness of each of these strategies. It is not putting forward an argument for one of the strategies being more "successful", more "Christian" or more "feminist" than the others. Neither is it intended as a concluding systematic overview and analysis of the strategies of feminist Christian encounter.

As has been stressed throughout this study, there are other possible strategies of encounter, and different versions of the strategies that have been focused on here, that might be identified and explored. The identification of three strategies, and the choice of theologians, is individual and personal to the intentions of this study. Some explanation and rationale can be given for the choice, but even this has to be recognised as grounded and specific, and based in a personal reading. For example, the first two theologians studied, Heyward and Schüssler Fiorenza, might in some key respects be described as traditional feminist informed theologians. Their significance to this study, and one of the reasons for focusing on their work, is the impact that their approach has had on the overall development of the field of feminist Christian encounter and especially as theologians who were active in the earlier days of feminist Christian encounters. But at the same time, their significance here is not limited to their earlier contribution, it is also the movement or development of method in terms of the critical base of feminisms within their feminist informed theologies, that are important. Which is a movement or development that is so vital when trying to get some sort of sense of the overall ways in which feminisms and Christianity are in dialogue and are encountering each other. Feminist Christian strategies it seems, if one accepts the claims made by some, are at some kind of critical crossroads in which questions of the viability and relevance of feminisms for Christianity are the determining agenda. The focus on the approach of Althaus-Reid in chapter five, again is bound up with authorial reading of the significance of her approach for the development of feminist Christian encounters. And in particular with the claim that her theology incorporates and announces some of the very radical implications of the critical crossroads that feminist Christian strategies find themselves at. Even so, despite the rationale for the choice of these three theologies for detailed focus in this study, there are many other theologies that might well present themselves as candidates for investigation here. Among those whose approaches to feminist Christian encounter might offer different perspectives and strategies of engagement are, Kwok Pui-lan, Mary McClintock Fulkerson, Katie Cannon, Letty Russell, Ada Isasi-Diaz, Elizabeth Johnson, Mercy Oduyoye, Rita Brock, Mary Grey and Sheila Greeve Davaney. For example, Kwok Pui-lan might be included for her postcolonial approach to feminist biblical interpretation among Asian Christian women; or Mary McClintock Fulkerson might be included for her poststructuralist feminist approach to the analysis of gender and gender difference, and her challenge to the universalising tendencies of feminist theologies. However, not withstanding the importance of such theologians to any understanding of the strategies of feminist Christian encounter, the questions that present themselves here relate specifically to the issues of how feminisms and Christianity encounter each other in the work of Heyward, Schüssler Fiorenza and Althaus-Reid.

The process of addressing such questions in this final chapter will include an overview of the strategies of the three theologians as unpacked in the previous chapters, drawing out key strategic aspects that enable and shape feminist Christian encounters in their theologies. Here, focus will specifically be on the relationships between Christianity and feminisms in their work. This will be approached by consideration first of the question of feminisms, tradition and authority, before focusing on the problematising of feminisms. This is effect constitutes a return to the centre of this study. It will ask of the relationship between feminisms and Christian traditions in the work of each of the theologians with reference to the closely related issue of the bases of authority in these theologies. It then focuses on the problematisation of feminisms and feminist informed theologies and the impact of this on the strategies of feminist Christian encounter. Here, the approaches of Heyward and Schüssler Fiorenza are revealed as incorporating important shifts in response to the changing perceptions of feminisms and the work of Althaus-Reid as representing a significant and distinctively different kind of feminist Christian encounter. This also relates to another important issue that needs to be taken into account, that of the challenges of poststructuralism and postmodernism in terms of questioning the 'truth' and 'liberation' agendas of modernist theologies, and shaping the work of some contemporary theologians. In all of this the strategies of Heyward, Schüssler Fiorenza and Althaus-Reid will be variously questioned for the place and understanding of Christianity in their theologies, and the kind of significance and role that feminisms have here. In asking such questions the function and authority of the different partners of feminisms and Christian theology will be interrogated in order to reveal the mechanisms of feminist Christian encounter in relation to the three strategies identified.

Tradition and authority

Questions of the critical bases of authority in the theologies of Heyward, Schüssler Fiorenza and Althaus-Reid relate to the place and function of feminisms and Christianity in each of these encounters. These do not constitute a return to questions of compatibility and incompatibility but rather arise out of and so question the dialogical relationship between feminisms and Christianity, or feminisms and tradition. Given the very different perspectives and approaches to Christianity and feminisms taken in the indecent theology of Althaus-Reid, the same questions in some senses do not really arise. However, the same questions can be put to her theology, not with the expectation of answering them in the same way as in relation to the theologies of Schüssler Fiorenza and Heyward but as a starting point for working out possible points of departure for feminist informed theologies. The kinds of questions that might be asked of these theologies, and specifically of the relationship between feminisms, tradition and authority in these theologies include:

1. What are the guiding principles or criteria of each of these theologies?
2. What determines the shape, inclusion and focus of these theologies?
3. What criteria of appropriateness or perhaps even "orthodoxy" lie at the heart of different approaches?

However, the question that will be used to take this study forward to conclusion will be the simplistically framed: *how do each of the theologies investigated employ the radical insights of feminisms whilst at the same time maintain a clear relationship to the perceived Christian tradition?*

Carter Heyward and radical reinterpretation

Carter Heyward's strategy of radical reinterpretation was examined in chapter three in relation to her feminist informed reinterpretation of christology. In her theology she has developed a feminist informed and often necessarily radical, reinterpretation of Christian symbols and traditions. This approach, according to her own understanding, maintains a clear relationship to the traditions of Christianity whilst at the same time offers a feminist rereading or reinterpretation of the meaning and relevance of these traditions. As part of this she argues for a compassionate christology of mutual relationship, which is not just incidental to her understanding of justice, but as central to it. Injustice, according to her understanding, is not limited or confined to gender based injustice. Rather, she argues for a spectrum of human experiences of injustice that includes racism, sexism, classism, militarism, imperialism and anti-Semitism. However, despite this recognition of a diversity of human experiences of injustice, she seems to place with feminisms some kind of priority or special significance as a tool for seeking justice. This in part can be explained by her own experiences and, in particular, by the role that feminisms have played in uncovering and challenging the injustices that she has faced. From very early on in her formal theological training at seminary she encountered feminisms as an alternative explanation or worldview by which she could not only make sense of her own experiences of exclusion and marginalisation, relating to both gender and sexuality, but also as an alternative framework of justice to which she could make an authoritative appeal to challenge the traditional authorities threatening exclusion. This is effected through her understanding of the shared commitment of Christianity and feminisms to justice and mutuality.

Carter Heyward accepts that feminisms bring radical challenges to Christianity but sees such challenges as both acceptable and necessary. The challenges, as she understands them, are to the "traditions" of Christianity that have developed as a "stumbling block"[1] to Christian faith. In fact, rather than seeing feminist informed theology as threatening to the identity or traditions of Christianity, she sees it as traditional, and describes herself as a "traditionalist".[2] What she is doing here is to relocate the Christian tradition, and the criteria for identifying or locating Christianity here is justice, which can be discerned through the justice seeking tool of feminisms. Feminisms, then, rather than being a problem for Christianity, is in fact a tool of authentic, liberating Christianity, necessary because of historical distortions. She claims a very strong tradition of continuity between her own feminist informed experiences and the earliest Christian experiences, to the extent that she argues for "...continuity between the life and teachings of Jesus and contemporary events among women in the church".[3] As such, her theological concern in part is with Jesus, rather than the traditions of the Christian Church that have grown up around him.

Heyward's concept of a theology of mutual relation brings together her thinking on the religious or spiritual significance of Jesus and the political, theological significance of feminisms. It is also where the direct and uncompromising relationship that she claims for her theology with Jesus is to be found, through the shared commitment to mutuality and to relationality. She is very critical in her thinking of alienating or estranging theologies that stress distinction or separation between humanity and God. Her concern is with a theology of connection, in which God and humanity are "co-creative"[4] and where injustice is alienation from mutual relationship:

> The theological norm is the primary hermeneutical principle...the theological norm operative for me is right-relation or the love of ones neighbor as oneself. In the Old and New Testaments this is referred to as the 'second commandment'...[5]

Heyward's theology is a relational theology of justice informed by feminist values and methods that aims to overcome all forms of alienation and injustice through a particular focus on christology. Her sustained feminist critical focus on the traditions and images of Jesus brings a radical shift from a theology that stresses the unique revelatory and redemptive significance of Jesus to a theology that emphasises the possibilities of mutuality as evidenced in the life and teachings of Jesus. As was described earlier, Heyward develops a functional christology that is concerned with the actions rather than the nature of Jesus for what they can suggest or exemplify for humanity, seeing the Jesus' story as "a window into our own".[6] The significance of Jesus was in terms of his meaning for mutuality and relationality:

> JESUS' historical significance – his Christic, or redemptive, meanings – originated in his faith in the power that he experienced in relation to sisters and brothers. Thus, any discussion of JESUS is a discussion of power.[7]

Mutual relation is the source of liberation, and so theologies of mutual relation are liberation, justice seeking theologies in which the role of Jesus is revealing of the radical possibilities of mutual relationship, through which transformatory re-imaging possibilities exist. And Christianity is "...a revolutionary political call and a spiritual home.[8] So, it is through the development of her theology of mutual relation, and the central place within this that she gives to the central Christian figure and symbol of Jesus, that she is able to bring the often radical insights and critiques of feminisms to Christianity, whilst at the same time claim a clear relationship to the perceived Christian tradition. She renames or reconfigures a justice seeking Christianity in which there is a very definite continuity between the theology of mutual relation, Christ and feminist informed theology. In this way, then, in reflecting in *The Redemption of God* she rejects the description of her theological approach as "...a faulty hermeneutic given zealous voice by one confused woman",[9] claiming instead that it is "...a recurrent voice of orthodox Christians".[10]

Schüssler Fiorenza and feminist recovery and reconstruction

Elisabeth Schüssler Fiorenza's strategy of the historical location, recovery and reconstruction of "authentic Christianity" was explored in chapter four as the second strategy of feminist Christian encounter. It was explored specifically in relation to her feminist reconstructionist approach to the recovery and elaboration of the early Christian tradition. The hermeneutics of suspicion, central to her approach, challenges the traditional authority of biblical texts. This is underpinned by the feminist claim that as biblical texts have been used as tools to oppress and silence women they need now to be subjected to rigorous critical scrutiny before they can be accorded any kind of function or authority in the lives of women and men. Her theology is based on a reading of Christianity, or at least authentic Christianity, as inherently justice seeking or liberative. Christian theology for Schüssler Fiorenza is not only contextual and specific but has a particular commitment as an advocacy theology:

> Only when theology is on the side of the outcast and oppressed, as Jesus was, can it become incarnational and Christian. Christian theology, therefore, has to be rooted in emancipatory praxis and solidarity.[11]

From this she then appeals to an understanding of an original or authentic Christian message of equality that she argues has been marginalized and silenced by the patriarchal movements of recorded history and societal and religious development. She points back in historical terms to an original justice based Christian vision and praxis free from oppressive tendencies. Her feminist reconstructionist model aims to liberate the egalitarian impulses of the early Christian movement and engage them constructively in contemporary contexts. So, she claims historical credence for her reading or interpretation of Christianity as justice seeking, although the basis or evidence for this has been open to some criticism. Schüssler Fiorenza claims that the historical processes by which the initial or original Christian message was recorded, transmitted and developed were influenced by kyriarchal concerns and interests. As a result this means that the egalitarian Christian experience has largely been erased or marginalised to the extent that a radical approach of recovery or reconstruction is needed to piece together this largely lost tradition:

> Just as the woman in the parable sweeps the whole house in search of her lost coin, so feminist critical interpretation searches for the lost traditions and visions of liberation among its inheritance of androcentric biblical texts and their interpretations.[12]

So, the radicalism or feminisms in their reading, critique and reconstruction of Christianity are not only justified but necessary given the distorting historical processes of transmission and development. The egalitarian vision or discipleship of equals that Schüssler Fiorenza places at the centre of Christian history and at the centre of the Christian experience is incorporated and maintained by feminist visions and values. The critical process of discerning or uncovering this egalitarian Christian tradition is guided by women's experiences and feminist informed interpretation of this experience. In Schüssler Fiorenza's feminist approach to the early Christian traditions, then, women's experiences and feminist values are the determining factor in assessing what is and what is not liberating and so, according to her understanding, what is and what is not authentically Christian.

Like Carter Heyward, Schüssler Fiorenza does seem to place particular significance with the experiences of women and feminisms as tools for uncovering and challenging injustice. Mary McClintock Fulkerson in *Changing the Subject* (1994) has characterised Schüssler Fiorenza's approach granting, "...priority to the principle of the struggle for justice for women, a norm for revelation that is parallel to the norm of full humanity within Ruether's model".[13] Many analyses of the methods of feminist informed theologies distinguish very clearly between the approaches of Schüssler Fiorenza and Ruether, seeing the first in quite radical terms and second in more traditional and even neo-orthodox terms. And whilst there are some very important distinctions between the two theologians in terms of their feminist informed theologies, within this description of the strategies of feminist Christian encounter Ruether's approach and Schüssler Fiorenza's do share certain characteristics and tendencies, in that they both focus on a specific "historical based" aspect or element of the Christian tradition, which they identify, recover and develop through the use of feminist informed tools and then place this at the centre of their Christian theologies. For Ruether it is the prophetic messianic tradition and for Schüssler Fiorenza it is the egalitarian discipleship of equals. The discipleship of equals in Schüssler Fiorenza's theology is understood in the following way:

> The praxis and vision of Jesus and his movement is best understood as an inner-Jewish renewal movement that presented an *alternative* option to the dominant patriarchal structures rather than an oppositional formation rejecting the values and praxis of Judaism.[14]

From this the ekklesia of women, or ekklesia of wo/men, places women's experiences and feminist informed analysis and praxis at the centre of Christian theology. It stresses the historical continuity of the discipleship of equals and contemporary feminist informed Christian theology. And it is in this way that Schüssler Fiorenza can be seen to incorporate the radical insights of feminisms into theology whilst at the same time still claim a direct relationship to the perceived Christian tradition. The authority that she places with the experiences of women and feminist informed analysis determines or guides the theological process. Pamela Dickey Young in exploring the authoritative placing of women's experiences in feminist informed theologies has argued that Schüssler Fiorenza in effect establishes women experiences as "an alternative magisterium".[15]

Both Carter Heyward and Schüssler Fiorenza are concerned to stress the relationship of their feminist informed theologies to the Christian tradition. In the face of apparent radicalism emphasis is placed on continuity with tradition. For Schüssler Fiorenza this is through the feminist informed recovery and reconstruction of the authentic early Christian experience of the discipleship of equals, and for Carter Heyward through the feminist informed reinterpretation of the central Christian figure and symbol of Jesus. In this way the radicalism of feminisms is offset against the claimed direct relationship to authentic tradition or even orthodoxy, as understood in feminist informed terms. There is no doubt that both theologians accept the far-reaching and fundamental criticisms of feminist based analysis that Christianity has participated in and sustained gender based injustice. The feminist informed strategies or radical reinterpretation of the Jesus symbol and the recovery and reconstruction of authentic Christianity stress relationship to tradition whilst at the same time offer what for many amounts to a feminist informed reading of that tradition. In both approaches there is an important differentiation between authentic tradition and received tradition. Authority is with the feminist informed theological approaches adopted and orthodoxy, or orthopraxy, is related to justice. They interpret authentic, marginalised Christianity differently, and employ different feminist informed approaches to reinterpret and reconstruct this reading of Christianity.

Althaus-Reid and the radically contextual queering of Christianity

Marcella Althaus-Reid's indecent theology presents itself as a quite different theological project to the theologies of Carter Heyward and Schüssler Fiorenza, in that Althaus-Reid makes a quite different use of feminisms in her work. Feminisms are really not accepted as a liberal critique or ideology which are being brought into conversation with Christianity or to bear on Christianity as critical, corrective and, most clearly, value-based. In this sense, then, there are not two systems of values, whether competing or not, in encounter. As such, the question of the authoritative functioning of feminisms and Christianity in Althaus-Reid's indecent theology is misplaced, as her focus is not so much on the feminist informed transformation of Christianity as on the questioning and deconstruction of the functioning of Christian theology. It is a theological interruption, an indecent theological interruption that intends to uncover through the process of queering the constraining function of Christian theologies:

> The point is that the political and economic constructions of this world are based on sexual experience, or the interpretation of sexual experience. Theology is from that perspective a sexual act participating in the ideological construction of God from the idealist discourse of what it is supposed to be going to bed with God, the regulations and control discourses based on some heterosexual falsifications or alienations of what is due to reality, and to the people who live under the threats of the naturalisation of sexuality or decency codes in theology.[16]

In this sense, it is a moment of indecency rather than participation in any kind of constructive theological enterprise. It employs queer theory to uncover the participation of Christian theology in the repressive orders of decency and so to ask the question of the relative authoritative functioning of Christianity and feminisms is to misconceive of the project. It does not really participate, or at least hasn't so far, in any kind of constructive theological enterprise. And perhaps to ask of the relationship that it bears to the Christian tradition is to misconceive of the project. This again demonstrates the very different nature of Althaus-Reid's theology. However, the question of the place of feminisms in her theological approach can be asked, and should be asked. This is not to impose a definition of her work as "feminist" to suit a determined methodological framework but to capture something of the different ways in which feminisms are, and might be, participating in encounters with Christianity. As noted in chapter five, the underlying approach or methodological base of Althaus-Reid's indecent theology is queer theory, and not feminist theology as such. Like Heyward and Schüssler Fiorenza, she is very critical of feminist informed theologies in terms of their effectiveness as justice seeking tools, and is especially critical that feminisms and feminist informed theologies have not recognised or addressed the underlying sexual base of injustice, "The gap between a Feminist Liberation Theology and an Indecent Theology is one of sexual honesty".[17] Despite this, she does share some key feminist concerns relating to issues of gender and sexuality. She recognises the place of gender as a key factor in human injustice, as one category of human exclusion. She wants to challenge this exclusion, alongside many others within a Latin American context:

....problematises and undresses the mythical layers of multiple oppression in Latin America, a theology which, finding its point of departure at the crossroads of Liberation Theology and Queer Thinking, will reflect on economic and theological oppression with passion and imprudence. An Indecent Theology will question the traditional Latin American field of decency and order as it permeates and supports the multiple (ecclesiological, theological, political and amatory) structures of life in my country, Argentina, and in my continent.[18]

The critical bases of feminisms, although certainly not exclusive to feminisms, can perhaps been seen as part what informs Althaus-Reid's deconstructive task, to the extent that she is able to describe *Indecent Theology* "...as a critical continuation of Feminist Liberation Theology".[19]

So, the theologies of Schüssler Fiorenza and Heyward both accord very clear significance to feminisms as critical tools of liberation and also as value systems in and of themselves. Within both theologies the use of feminisms is becoming increasingly critical and expansive but there is a very clear commitment to the liberative agenda of feminisms per se. For Schüssler Fiorenza, feminisms are incorporated, in part, as the criteria of inclusion in the reclamation and reconstruction of the early justice seeking, liberative Christian experience. For Carter Heyward, feminisms underpin her theology of mutual relation and her reinterpretation of the figure and symbol of Jesus within this. Within Althaus-Reid's indecent theology the place of feminisms is more ambiguous, but can perhaps be best described as one tool informing the deconstructive indecenting of Christian theology. Both Carter Heyward's and Elisabeth Schüssler Fiorenza's feminist informed theologies in many ways can be seen as shaped by the concerns of modernity. And whilst Althaus-Reid's approach is clearly underpinned by a liberation theological agenda, in methodological terms at least, there is a definite move away from a value based constructive theological project to a more deconstructive, interruptive approach. In many ways questions about the place of feminisms in Christian theology when raised in this way are tied up with the issue of the shape and identities of feminist informed theologies in a postmodern age. And in particular, how do feminist informed theologies make appropriate claims for their justice seeking concerns and visions when many of the problems of feminist informed theologies and feminisms that have so far been uncovered seem to relate to the modernity driven concern with absolutes and possibly with commitment to a liberation agenda?

The problematisation of feminisms and feminist informed theologies

All three of the theologians whose use of the identified strategies has been examined share, to various extents, the recognition of the problematic nature of feminisms, and have incorporated into their work a specific concern with the limitations of feminist informed theologies. And any consideration of the strategies of feminist Christian encounter in the late twentieth century and early twenty-first century needs to give recognition to this increasing reflexivity and critical questioning of feminisms and feminist theologies and the influence that this is having on the strategies of feminist Christian encounter. What can be said is that today the state and place of feminisms in the world is uncertain, they are subject to extensive questioning about their suitability and effectiveness in understanding and challenging gender based difference and inequity. Feminisms and feminist informed theologies are increasingly being seen as problematic in terms of the way in which they have understood and represented themselves and the way in which they understood and represented women. This brings both feminisms and feminist informed theologies to some kind of intense testing ground in which the key factors are questions of relevance, attentiveness to diversity and the challenges of self-reflexivity. The history of feminisms and feminist theologies details a history of fierce expectation followed by limited effectiveness, and often great disappointment. If we listen to some of the voices of discontent and dissatisfaction to be heard in recent years, and there are very strong compulsions to do exactly this, the initial visions of feminisms and feminist theologies seem not to have been realised in any substantial way. Such critical questioning of the effectiveness and validity of feminisms and feminist informed theologies as tools for addressing and overcoming injustice is by no means a new thing. However, in the last few years this has intensified to the extent that there is talk now of a discernible crisis facing feminisms and feminist informed theologies. And the charges against feminisms and feminist informed theologies not only relate to ineffectiveness in failing to adequately address and overcome gender based injustice but relate also to the claim that they have themselves been the cause of further injustices.

Such concerns and criticisms are seen for example in the discourses of women of colour, women of varied and fluid sexualities, and women working out of colonial and post-colonial contexts, some of whom from the beginnings of the explicit second-wave feminist presence in the 1960s have argued that feminism is largely a movement and discourse of limited validity. And more specifically, as a discourse of and for western white, middle-class, and well-educated women, arising out of the experiences of a small group of women but claiming validity for all women. Criticisms have been made of the location, representation and translation of women's experiences, and increasingly, experience has been shown to be an intrinsically unstable aspect of feminisms and so of feminist informed theologies. Mary McClintock Fulkerson has referred to this as "the false universal in feminist appeals to women".[20] And some would argue that the same patterns of exclusion and marginalisation that have been identified in traditional theology have tainted the liberationist project of feminist informed theologies. The implications of the oppressive nature of feminisms and feminist informed theologies, if accepted, are striking. Weisser and Fleischner have argued, for example, that the "Feminist reluctance to come squarely to grips with women's oppression of other women has virtually handed over the problem to critics unsympathetic to feminism".[21]

In feminist informed theologies experiences are increasingly being understood as determinate of theological perspective and criteria. Maria Pillar Aquino in talking of the experiences of Latin Americana feminist theology, points out that:

> For us indigenous women, mestizas, or Afro-Caribbean women, it is radically impossible to disregard the fact that we sprang from a conquered and colonized continent. Our ways of looking at life, understanding our own existence, and interpreting our faith-experience are all indelibly marked by this fact, regardless of whether it results in the perpetuation of an oppressive reality or brings forth emancipatory experiences. Even today the consequences of this historical fact are very much present in our daily life and affect not only how we understand ourselves but also how we do theology what criteria we select for our theologizing, what theological themes we emphasize, and what the ultimate purpose of our theology is.[22]

Kate Coleman also demonstrates such a concern with the importance of recognising the specificity of women's experiences in her explorations of the emergence of British womanist theology, reflecting that just as white feminisms cannot claim to represent all women so black African-American womanist theology cannot claim to speak for British women:

> As Black British women we cannot simply depend upon our insights of our African-American cousins. Our voices must also be heard if we are to achieve liberation. This we require that we dispense with an essentialized concept of Black womanhood and with the idea of monolithic Black identity and instead recognize that there are many and varied models of Black womanhood.[23]

Perhaps one reason why the diversity of women's experiences, the diversity of feminisms and so the diversity of feminist informed theologies have been so difficult to face up to is the concern that in recognising both the particular and the diverse nature of experiences a challenge is in effect made to the self-identity and internal coherence of feminist discourse. In that if it is accepted that different women have different needs, have different experiences of injustice and so different justice needs, then feminisms, as tools of such justice, will by definition need to be diverse. The wider the experiences of women, the more fluid and potentially incoherent feminisms become. But whatever the reason behind this reluctance, recognition of the specific and particular nature of experience must be key here in addressing such problems.

There is clearly no agreement about the state of play of feminisms and feminist informed theologies today, especially in terms of the successes, failures and continuing relevance of feminisms. For some, feminisms have achieved what they set out to, others, however, predict that the goals of feminisms are far from being achieved, and others still talk of a backlash against feminisms, an antifeminist push that challenges and rejects the aims and methods of feminisms. Susan Faludi's *Backlash: The Undeclared War Against Women*,[24] set out clearly in 1991 what was being interpreted as a new antifeminist assault on women. Emilie Townes argues that feminist informed theologies need to recognise the extent and manifestations of the backlashes that women face, and that for black women it takes on particular forms, "The backlash has within it a hierarchy based on race, class, and sexual orientation that has yet to be considered fully".[25] Some interpret this perceived backlash as clear evidence of the continuing injustices that women face. Carter Heyward and Beverly Harrison, for example, claim that:

> Backlash has awakened many women, relieving us of the last vestiges of liberal belief that the struggle for women's liberation is well on the road to victory. Backlash confirms that the situations of women really are as bad as our deepest intuitions lead us to believe. It enables us to value the gains some women have made, some of the rights won – to be doctors, pastors, generals; to own land, homes, businesses; to name ourselves and our children; to choose whom we love, sexually and otherwise; to raise children in partnerships and communities in which new values can be fostered. But backlash also enables us to see that such gains, far from freeing women from violence, also stir men's rage and increase their resistance to what we seek in both the public and private domains of our lives.[26]

Coward offers a different perspective on the concept of backlash as articulated by Faludi, claiming that it "threw feminism a lifeline just when it might have sunk".[27]

As well as questions being raised about the limitations of feminist understandings of women's experiences and their associated exclusions, some of those who have previously articulated a feminist informed position, who have employed feminist based critiques and used the term "feminist" in description of their approach, are now questioning its continuing validity and in fact asking questions as to whether it was ever really effective. Susan Faludi, Camilla Paglia, Naomi Wolf and Rosalind Coward are all influential voices in the articulation of this dissatisfaction. Rosalind Coward, for example, in *Sacred Cows: Is Feminism Relevant to the New Millennium?* claims that the success of the feminist movement has in effect changed the agenda for women. And whilst she recognises that gender based injustices still exist the picture is essentially much more complex now than before. As a result she argues that "Over the last few years...I found it increasingly difficult to say I was a feminist...I had become disenchanted with the idea of being 'a feminist' in such times".[28] And yet she notes the reluctance among those employing feminisms to submit it to what she calls "an audit".[29] She seems to be arguing that feminisms need a different kind of place in the world because of its successes and this leads her to the following claim, that, "Feminism no longer has to be reiterated but simply breathed"[30] and what she seems to be suggesting here is the need for a very different kind of feminism. This however, as Coward acknowledges, will not be easy:

> ...feminism has succeeded beyond the wildest dreams of the brave women who fought its first battles. Its future in the new millennium is to face up to the problems of its success, and to see gender as just one possible reason for social and personal conflicts rather than an all-encompassing cause. But if it is going to be capable of making these changes, it will first have to let go of its sacred cows.[31]

This sense of having to move on to something else was also captured in 1999 in an article published in *Feminist Review*[32] where the concept of snakes and ladders was offered as a metaphor for the situation facing feminisms. Where it was argued that there was a need to move beyond identity politics but a concern with how, given this recognition, feminisms might go forward and how might they be the continued basis of transformatory engagement?,[33] again, a different kind of feminisms was being envisaged.

With such concern over the current state of feminisms and feminist informed theologies there has been increasing talk in recent years of "postfeminism"and the claim that we have moved beyond feminism, or have somehow outgrown feminisms. There is still a certain lack of clarity about what "postfeminism" actually means but clearly for some it has come to be seen as the end of feminisms. For others, the announcement of "postfeminism" offers more hope, and in fact constitutes a significant development in feminisms, Brookes in *Postfeminisms: Feminism, Cultural Theory and Cultural Forms* argues that postfeminisms represents:

> ...feminism's "coming of age", its maturity into a confident body of theory and politics, representing pluralism and difference and reflecting on its position in relation to other philosophical and political movements similarly demanding change.[34]

She argues that postfeminism marks the moving of...feminist theory into a position that she sees as "resisting closure of definition".[35] Such a proposal as is made by Brookes here of the place of feminist theory brings in another important issue in the destabilising and possible reconfiguration of feminisms and feminist informed theologies. To do with constraints about what actually constitutes a feminist or feminist informed approach. As noted in chapter four, Schüssler Fiorenza has faced criticisms by feminists for the way in which she has included serious methodological and theoretical engagement in her theological approach:

> Even today, feminist students will occasionally accuse me of "male scholarship" because my book *In Memory of Her* is full of footnotes and written in a "logical-linear" style. Although I can understand such a sentiment, given the bad experiences women have had in academic institutions, I could never share this view. It tends to replicate the cultural stereotype that restricts logical thinking and disciplined intellectual work to men and thereby prohibits women from producing knowledge and from defining the world.[36]

Related to this, a suspicion of theory has also claimed a shaping presence in specifically theological feminist discourse to date. And given some of the important ways in which feminisms and feminist informed theologies are reconsidering themselves, such a suspicion is problematic, as is the whole question of development and change in feminisms and feminist informed theologies. For example, Emily Neill, in a 1999 article,[37] reflecting on the publication of *Horizons in Feminist Theology* refers to the "theoretical wrangling"[38] of the collection. She claims, that this work "seems almost completely void of a feminist commitment to use theory and the construction of knowledge to transform structures of oppression and domination".[39] Neill also talks of "a disheartening trend among feminist scholars in religion and theology",[40] and is deeply critical of what she interprets as the progressive depiction of the development of feminist theological theory. For

Neill, this is an understanding in which the value given to the early writers of feminist theology is minimal, and concern here is with a generational split among Christian feminist theologians. She envisages and is critical here of a progressive understanding of new generation feminists which goes beyond, and in a sense diminishes, the significance of, the work of the earlier Christian feminist theologians, what Marla Brettschneider has referred to as "kill the mother syndrome".[41] Neill's concern is important because the issue of feminists criticising other feminists' work is crucial. Emily Culpepper as long ago as 1987 claimed that:

> One of the challenges facing present feminist theory is how to raise overall observations.... without turning them into scapegoating attacks of any particular woman's work. Of course, we must criticize, and these are subjects about which passions run high. But we do not fully reach new ground if our criticisms replicate the patriarchal pattern of horizontal hostility.[42]

It seems that feminist informed theologies, and perhaps feminisms in general, are still quite a way from comfortable acceptance and recognition of the integrity and necessity of detailed critical analysis and deconstruction of themselves. Teresa Ebert in her feminist materialist critique of postmodernism, poststructuralism and feminist discourses, *Ludic Feminism and After: Postmodernism, Desire and Labor in Late Capitalism*,[43] offers another perspective in exploring the issue of feminist informed criticism of feminisms, arguing that:

> We thus need to ask why critique, when aimed at other feminists, is misrecognized as trashing, as uncorteous demolition. What is at stake in this misreading, and can critique be understood in more productive terms?"[44]

For many, at a time in which questions are being asked of the location, future and critical edge of both feminisms and feminist informed theologies, such an interaction is vital. Recent studies such as *Horizons in Feminist Theology* mark the emergent questioning of the theoretical identity and perspectives of feminist informed theologies, along with recognition of the ambiguous status of such a questioning. This collection voices and explores issues of gender, theory, norms, practice and experience in the context of the patterns and identity of feminist theological discourse, and may prove to be a very important text for the development of feminist theological discourse. As Davaney argues:

> Many feminists, including the contributors to this volume, have been exploring theoretical issues and rehabilitating the category of theory in general.
> ...a turn to theory is not a covert return to the grand theories of old but a commitment to critical analysis that seeks to make clear the often implicit and unacknowledged presuppositions that shape our feminist proposals.
> ...Trafficking with theory is thus not, for the contributors of this volume, an exercise in abstract thinking, disengaged from the real concerns of feminist work, but the self-conscious attempt to confront and take responsibility for the assumptions we hold and the repercussions that flow from them.[45]

It is being recognised by many that theory offers much, in terms of analysis, promise and possibility and in a similar way, feminist based criticism of feminisms brings an essential critical edge to feminisms and feminist informed theologies. It helps to avoid the normative positioning of any one woman's or any one group of women's experiences. Part of the task now facing feminist informed Christian theologies is to simply acknowledge that feminist theory has, and continues to have, a key role in the shaping of such theologies. The collection *Transfigurations: Theology and the French Feminists*[46] edited by Maggie Kim, Susan M. St. Ville and Susan M. Simonaitis has contributed to this important recognition. By focusing on the work of Luce Irigaray, Hélène Cixous and Julia Kristeva, the contributors have addressed issues of how French feminisms can inform contemporary feminist theological discourse. The papers in this collection are informative and intriguing in the possibilities opened up by a direct, specific conversation between feminist informed Christian theology and French gender based theory.

The place of theory in feminisms and feminist informed theologies is clearly complex, but important. Andrea Nye argues that "Contemporary feminist theory is a tangled and forbidding web"[47] and yet also acknowledges that, "...women urgently require the answers that feminist theory promises".[48] The movement and responses of theory, and reflection on theory, are intrinsic aspects of feminisms and feminist informed theologies, which require self-conscious recognition and exploration. Contemporary theology exists neither in a state of isolation nor privilege and the study of theology is an increasingly diverse activity. Those engaged with feminist informed theologies in a variety of guises have an array of relationships and defining motivations that may be a fruitful resourcing of such engagement. And a key part of the contemporary challenge to feminist informed theologies is to reflect on, and respond to, the ever-expanding concerns and participants on theology. For feminisms generally, there is clearly evident a tension between theory and praxis, however, this tension is seen by some in more creative terms, and so concern does not have to be with the resolution of this tension. Rather than problematic, critical explorations in theory are, potentially, a massive resource for feminisms and feminist informed theologies.

Strategic options where now?

Having outlined some concerns and problems with the viability of feminisms and feminist informed theologies as tools or mechanisms for overcoming gender based injustice the question arises as to whether feminisms really do have a future in relation to such tasks? This is not an easy question either to ask or to answer, but what is clear is that more than ever feminisms are diverse in form, address and context. One of the problems when talking about the failure of feminisms and about whether feminisms are any longer relevant, is that despite the critical work that has been carried out, in some ways feminisms are still being seen as homogenous, as one thing with one aim. When clearly, for many different people feminisms have meant many different things. Returning to the specific theologies examined in depth in this study, for example, Heyward, Schüssler Fiorenza and Althaus-Reid have all to some extent recognised the problems that feminisms and feminist informed theologies present in terms of exclusions. Exclusions seem to be linked to processes of normalisation whereby particular feminist informed critiques, visions theologies etc. become authoritative in and of themselves. And one of the factors that influences such tendencies is the kinds of roles that feminisms are actually given. Which is linked to questions of what exactly, especially in the context of examining feminist informed Christian theologies, the feminist base actually is? Is it a social movement, a set of values, a worldview, or a critical force? As has already been seen, feminisms and feminist informed theologies, clearly cannot claim to know or understand either injustice or the justice needs of women in any kind of definitive way, and when they do, they tend to exclude and to close themselves down. Problems emerge precisely when feminisms have become normative or prescriptive and become concerned with the articulation of a set vision rather than visionary. Understandings of the sites of injustice and the possibilities of justice need to remain fluid. It seems that a fuller but also consistently open picture is needed and self-reflexive feminisms and accompanying critical questioning of feminisms is entirely appropriate and in fact essential.

As the theologies of Heyward and Schüssler Fiorenza suggest, and the theology of Althaus-Reid very strongly announces recognition of the problems of feminisms have very definite implications for feminist informed theologies. And given the radically contextual approach to understanding and responding to gender based injustice questions need to be asked about what this amounts to for feminist informed theologies. Is it the end of such theologies? In one sense, yes, because it is the end of feminist theology in its singularity but this could also mean that what we understand as feminisms or feminist informed theologies will constantly be broken down, as is perhaps being seen in the theology of Althaus-Reid. And through such expansion in the end different feminist informed theologies may well bear no clear or coherent relationship to each other. The guiding factor to the engagement and validity of feminisms, feminist and womanist theologies, is contextual needs and one example of how a radically contextual theology or response to injustice might engage feminism as a tool of critical disclosure and move towards justice illustrates the possibilities here. Explorations in the contemporary viability of feminism as tools of justice seem to raise many questions and offer very few clear pathways for action and analysis. However, the questions that do emerge seem to underpin the very heart of feminist justice projects and to indicate something of the challenges and radical possibilities for social transformation if addressed with openness. Perhaps feminisms should be seen as something much less stable and as open to multiple definitions and developments, as a movement towards critical interrogation and analysis, and not as the substantive point of reference. As functional, as a tool of critical analysis or critical disclosure and not the solution in and of itself. Feminism needs to constantly subvert itself and this may well result in a fragmentation in which what is left is not discernibly feminist from what we have understood as feminist so far. The 1999 publication *Is There a Future for Feminist Theology?*[49] edited by

Deborah Sawyer and Diane Collier raised some important issues in relation to the way in which feminist informed theologies in the new millennium might reconstitute themselves. Ursula King in her contribution to the collection "Feminist Theologies in Contemporary Contexts"[50] laid down a comprehensive challenge to those engaged with feminist informed theologies:

> In spite of all that has been achieved there is still a need for feminist theologians to get out of their own isolation − whether institutionally imposed or intellectually adopted − and develop a more fully dialogical approach, not only among themselves in different parts of the world or with women of many different faith traditions, but also through reflecting from their experience of solidarity and sisterhood on some of the burning questions of our time.[51]

At the heart of such an analysis of the continuing relevance of feminisms is the conviction that the shifting nature of society, culture and critical understanding means that many forms of feminisms and feminist informed theologies can no longer, if in fact they ever really did, meet the needs of many of those seeking to overcome perceived injustices surrounding issues of gender and sexualities. Also, that if feminisms are to have validity or relevance at this stage in the twenty-first century as a tool of critical disclosure pushing towards justice seeking practices, then a solid revisioning of feminism, based in contextual needs and forms, is needed. And beyond this, it is in fact very difficult to say anything fixed about feminisms and feminist theologies if they are not to slide again towards ineffectiveness through stasis.

Many of the issues and questions that have emerged from this study of the strategies of feminist Christian encounter relate to issues of authority, even orthodoxy, and tradition. Feminisms are accorded authority in feminist informed Christian theologies alongside the Christian tradition, in a complex interplay of dependent relationships, where in some cases authentic Christianity is only really known, or can only really be discerned, through the critical lens of feminisms and feminist interpreted experiences. The authoritative place of feminisms and Christianity within the overall scheme of feminist informed theologies then is crucial to understanding the mechanisms of feminist Christian encounter. Feminist informed theologians such as Schüssler Fiorenza and Heyward accord authority, although in different ways, to both feminisms and the Christian tradition (as they understand it in its authentic or original forms). As Serene Jones has argued, "When feminists attempt to reconceive of the nature of theological sources, they immediately confront the question of authority. How does one determine which texts are normatively illustrative of a given tradition and which texts are marginal to the development of a historical theology?"[52] and from this she notes "...feminists have discovered new norms, alternative boundaries".[53]

Major shifts are apparent in the work of some theologians such as Althaus-Reid as they try to take on board some of the insights and critiques that are being levelled at feminisms and feminist informed theologies. Such critiques amount to a challenge to the underlying liberation agenda and claims to truth of feminisms and feminist informed theologies. Grace Jantzen in *Becoming Divine*[54] questions such a concern with truth and is interested in a more pragmatic ethical theological focus. Kwok Pui-lan is very clear on the problems facing feminist informed theologies in the twenty-first century, and argues that they face significant challenges to relevancy:

> Much of contemporary feminist theology in the West is premised on the liberal project of the assertion of an individualist female subject and of achieving equality between the sexes based on the Enlightenment ideals of equality and liberty. Such a narrow and individualistic theoretical framework proves to be ill equipped to meet the challenges of colonialism and post-war development, and will not provide adequate tools to analyse the newest stage of global capitalism. In the past, much energy has been devoted to reinterpreting sexist biblical and theological texts, inclusive language in worship, re-evaluating church teachings on sexuality, and on the ordination of women. Whilst these struggles are clearly necessary, feminist theology in the twenty-first century must have a broader vision to develop a new theoretical discourse to analyse how economic domination intersects with cultural and religious production, and to articulate ways women can participate in shaping their future in the age of globalization.[55]

Susan Parsons in *Challenging Women's Orthodoxies in the Context of Faith* (2000) also recognises some of the problems that face feminist informed theologies as she reflects on the "established orthodoxies of what have been become feminisms and feminist theologies".[56] She comes to speak of feminist theologies as fundamental theology[57] and asks questions about what a "renewed orthodoxy"[58] in feminist informed theologies might be. Parsons in her reflections names one of the challenges for feminisms as follows:

> So feminism is challenged to explain why it cannot be dissolved without residue into pragmatism, and herein lie some difficult questions about feminist collusions in a culture of technique, and in a theological and philosophical thinking the human person that fixes the horizon of our transcending at the limits of the technically possible, the do-able.[59]

Harriet Harris claims that the postmodern rejection of certainty should not be on the feminist agenda, and argues that "...we must not give up on truth...we should work to disclose truth".[60] For Harris truth is not the misguided concern of the epistemologist but a moral, spiritual task. The problem seems to be one of how a project that very much has its roots in the Enlightenment can respond to the criticisms of poststructuralism and postcolonialism. And if it can and does respond and transform itself accordingly and perhaps inevitably lose its liberal, modern agenda then surely there will no longer be any need for it.

Some theologians are questioning the most challenging outworkings of the postmodern critique, whilst accepting some of its insights. For example, Schüssler Fiorenza in responding to the issues of how feminisms and feminist informed theologies can operate in a postmodern age, challenges the postmodern doubting that authentic "working across borders" can really happen and claims that it has been happening in feminisms. She calls on feminist informed theologies to engage likewise and despite all of the advancements made in the area in respect of attention to diversity and recognition of the problematization debate is still very critical of some of the workings of feminist informed theologies:

> The slogan "think globally, act locally" has become a clarion call for feminist grassroots movements and theorists alike in their struggle against neoliberal capitalist globalization. However, feminist theologians and scholars in religion have not paid sufficient attention to this intellectual and political context. In my experience feminist discourses in religion tend to continue to draw exclusive boundaries between theology and religious studies, between the various subdisciplines of theology, between the West and the Rest, between Christians and members of other religions, and between the academic study of religion and feminist movements in religion. Moreover, although feminists in religion have problematized race, gender, class and colonialism, very little attention has been paid to nationalism and its impact on wo/men in religion as well as on the academic study of religion and theology.[61]

In many ways the kinds of criticisms that feminisms and feminist informed theologies are facing, and the kinds of responses that are beginning to be made to these critiques, seem to be pointing towards a different kind of place and use for feminisms in the contemporary world. As Susan Gubar in *Critical Condition*[62] asks "Do our disputes prove that feminist criticism is self-destructing or that it is going through a transition that will issue in innovative modes of inquiry?".[63] These innovative models of enquiry that Gubar is referring to may well be glimpsed in the work of theologians such as Marcella Althaus-Reid, Mary McClintock Fulkerson and Sheila Greeve Davaney. Where there is a discernible shift away from values and truth to a more functional or pragmatic theological use for feminisms.

Notes

[1] Heyward, C., (1999b), *A Priest Forever*, Cleveland, Ohio: The Pilgrim Press, p.5.
[2] Heyward, 1999b:5.
[3] Heyward, 1984:8.
[4] Heyward, 1982:2.
[5] Heyward, 1982:15.
[6] Heyward, 1999a: 10.
[7] Heyward, 1999a: 66.
[8] Heyward, 1999a: 36.
[9] Heyward, 1982:xvii.
[10] Heyward, 1982:xvii.
[11] Schüssler Fiorenza, 1975:616.
[12] Schüssler Fiorenza, 1984:16.
[13] McClintock Fulkerson, M., (1994), *Changing the Subject: Women's Discourses and Feminist Theology*, Minneapolis: Fortress Press, pp.34-35.
[14] Schüssler Fiorenza, 1983:105.
[15] Young, P.D., (1990), *Feminist Theology/Christian Theology: In Search of Method*, Eugene, OR: Wipf and Stock Publishers, p.81.

[16] Althaus-Reid, 2000:23-24.
[17] Althaus-Reid, 2000:7.
[18] Althaus-Reid, 2000:2.
[19] Althaus-Reid, 2000:7.
[20] S.G. Davaney in Rebecca S. Chopp, and Davaney, S.G., (eds.), (1997), *Horizons in Feminist Theology: Identity, Tradition and Norms* Minneapolis: Fortress Press, p.99.
[21] Weisser, S., and Fleischner, J., (eds.), (1994), *Feminist Nightmares: Women at Odds - Feminism and the Problem of Sisterhood*, New York and London: New York University Press, p.5.
[22] Aquino, M.P., in Isasi-Diaz, A.M. and Segovia, F.F., (eds.), (1996), *Hispanic/Latino Theology: Challenge and Promise* Fortress Press, pp.240-241.
[23] Coleman, K., "Black theology and black liberation: a womanist perspective" in *Black Theology*, 1, (1998), p.68.
[24] Faludi, S., (1991), *Backlash: The Undeclared War Against Women*, Random House.
[25] Townes, E.M., in Harrison, B.W., Heyward, C., Hunt, M.E., Townes, E.M., Starhawk, Barstow, A.L., and Cooey, P.M., (1994), Roundtable discussion: backlash", *Journal of Feminist Studies in Religion*, 10(1), p.102.
[26] Harrison, B.W., and Heyward, C., in Harrison, B.W., Heyward, C., Hunt, M.E., Townes, E.M., Starhawk, Barstow, A.L., and Cooey, P.M., (1994), "Roundtable discussion: backlash", *Journal of Feminist Studies in Religion*, 10(1), p.94.
[27] Coward, R., (1999), *Sacred Cows: Is Feminism Relevant to the New Millennium?* London: HarperCollins Publishers, p.10.
[28] Coward, R., (1999), *Sacred Cows: Is Feminism Relevant to the New Millennium?* London: HarperCollins Publishers, p.4.
[29] Coward, 1999:7.
[30] Coward, 1999:7.
[31] Coward, 1999:14.
[32] Hall, C., O'Sullivan, Phoenix, A., Thomas, L., and Whitehead, A., (1999), "Snakes and ladders: reviewing feminisms at century's end", *Feminist Review*, 61, pp.1-3.
[33] Hall, C., et al, 1999:1.
[34] Brookes, A., (1997), *Postfeminisms: Feminism, Cultural Theory and Cultural Forms* London: Routledge, p.1.
[35] Brookes, 1997:5.
[36] Schüssler Fiorenza, 1990:798.
[37] Neill, E.R., Brettschneider, M., Grunenfelder, R., Grace Ji-Sun Kim, Martinez, P.A., Witte, K., Iwamura, J.N., Washington, D., "Roundtable discussion: from generation to generation horizons in feminist theology or reinventing the wheel?", *Journal of Feminist Studies in Religion*, 1999, 15(1), pp.102-138.
[38] Neill in Neill, et al, 1999:104.
[39] Neill in Neill, et al, 1999:104-5.
[40] Neill in Neill, et al, 1999:102.
[41] Brettschneider, M., in Neill, E., et al, 1999:111.
[42] Culpepper in Atkinson, C.W, Buchanan, C.H., and Miles, M., (eds.), 1987:53.
[43] Ebert, T.L., (1996), *Ludic Feminism and After: Postmodernism, Desire, and Labor in Late Capitalism*, The University of Michigan Press.
[44] Ebert, 1996:4.
[45] Davaney, S.G., in Chopp, R.S., and Davaney, S.G., (eds.) (1997), *Horizons in Feminist Theology: Identity Tradition and Norms*, Minneapolis: Fortress Press, pp.2-3.
[46] Kim, M.C.W., St. Ville, S.M., and Simonaitis, S., (eds.), (1993), *Transfigurations: Theology and the French Feminists*, Minneapolis: Fortress Press.

⁴⁷ Nye, A., (1988), *Feminist Theories and the Philosophies of Man*, Routledge, p.1.
⁴⁸ Ibid.
⁴⁹ Sawyer, D.F., and Collier, D.M., (eds.), (1999), *Is There a Future for Feminist Theology?*, Sheffield: Sheffield Academic Press.
⁵⁰ King, U., (1999), "Feminist Theologies in Contemporary Contexts" in Sawyer, D.F., & Collier, D.M., (eds.), (1999), *Is There a Future for Feminist Theology?*, Sheffield: Sheffield Academic Press, pp.100-114.
⁵¹ King, (1999), in Sawyer, D.F., and Collier, D.M., (eds.), p.111.
⁵² Jones, in Russell, L., and Shannon, J., (ed.), (1996), *Dictionary of Feminist Theologies*, London: Mowbray, p.291.
⁵³ Jones, in Russell, L., and Shannon, J., (ed.), 1996:292
⁵⁴ Jantzen, G.M., (1998), *Becoming Divine: Towards a Feminist Philosophy of Religion*, Manchester: Manchester University Press.
⁵⁵ Pui-lan, K., (2001), "Feminist theology at the dawn of the millennium", *Feminist Theology*, 27, p.11.
⁵⁶Parsons, S., in Parsons, S., (ed.), (2000), *Challenging Women's Orthodoxies in the Context of Faith*, Aldershot: Ashgate, p.4.
⁵⁷ Parsons, in Parsons, S., (ed.), 2000:5.
⁵⁸ Parsons, in Parsons, S., (ed.), 2000:19.
⁵⁹ Parsons, in Parsons, S., (ed.), 2000:15-16.
⁶⁰ Harris, H.A., (2001), "Struggling for truth", *Feminist Theology*, 28, p.40.
⁶¹ Schüssler Fiorenza, E., (2002), "Thinking and working across borders: the Feminist Liberation Theologians, Activists, and Scholars in Religion Network", *Journal of Feminist Studies in Religion*, 2002, 18(1), pp.71-72.
⁶² Gubar, S., (2000), *Critical Condition: Feminism at the Turn of the Century*, New York: Columbia University Press.
⁶³ Gubar, 2000:7.

Bibliography

Abraham, W.J., (1998), *Canon and Criterion in Christian Theology: From the Fathers to Feminism*, Oxford: Clarendon Press.

Adler, M., (1986), *Drawing Down the Moon: Witches, Druids, Goddess-Worshippers, and Other Pagans in America Today*, Boston: Beacon.

Allen, C., and Howard, J.A., (eds.), (2000), *Provoking Feminisms*, Chicago: University of Chicago Press.

Alsop, R., Fitzsimons and Lennon, K., (2002), *Theorizing Gender*, Cambridge: Polity.

Althaus-Reid, M, (1994), "When God is a rich white woman who does not walk", The hermeneutical circle of Mariology in Latin America", *Theology and Sexuality*, 1, pp.55-72.

Althaus-Reid, M, (1997), "Sexual Strategies in Practical Theology. Indecent Theology and the Plotting of Desire With Some Degree of Success", *Theology and Sexuality*, 7, pp.45-52.

Althaus-Reid, M, (1999a), "Sexual Strategies in Practical Theology: Indecent Theology with Some Degree of Success", *Theology and Sexuality*, Vol.7. pp.45-52.

Althaus-Reid, M, (1999b), "On Using Skirts without Underwear. Indecent Theology Contesting the Liberation Theology of the Pueblo: Poor Women Contesting Christ", *Feminist Theology*, 20, pp.39-51.

Althaus-Reid, M., (2000), *Indecent Theology: Theological Perversions in Sex, Gender and Politics*, Routledge.

Althaus-Reid, M., (2001a), "Outing Theology: Thinking Christianity out of the Church Closet, *Feminist Theology*, 27, pp.57-67.

Althaus-Reid, M., (2001b), "Sexual Salvation: The Theological Grammar of Voyeurism and Permutations", *Literature and Theology*, Vol.15 (3), pp.241-248.

Althaus-Reid, M., (2003), "On Non-Docility and Indecent Theologians: A Response to the Panel for *Indecent Theology*", *Feminist Theology*, Vol.11 (2), pp.182-189.

Althaus-Reid, M., The University of Edinburgh Website (no date). Retrieved on 1 June 2003, from the World Wide Web: http://www.div.ed.ac.uk/contact/staff_pages/m_althaus-reid.htm.

Aquino, M.P., and Schüssler Fiorenza, E., (eds.), (2000), *In the Power of Wisdom: Feminist Spiritualities of Struggle*, London: SCM Press.

Armour, E., (1999), *Deconstruction, Feminist Theology, and the Problem of Difference: Subverting the Race/Gender Divide*, Chicago: The University of Chicago Press.

Batsone, D., Mendieta, E., Lorentzen, Hopkins, D, (eds.), (1997), *Liberation Theologies, Postmodernity, and the Americas*, London and New York: Routledge.

Benedict, R., (1935), *Patterns of Culture*, London: Routledge and Kegan Paul.
Benhabib, S., Butler, J., Cornell, D., and Fraser, N., (1995), *Feminist Contentions: A Philosophical Exchange*, New York and London: Routledge.
Berlis, A. et al, (1995), *Women Churches: Networking and Reflection in the European Context*, Kampen: Kok Pharos Publishing House.
Børresen, K., (1968), *Subordination and Equivalence*, Oslo: Oslo University Press.
Braidotti, R., (1994), *Nomadic Subjects: Embodiment and Sexual Difference in Contemporary Feminist Thought*, New York: Columbia University Press.
Braidotti, R., (2002), *Metamorphoses: Towards a Materialist Theory of Becoming*, Cambridge: Polity.
Brooks, A., (1997), *Postfeminisms: Feminism, Cultural Theory and Cultural Forms*, London and New York: Routledge.
Butler, J., (1990), *Gender Trouble: Feminism and the Subversion of Identity*, New York: Routledge.
Cady Stanton, E., (1999), *The Woman's Bible*, U.S.: Prometheus Books.
Campbell, J., (2000), *Arguing With the Phallus: Feminist, Queer and Postcolonial Theory: A Psychoanalytic Contribution*, London and New York: Zed Books.
Cannon, K.G., (1987), "Hitting a straight lick with a crooked stick: the womanist dilemma in the development of a Black liberation ethic", *Annual of the Society of Christian Ethics*, pp.165-177.
Cannon, K.G., (1988), *Black Womanist Ethics*, Ga: Scholars Press.
Cannon, K.G., (1995), *Katie's Canon: Womanism and the Soul of the Black Community*, New York: Continuum.
Carmody, D.L. (1995) *Christian Feminist Theology: A Constructive Response*, Oxford: Blackwell Publishers.
Carr, A., and Schussler Fiorenza, E., (eds.), (1987), *Women, Work and Poverty ("Concillium")*, Edinburgh, T & T Clark.
Carr, A.E., (1988), *Transforming Grace: Christian Tradition and women's Experience*, San Francisco: Harper and Row.
Carrette, J., (2001), "Radical heterodoxy and the indecent proposal of erotic theology: critical groundwork for sexual theologies", *Literature and Theology*, Vol.15(3), 2001, pp.286-298.
Castelli, E.A., (1994), "Heteroglossia, Hermeneutics, and History: A Review Essay of Recent Feminist Studies of Early Christianity", *Journal of Feminist Studies in Religion*, 10(2), pp.73-98.
Chapman, M.D., (ed.), (2002), *The Future of Liberal Theology*, Aldershot:Ashgate.
Chopp, R., (1995), *Saving Work: Practices of Theological Education*, Westminster John Knox Press.
Chopp, R.S., and Davaney, S.G., (eds.), (1997), *Horizons in Feminist Theology: Identity, Tradition and Norms*, Minneapolis: Fortress Press.
Christ, C., (1975) "Spiritual quest and women's experience", *Anima*, 1(2), pp.4-15.
Christ, C., (1977), "The new feminist theology: a review of the literature", *Religious Studies Review*, 3(4), pp.203-212.

Christ, C., (1978), "Expressing anger at God: an essay in story theology", *Anima*, 5(3), pp.3-10.
Christ, C., (1980) *Diving Deep and Surfacing: Women Writers on Spiritual Quest*, Beacon Press.
Christ, C., (1985) "What are the sources of my theology?", *Journal of Feminist Studies in Religion*, 1(1), pp.120-122.
Christ, C., (1989), "Embodied thinking: reflections on feminist thealogical method", *Journal of Feminist Studies in Religion*, 5(14), pp.7-15.
Christ, C., (1995), *Odyssey with the Goddess: A Spiritual Quest in Crete*, New York: Continuum.
Christ, C., (1997), *Rebirth of the Goddess: Finding meaning in Feminist Spirituality*, New York: Routledge.
Christ, C., and Plaskow, J., (eds.), (1992), *Womanspirit Rising: A Feminist Reader in Religion*, San Francisco: Harper SanFrancisco.
Chung, Hyun Kyung, (1991), *Struggle to be Sun Again: Introducing Asian Women's Theology*, London: SCM Press.
Coakley, S., (2002), *Powers and Submissions: Spirituality, Philosophy and Gender*, Oxford: Blackwell.
Coll, R.A., (1998), *Christianity and Feminism in Conversation*, Mystic, Connecticut: Twenty-Third Publications.
Collins, R.F., (1978), "The Bible and sexuality II", *Biblical Theology Bulletin*, 8(1), pp.3-18.
Collins, S.D. (1974), *A Different Heaven and Earth: A Feminist Perspective on Religion*, Judson Press.
Cooey, P.M., Farmer, S.A., and Ross, M.E., (eds.), (1987), *Embodied Love: Sensuality and Relationship as Feminist Values*, San Francisco: Harper and Row.
Cornell, J.C., (2000), *Women Priests, Assimilation and Transformation*, Oxford: Oxford Brookes University.
Coward, R., (1999), *Sacred Cows: Is Feminism Relevant to the New Millennium?* London: HarperCollins Publishers.
Crook, M.B., (1964) *Women and Religion*, Boston: Beacon Press.
Culpepper, E., (1988), "New tools for theology: writings by women of color", *Journal of Feminist Studies in Religion*, 4, pp.39-50.
Culver, E. (1967) *Women in the World of Religion*, Garden City, New York: Doubleday.
Daggers, J., (2002), *The British Christian Women's Movement: A Rehabilitation of Eve*, Aldershot: Ashgate.
Daly, L., (ed.), (1994), *Feminist Theological Ethics: A Reader*, Louisville, Kentucky: Westminster John Knox Press.
Daly, M., (1965), "A built in bias", *Commonweal*, 81, pp.308-311.
Daly, M., (1971), "The courage to see", *Christian Century*, 88(38), pp.1108-1111.
Daly, M., (1972), "The spiritual revolution: women's liberation as theological Reeducation", *Andover Newton Quarterly*, 12(4), pp.163-176.
Daly, M., (1984), *Gyn/Ecology: The Metaethics of Radical Feminism*, London: The Women's Press.

Daly, M., (1985) [1968] *The Church and the Second Sex*, Boston: Beacon Press.
Daly, M., (1986), [1973], *Beyond God the Father: Towards a Philosophy of Women's Liberation*, London: The Women's Press.
Daly, M., (1988), *Webster's First New Intergalactic Wickedary of the English Language*, London: The Women's Press.
Daly, M., (1993), *Outercourse: The Be-Dazzling Voyage*, London: The Women's Press.
Daly, M., (1998), *Quintessence....Realizing the Archaic Future: A Radical Elemental Feminist Manifesto*, Boston: Beacon Press.
Davaney, S.G., (1989), "The limits of the appeal to women's experience", in Atkinson, C., Buchanan, C., and Miles, M., (eds.), *Shaping New Vision: Gender and Values in American Culture*, Ann Arbor: University of Michigan Research Press.
Davaney, S.G., (1991), "Directions in historicism", *Zygon*, 26(2), pp.201-220.
Davaney, S.G., (2000), *Pragmatic Historicism: A Theology for the Twenty-First Century*, New York: State University of New York Press.
De Beauvoir, S., (1981), The *Second Sex*, (translated and edited by H.M. Parshley), Penguin Books.
Doely, S.B., (ed.), (1970) *Women's Liberation and the Church: The New Demand For Freedom in the Life of the Christian Church*. Association Press.
Douglas, K.B., (1994), *The Black Christ*, Maryknoll, New York: Orbis Books.
Doyle, L., (2001), *The Surrendered Wife: A Practical Guide for Finding Intimacy, Passion, and Peace With a Man*, London: Simon and Schuster.
Ebert, T.L., (1996), *Ludic Feminism and After: Postmodernism, Desire, and Labor In Late Capitalism*, The University of Michigan Press.
Eller, C., (1993), *Living in the Lap of the Goddess: The Feminist Spirituality Movement in America*, New York: Crossroad.
Elwes, T., (ed.), (1992), *Women's Voices: Essays in Contemporary Feminist Theology*, London: Marshall Pickering.
Erickson, J.Q., (1983), "What difference? The theory and practice of feminist criticism", *Christianity and Literature*, 33(1), pp.65-74.
Faludi, S., (1991), *Backlash: The Undeclared War Against Women*, Random House.
Faludi, S., (1999), *Stiffed: The Betrayayl of the Modern Man*, London: Chatto and Windus.
Farnham, C., (ed.), (1987), *The Impact of Feminist Research in the Academy*, Bloomington: Indiana University Press.
Field-Bibb, J. (1989) " From *The Church to Wickedary*: the theology and philosophy of Mary Daly", *Modern Churchman*, NS, XXX(4), pp.35-41.
Frascati-Lochhead, M., (1998), *Kenosis and Feminist Theology: The Challenge of Gianni Vattimo*, New York: State University of New York Press.
Freidan, B., (1963), *The Feminine Mystique*, WW Norton and Co.
Fulkerson, M.M., (1994), *Changing the Subject: Women's Discourses and Feminist Theology*, Minneapolis: Fortress Press.
Gage, M.J. (1980) [1893] *Woman, Church and State*, Watertown, Massachusetts: Persephone Press.

Gamble, S., (ed.), (2001), *The Routledge Companion To Feminism and Postfeminism*, London and New York: Routledge.
Gardiner, A.M., (ed.), (1976) *Women and Catholic Priesthood: An Expanded Vision*, Paulist Press.
Giles, J., and Middleton, T., (1999), *Studying Culture: A Practical Introduction*, Oxford: Blackwell Publishers.
Gill, R., (ed.), (1995), *Readings in Modern Theology: Britain and America*, London: SPCK, pp.198-214.
Goldenberg, N., (1979), *Changing of the Gods: Feminism and the End of Traditional Religion*, Boston: Beacon Press.
Goldenberg, N., (1990), *Returning Words to Flesh: Feminism and the End of Traditional Religion*, Boston: Beacon Press.
Goldenberg, N., (1990), Resurrecting the Body: Feminism, Religion and Psychoanalysis, Diane Pub Co.
Goodin, R.E., and Petit, R., (1993), *A Companion to Contemporary Political Philosophy*, Blackwell.
Goss, R.E., (1993), *Jesus ACTED UP: A Gay and Lesbian Manifesto*, San Francisco: Harper SanFrancisco.
Goss, R.E., (2002), *Queering Christ: Beyond Jesus Acted Up*, Cleveland: The Pilgrim Press.
Graham, E.L., (1995), *Making the Difference: Gender, Personhood and Theology*, London: Mowbray.
Graham, E.L., (1996), *Transforming Practice: Pastoral Theology in an Age of Uncertainty*, London: Mowbray.
Grant, J., (1989), *White Women's Christ and Black Women's Jesus: Feminist Christology, a Womanist Response*, Atlanta Georgia: Scholar's Press.
Green, C., (1974), "Liberation theology? Karl Barth on women and men", *Union Seminary Quarterly Review*, 29(3/4), pp.221-231.
Greenberg, B., (1977), "Jewish women: coming of age", *Tradition*, 16(4), pp.79-94.
Greer, G., (1991), [1970], *The Female Eunuch*, London: Paladin.
Grey, M., (1989), *Redeeming the Dream: Feminism, Redemption and Christian Tradition*, London: SPCK.
Grey, M., (1993), *The Wisdom of Fools: Seeking Revelation for Today*, London: SPCK.
Grey, M., (1997), *Beyond the Dark Night: A Way Forward for the Church*, Cassell.
Grey, M., (2001), *Introducing Feminist Images of God*, Cleveland, Ohio: The Pilgrim's Press.
Grey, M., (2003), *Sacred Longings: Ecofeminist Theology and Globalisation*, London: SCM Press.
Gross, R.M., (2000), "Feminist theology: religiously diverse neighborhood or Christian ghetto?", *Journal of Feminist Studies in Religion*, 16(2), 73-78.
Gubar, S., (2000), *Critical Condition: Feminism at the Turn of the Century*, New York: Columbia University Press.
Hall, C., O'Sullivan, Phoenix, A., Thomas, L., and Whitehead, A., (1999), "Snakes and ladders: reviewing feminisms at century's end", *Feminist Review*, 61, 1-3.

Hampson, D., (1990), *Theology and Feminism*, Oxford: Basil Blackwell.
Hampson, D., (1996), *After Christianity*, Continuum International Publishing Group.
Hampson, D., (ed.), (1996), *Swallowing a Fishbone?: Feminist Theologians Debate Christianity*, London: SPCK.
Hampson, D., (1998), "On not remembering her", *Feminist Theology*, 19, pp.63-83.
Hampson, D., (2002), *After Christianity (Second Edition)*, London: SCM Press.
Hampson, D., and Ruether, R.R., (1987), "Is there a place for feminists in the Christian Church?" *New Blackfriars*, 68, pp.7-24.
Hardesty, N. et al, (1979), "Women clergy: how their presence is changing the Church", *Christian Century*, 96(5), pp.122-128.
Harding, S., (ed.), (1987), *Feminism and Methodology: Social Science Issues*, Open University Press.
Harris, H.A., (2001), "Struggling for truth", *Feminist Theology*, 28, pp.40-56.
Harrison, B.W., (1975), "The early feminists and the clergy: a case study in the dynamics of secularisation", *Review and Expositor*, 72(1), pp.41-52.
Harrison, B.W., Heyward, Hunt, C., Townes, E.M., Starhawk, Barstow, A.L. and Cooey, P.M., (1994), "Roundtable discussion: backlash", *Journal of Feminist Studies in Religion*, 10(1), pp.91-111.
Hayes, M.A., Porter, W., and Tombs, D., (eds.), (1998), *Religion and Sexuality*, Sheffield: Sheffield Academic Press.
Height, D.I., (1979), "The new black woman", *Journal of Ecumenical Studies*, 16(1), pp.166-169.
Hewitt, M.A., (1995), *Critical Theory of Religion: A Feminist Analysis*, Minneapolis: Fortress Press.
Heyward, C., (1979), "Speaking and sparking, building and burning: Ruether and Daly, theologians", *Christianity and Crisis*, 39(2), pp.66-72.
Heyward, C., (1982), *The Redemption of God: A Theology of Mutual Redemption*, University Press of America.
Heyward, C., (1984), *Our Passion for Justice: Images of Power, Sexuality and Liberation*, New York: Pilgrim Press.
Heyward, C., (1989), *Speaking of Christ: A Lesbian Feminist Voice*, New York: Pilgrim Press.
Heyward, C., (1995), *Staying Power: Reflections on Gender, Justice, and Compassion*, Cleveland, Ohio: Pilgrim Press.
Heyward, C., (1999a), *Saving Jesus From Those Who Are Right: Rethinking What it Means to be Christian*, Minneapolis: Fortress Press.
Heyward, C., (1999b), *A Priest Forever*, Cleveland, Ohio: The Pilgrim Press.
Heyward, C., (1999c), *When Boundaries Betray Us*, Cleveland, Ohio: Pilgrim Press.
Heyward, C., and Davis, E.F., (eds.), (1989), *Speaking of Christ: A Lesbian Feminist Voice*, Cleveland, Ohio: Pilgrim Press.
Hirsch, P., (1998), *Barbara Leigh Smith Bodichon*, London: Random House.
Hoagland, S.L., and Frye, M., (eds.), *Feminist Interpretations of Mary Daly*, Pennsylvania: The Pennsylvanian State University Press.

Holm, J., (ed), (1994), *Women in Religion*, London: Pinter Publishers.
Hopkins, J., (1995), *Towards a Feminist Christology: Jesus of Nazareth, European Women and the Christological Crisis*, London: SPCK.
Humm, M., (ed.), (1992), *Feminisms: A Reader.* London: Harvester Wheatsheaf.
Irigaray, L., (1993), *je, tu, nous: Toward a Culture of Difference*, (trans. Alison Martin), Routledge.
Irigaray, L., (1997), "Equal to whom?", in Ward, G., (ed.), *The Postmodern God: A Theological Reader*, Oxford: Blackwell Publishers Ltd, pp.198-213
Isasi-Diaz, A.M., (1979), "Silent women will never be heard", *Missiology*, 7(3), pp.295-301.
Isasi-Diaz, A.M., (1997), *Mujerista Theology: A Theology for the Twenty-First Century*, New York: Maryknoll.
Isherwood, L., and Stuart, E., (1998), *Introducing Body Theology*, Sheffield: Sheffield Academic Press.
Isherwood, L., (ed.), (2000), *The Good News of the Body: Sexual Theology and Feminism*, Sheffield: Sheffield Academic Press.
Isherwood, I., (2001), *Introducing Feminist Christologies*, Sheffield: Sheffield Academic Press.
Jantzen, G. M., (1998), *Becoming Divine: Towards a Feminist Philosophy of Religion*, Manchester: Manchester University Press.
Japinga, L., (1999), *Feminism and Christianity: An Essential Guide,* Nashville: Abingdon Press.
Jones, S., (2000), *Feminist Theory and Christian Theology: Cartographies of Grace*, Minneapolis: Fortress Press.
Kanyoro, M.R.A., (2002), *Introducing Feminist Cultural Hermeneutics*, Sheffield: Sheffield Academic Press.
Kelly, C.M., (1992), *The Enemy Within: Radical Feminism in the Christian Church,* Milton Keynes: Family Publications.
Kemp, S., and Squires, J., (eds.), (1997), *Feminisms*, Oxford: Oxford University Press.
Kim, C.W.M., St. Ville, S.M., and Simonaitis, S.M., (eds.), (1993), *Transfigurations: Theology and the French Feminists*, Minneapolis: Fortress Press.
King, U., (ed.), (1987), *Women in the World's Religions, Past and Present*, New York: Paragon House.
King, U., (1993), *Women and Spirituality: Voices of Protest and Promise,* 2nd Edition, Macmillan Press.
King, U., (ed.), (1994), *Feminist Theology from the Third World: A Reader*, London: SPCK.
King, U., (ed.), (1995), *Religion and Gender*, Oxford: Blackwell.
King, U., (ed.), (1998), *Faith and Praxis in a Postmodern Age*, London: Cassell.
King, U., (ed.), (2001), *Spirituality and Society in the New Millennium*, Brighton: Sussex Academic Press.
LaCugna, C.M., (ed.), (1993), *Freeing Theology: The Essentials of Theology in Feminist Perspective*, Harper SanFrancisco.
Lauer, R., (1966), Women clergy for Rome? *The Christian Century*, pp.1107-1110.

Leonard, E., (1990), "Experience as a source for theology: a Canadian and feminist perspective", *Studies in Religion/Sciences religieuses*, 19(2), pp.143-162.
Lindley, S.H. (1979), "Feminist theology in a global perspective", *Christian Century*, 96(15), pp.465-469.
Linzey, A., and Wexley, P., (eds.), (1991), *Fundamentalism and Tolerance: An Agenda for Theology and Society*, London: Bellew Publishing.
Litfin, A.D., (1979), "Evangelical feminism: why traditionalists reject it", *Bibliotheca Sacra*, 136(543), pp.258-271.
McClintock Fulkerson, M., (1994), *Changing the Subject: Women's Discourses and Feminist Theology*, Minneapolis: Fortress Press.
McKim, D.K., (ed.), (1986), *A Guide to Contemporary Hermeneutics: Major Trends in Biblical Interpretation*, Grand Rapids, Michigan: William B. Eerdmans Publishing Company.
Mackinnon, H. and McIntyre, M., (eds.), (1980), *Readings in Ecology & Feminist Theology,* Kansas City: Sheed & Ward.
Maitland, S., (1983), *A Map of the New Country: Women and Christianity*, London: Routledge & Kegan Paul.
McLaughlin, E.L., (1975), "The Christian past: does it hold a future for women?", *Anglican Theological Review*, 57(1), pp.36-56.
May, M., (1995), *A Body Knows: A Theopoetics of Death and Resurrection*, New York: Continuum.
Mernissi, F., (1975), *Beyond the Veil: Male-Female Dynamics in a Modern Muslim Society,* Cambridge, Mass.: Schenkman.
Metz, K., (1990), "Passionate differences: a working model for cross-cultural Communication", *Journal of Feminist Studies in Religion*, 6(1), pp.131-151.
Millett, K., (1977), [1970], *Sexual Politics*, London: Virago.
Moi, T., (1999), *What is a Women? And Other Essays*, Oxford: Oxford University Press.
Mollenkott, V.R., (1974), "The women's movement challenges the Church", *Psychology and Theology*, 2(4), pp.298-321.
Moltmann-Wendel, E., (1975), "The women's movement in Germany", *Lutheran World*, 22(2), pp.122-1309.
Morny, J., and Neumaier-Dargyay, E.K., (1995), *Gender, Genre and Religion: Feminist Reflections*, Ontario, Canada: Wilfred Laurier University Press.
Morton, N., (1972), "The rising woman consciousness in a male language structure", *Anderton Newton Quarterly*, 12(4), pp.177-190.
Murray, M.A., (1963), *The Genesis of Religion*, London: Routledge & Kegan Paul.
Neill, E.R., Brettschneider, M., Grunenfelder, R., Grace Ji-Sun Kim, Martinez, P.A., Witte, K., Iwamura, J.N., Washington, D., "Roundtable discussion: from generation to generation horizons in feminist theology or reinventing the wheel?", *Journal of Feminist Studies in Religion*, 1999, 15(1), pp.102-138.
Nelson, J.B., (1978), *Embodiment: An Approach to Sexuality and Christian Theology*, Minneapolis, Minnesota: Augsburg Publishing Press.

Nelson, J.B., (1992), *Body Theology*, Louisville, Kentucky: Westminster/John Knox Press.
Nelson, J.B., (1995), "On doing body theology", *Theology and Sexuality*, 2, pp.38-60.
Nelson, J.B., Longfellow, S.A., (eds.), (1994), *Sexuality and the Sacred: Sources For Theological Reflection*, London: Mowbray.
Northup, L., (1998), "Bitten from behind: babies, big institutions, and backlash", *Feminist Theology*, 17, pp.103-120.
Oakley, A., (2002), *Gender on Planet Earth*, Cambridge: Polity.
O'Neill, M., (1990), *Women Speaking, Women Listening: Women in Interreligious Dialogue*, Maryknoll, NY: Orbis Books.
Parsons, S., (1998), *Feminism and Christian Ethics*, Cambridge University Press.
Parsons, S., (ed.), (2000), *Challenging Women's Orthodoxies in the Context of Faith*, Aldershot: Ashgate.
Parsons, S., (ed.), (2002), *The Cambridge Companion to Feminist Theology*, Cambridge: Cambridge University Press.
Parsons, S., (2002), *The Ethics of Gender*, Oxford: Blackwell.
Parvey, C., (1969), "Ordain her, ordain her not", *Dialog*, 8(3), pp.203-208.
Parvey, C.F., (1975), "Women in the ordained clergy: entering an historically male role", *Lutheran World*, 22(1), pp.32-40.
Pears, A., (2001), "Mechanisms of disclosure: reconfiguring critical analysis of Christian feminist theological discourse", in *Feminist Theology: The Journal of the Britain and Ireland School of Feminist Theology*, 26, pp.8-20.
Pears, A., (2002), "When Leaving is Believing: The Feminist Ethical Imperative of Mary Daly's Rejection of Traditional Religion", *Feminist Theology: The Journal of the Britain and Ireland School of Feminist Theology*, 29, pp.7-18.
Pears, A., (2002), "Divine Wisdom: A Discourse of Christian Feminist Theology", in Joynes, C.E., (ed.), (2002), *The Quest for Wisdom: Essays in Honour of Philip Budd*, Cambridge: Orchard Academic.
Pears, A., (2003), "Re-Visioning Feminisms", *Feminist Theology: The Journal of the Britain and Ireland School of Feminist Theology*, 11(3), pp.281-291.
Plaskow, J., (1978), "Christian feminism and anti-Judaism", *Cross Currents*, 28(3), pp.306-309.
Plaskow, J., and Christ, C.P., (1989), *Weaving the Visions: New Patterns in Feminist Spirituality*, San Francisco: Harper and Row.
Plaskow, J., et al, (2000), "Publish not perish: celebrating 15 years of struggle", *Journal of Feminist Studies in Religion*, 16(1), 95-125.
Pritchard, E.A., (1999), "Feminist theology and the politics of failure", *Journal of Feminist Studies in Religion*, 15(2), pp.50-72.
Pui-lan, K., (2000), *Introducing Asian Feminist Theology*, Continuum International Publishing Group.
Pui-lan, K., (2001), "Feminist theology at the dawn of the millennium", *Feminist Theology*, 27, pp.6-20.
Pui-lan, K., (2003), "Theology as a sexual act?", *Feminist Theology*, 11(2), 149-156.
Raphael, M., (1996), *Thealogy and Embodiment: The Post-Patriarchal Reconstruction of Female Sacrality*, Sheffield: Sheffield Academic Press.

Richlin, A., (1998), "Teaching religion and feminist theory to a new generation", *Journal of Feminist Studies in Religion*, 14(2), pp.124-131.
Roof, J., and Wiegman, R., (eds.), (1995), *Who Can Speak? Authority and Critical Identity*, Urbana and Chicago: University of Illinois Press.
Ross, S.A., (2001), *Extravagant Affections: A Feminist Sacramental Theology*, New York: Continuum International Publishing Group.
Rowland, C., (ed.), (1999), *The Cambridge Companion to Liberation Theology*, Cambridge: Cambridge University Press.
Ruether, R.R., (1965), "Is Roman Catholicism reformable?", *Christian Century*, 82(38), pp.1152-1154.
Ruether, R.R., (1967), "The woman intellectual and the Church: a Commonweal Symposium", *Commonweal*, pp.446-458.
Ruether, R.R., (1969), "A perspective on a radical ecclesiology", *Dialog*, 8(3), pp.209-213.
Ruether, R.R., (1969), "New wine, maybe new wine-skins, for the Church", *Christian Century*, 86(14), pp.445-449.
Ruether, R.R., (1971), "Male chauvinist theology and the anger of women", *Cross Currents*, pp.173-185.
Ruether, R.R., (1974), *Faith and Fratricide: The Theological Roots of Anti-Semitism*, New York: Seabury Press.
Ruether, R.R., (1977), *Mary, the Feminine Face of the Church*. Philadelphia: Westminster Press.
Ruether, R.R., (1975), *New Woman New Earth: Sexist Ideologies and Human Liberation*, New York: The Seabury Press.
Ruether, R.R., (1976), "What is the task of theology?", *Christianity and Crisis*, 36, pp.121-125.
Ruether, R.R., (1981), *To Change the World: Christology and Cultural Criticism*, London: SCM Press Ltd.
Ruether, R.R., (1997), *Women and Redemption: A Theological History*, London: SCM Press Ltd.
Ruether, R.R., (ed.), (1974), *Religion and Sexism: Images of Woman in the Jewish and Christian Traditions*, New York: Simon and Schuster.
Ruether, R.R., (ed.), (2002), *Gender, Ethnicity, and Religion: Views From the Other Side*, Minneapolis: Fortress Press.
Russell, L., (ed.), (1985), *Feminist Interpretation of the Bible*, Philadelphia: Westminster Press.
Russell, L., and Shannon, J., (ed.), (1996), *Dictionary of Feminist Theologies*, London: Mowbray.
Saiving, V., (1960), "The human situation: a feminine view", *Journal of Religion*, 1960, 40(2), pp.100-112.
Saiving, V., (1995), "The human situation; a feminine view", in Mackinnon, M.H., and McIntyre, M., (eds.), *Readings in Ecology & Feminist Theology*. Kansas City: Sheed & Ward.
Sawyer, D.F., and Collier, D.M., (eds.), (1999), *Is There a Future for Feminist Theology?*, Sheffield: Sheffield Academic Press.

Scanzoni, L., and Hardesty, N., (1974), *All We're Meant to Be: A Biblical Approach to Women's Liberation*, Word Books.
Schneider, L.E., (1998), *Re-Imagining the Divine: Confronting the Backlash Against Feminist Theology*, Cleveland, Ohio: The Pilgrim Press.
Schottroff, L., (1995), *Lydia's Impatient Sisters: A Feminist Social History of Early Christianity*, London: SCM Press Ltd.
Schüssler Fiorenza, E., (1975), "Feminist theology as a critical theology of Liberation", *Theological Studies*, 36(4), pp.605-626.
Schüssler Fiorenza, E., (1978) "Women in the pre-Pauline Churches", *Union Seminary Quarterly Review*, 33(3&4), pp.153-166.
Schüssler Fiorenza, E., (1979) "Towards a liberating and liberated theology: women theologians and feminist theology in the USA", *Concilium*, 115, pp.22-32.
Schüssler Fiorenza, E., (1983), *In Memory of Her: A Feminist Theological Reconstruction of Christian Origins*, SCM Press Ltd.
Schüssler Fiorenza, E., (1984) *Bread Not Stone: The Challenge of Feminist Biblical Interpretation*, Boston: Beacon Press.
Schüssler Fiorenza, E., (1990), "Changing the paradigms", *The Christian Century*, 1990, Sept.5-12, pp.796-800.
Schüssler Fiorenza, E., (1992), *But She Said: Feminist Practices of Biblical Interpretation*, Beacon Press: Boston.
Schüssler Fiorenza, E., (1993), *Discipleship of Equals: A Critical Feminist Ekklesia-ology of Liberation*, London: SCM Press Ltd.
Schüssler Fiorenza, E., (1994), *Jesus, Miriam's Child, Sophia's Prophet: Critical Issues in Feminist Christology*, London: SCM Press.
Schüssler Fiorenza, E., (1995), "Commitment and critical inquiry", in Gill, R., (ed.), *Readings in Modern Theology: Britain and America*, London: SPCK, pp.267-277.
Schüssler Fiorenza, E., (1998), *Sharing Her Word: Feminist Biblical Interpretation in Context*, Edinburgh: T&T Clark.
Schüssler Fiorenza, E., (1999), *Rhetoric and Ethic: The Politics of Biblical Studies*, Minneapolis: Fortress Press.
Schüssler Fiorenza, E., (2000), "Speaking out: toward the millennium of wo/men", *Journal of Feminist Studies in Religion*, 16(1), pp.91-94.
Schüssler Fiorenza, E., (2002), "Thinking and working across borders: The Feminist Liberation Theologians, Activists, and Scholars in Religion Network", *Journal of Feminist Studies in Religion*, 2002, 18(1), pp. 71-74.
Schüssler Fiorenza, E., (ed.), (1993), *Searching the Scriptures, Volume One: A Feminist Introduction*, New York: Crossroad.
Schüssler Fiorenza, E, (ed.), (1994), *Searching the Scriptures, vol.2: A Feminist Commentary*, New York: Crossroad.
Schüssler Fiorenza, E., (ed.), (1996), *The Power of Naming: A Concilium Reader in Feminist Liberation Theology*, Maryknoll, NY: Orbis Books.
Schüssler Fiorenza, E., and Kwok Pui-Lan, (eds.), (1998), *Women's Sacred Scriptures*, Concilium, 1998/3, Maryknoll, N.Y.: Orbis Books.
Segal, L., (1987), *Is the Future Female? Troubled Thoughts on Contemporary Feminism*, London: Virago.

Segovia, F., (ed.), (2000), *Interpreting Beyond Borders*, Sheffield: Sheffield Academic Press.
Selling. J.A., (ed.), *Embracing Sexuality: Authority and Experience in the Catholic Church*, Ashgate Publishing Limited.
Sheldrake, P., (1994), *Befriending Our Desires*, Darton, Longman and Todd.
Shepherd, L.M., (2002), *Feminist Theologies for a Postmodern Church: Diversity, Community, and Scripture*, New York: Peter Lang.
Sigal, P., (1974), "Women in a prayer quorum", *Judaism*, 23(2), pp.174-182.
Stanley, L., (ed.), (1997), *Knowing Feminisms: On Academic Borders, Territories and Tribes*, London: Sage Publications.
Stanley, L., and Wise, S., (1993), *Breaking Out Again: Feminist Ontology and Epistemology*, London and New York: Routledge.
Starhawk, (1979), *The Spiral Dance: The Rebirth of the Ancient Religion of the Goddess*, San Francisco: Harper and Row.
Stevens, M., (ed.), *Reconstructing the Christ Symbol: Essays in Feminist Christology*, New York: Paulist Press.
Stuart, E., and Thatcher, A., (1997), *People of Passion: What the Churches Teach About Sex*, London: Mowbray.
Stuart, E,. (et al), (1997), *Religion is a Queer Thing: A Guide to the Christian Faith for Lesbian, Gay, Bisexual and Transgendered People*, London and Washington: Cassell.
Suchocki, M., (1980), "The Challenge of Mary Daly", *Encounter*, 41, pp.307-317.
Sugirtharajah, R.S., (ed.), (1991), *Voices From the Margin: Interpreting the Bible in the Non-Biblical World*, London: SPCK.
Swidler, L., (1971), "Jesus Was a Feminist", *Catholic World*, January 1971, pp.177-83.
Tavard, G., (1973), *Women in the Christian Tradition*, University of Notre Dame Press.
Thatcher, A., (1993), *Liberating Sex: A Christian Sexual Theology*, London: SPCK.
Thatcher, A., and Stuart, E., (eds.), (1996), *Christian Perspectives on Sexuality and Gender*, Gracewing.
Thorne, H., (2000), *Journey to Priesthood: An in-depth study of the first women priests in the Church of England*, Bristol: Centre for Comparative Studies in Religion and Gender.
Trible, P., (1975), "Biblical theology as women's work", *Religion in Life*, 44(1), pp.7-13.
Trible, P., (1978), God and the Rhetoric of Sexuality, Fortress Press.
Ward, G., (2000), *Theology and Contemporary Critical Theory*, Macmillan Press, Ltd.
Ward, G., (ed.), *The Postmodern God: A Theological Reader*, Oxford: Blackwell Publishers Ltd.
Weed, E., and Schor, N., (eds.), (1997), *Feminism Meets Queer Theory*, Bloomington and Indianapolis: Indiana University Press.
Weeks, J., (1985), *Sexuality and its Discontents: Meanings, Myths and Modern Sexualities*, London and New York: Routledge.

Welch, S., (2000), *A Feminist Ethic of Risk*, Augsberg Fortress Publishers.
Whelehan, I., (1995), *Modern Feminist Thought, Edinburgh: Edinburgh University Press.*
Young, P.D., (1990), *Feminist Theology/Christian Theology: In Search of Method,* Eugene, OR: Wipf and Stock Publishers.

Index

Abraham, William 124-125
Althaus-Reid, Marcella 2-3, 6-7, 134-161, 163-181
Aquino, Maria Pilar 33, 122, 172-173

Backlash 174
Body theology 74, 79-80, 137, 142-143
Brenner, Athalya 123
Brettschneider, Marla 176
Brock, Rita Nakashima 34
Butler, Judith 151

Cady Stanton, Elizabeth 10-11
Callahan, Sidney Cornelia 15-16
Cannon, Katie 30, 33
Carr, Anne 29
Chopp, Rebecca 31
Christ, Carol 13, 23-25, 28-29, 31, 55-59
Christa 97
Christology 71, 82, 84-94, 147, 157, 165-167
Chung, Hyun Kyung 34, 86
Coakley, Sarah 63
Coleman, Kate 33, 173
Coward, Rosalind 174
Crook, Margaret Brackenbury 14
Culpepper, Emily 25, 30, 176

Daly, Mary 16-20, 25, 43-61, 64, 69
Daggers, Jenny 28, 75
Davaney, Sheila Greeve 31-32, 51, 164, 176, 181
De Beauvoir, Simone 17-18, 41-43

Ebert, Teresa 176
Eller, Cynthia 43-44

Faludi, Susan 173-174

Feminist hermeneutics 11, 22-24, 112, 114, 120-122, 125, 128, 157, 168
Feminist informed theologies
  and authority 11, 15-16, 18, 23-24, 54-56, 58, 62-65, 72-76, 96, 112, 116, 118
  and God 42, 46, 54, 57, 62, 72, 80, 82-83
Feminist method 101, 104, 108-112, 120, 125
Feminist rejections of Christianity 40-67
Fulkerson, Mary McClintock 29, 164, 169, 172, 181

Gage, Matilda Joslyn 10, 11
Goldenberg, Naomi 24-26, 54-56
Goss, Robert 137, 144, 157
Grant, Jacquelyn 85
Grey, Mary 28, 33, 81, 120
Gross, Rita 34
Gubar, Susan 181

Halkes, Catharina 33
Hampson, Daphne 12, 59-63, 104, 119, 120
Harrison, Beverley 174
Heyward, Carter 71-104, 163-169, 178-179
Hewitt, Marsha Aileen 51-53
Hopkins, Julie 63, 85, 86
Horizons in Feminist Theology 4, 31
Hunt, Mary 127

Irigaray, Luce 44
Isasi-Diaz, Ada Maria 26, 31, 34
Isherwood, Lisa 32, 80, 86, 93, 144

Jantzen, Grace 33, 120-121, 179

Johnson, Elizabeth 85

Kanyoro, Musimbi 33-35
King, Ursula 12, 27, 28, 179
Kwok Pui-lan 31, 33-35, 107, 151, 164, 180
Kyriarchy 125-127

Liberation theology 129, 135-140, 148, 155
Leonard, Ellen 29
Loades, Ann 28, 33, 43, 49
Lorde, Audre 29, 52

Maitland, Sarah 28, 82
McFague, Sallie 54
Meo, Lisa 33
Mujerista theology 26, 31, 34

Neill, Emile 175
Nelson, James 79-80, 136, 142, 145

Oduyoye, Mercy 33, 164
Ordination 72-75, 76, 82, 180

Parvey, Constance 15
Parsons, Susan 33, 180
Plaskow, Judith 13, 23, 26-27, 29
Postfeminisms 175
Post-traditional feminisms 24-26, 57, 59, 61, 65

Queer theology 134, 136, 140, 144, 145, 149, 151, 156-159, 170, 171

Rich, Adrienne 136
Ruether, Rosemary 15, 19-21, 27, 60-61, 142

Ross, Susan 86
Russell, Letty 164

Saiving, Valerie 12-13, 28
Sawyer, Deborah 179
Schüssler Fiorenza, Elisabeth 15, 21-23, 28, 101-130, 163-165, 167-169, 171, 178-179, 180
Segal, Lynne 50
Sheldrake, Philip 144-145
Slee, Nicola 33, 63
Soskice, Janet 33, 63
Stuart, Elizabeth 137, 144-145
Suchocki, Marjori 48, 52
Swidler, Leonard 85

Thealogy 56-58
Theology of mutuality 69, 71, 78-81, 91-92, 94, 97
Thorne, Helen 75-76
Townes, Emile 173
Trible, Phyllis 23

Virgin Mary 138, 154-159

Williams, Delores 30
Womanist theologies 30-31, 173, 178

Young, Pamela Dickey 3, 31, 169

For Product Safety Concerns and Information please contact our EU
representative GPSR@taylorandfrancis.com
Taylor & Francis Verlag GmbH, Kaufingerstraße 24, 80331 München, Germany

www.ingramcontent.com/pod-product-compliance
Lightning Source LLC
Chambersburg PA
CBHW052118300426
44116CB00010B/1707